Family Engagement in the Digital Age

Family Engagement in the Digital Age: Early Childhood Educators as Media Mentors explores how technology can empower and engage parents, caregivers, and families and the emerging role of media mentors who guide young children and their families in the twenty-first century. This thought-provoking guide to innovative approaches to family engagement includes Spotlight on Engagement case studies, success stories, best practices, helpful hints for media mentors, and "learn more" resources woven into each chapter to connect the dots between child development, early learning, developmentally appropriate practice, family engagement, media mentorship, and digital age technology. In addition, the book is driven by a set of best practices for teaching with technology in early childhood education that are based on the National Association for the Education of Young Children (NAEYC) and Fred Rogers Center joint position statement on technology and interactive media.

Please visit the Companion Website at http://teccenter.erikson.edu/family-engagement-in-the-digital-age.

Chip Donohue, Ph.D., is Dean of Distance Learning and Continuing Education, and Director of the Technology in Early Childhood (TEC) Center at Erikson Institute, USA.

Family Engagement in the Digital Age

Early Childhood Educators as Media Mentors

Edited by Chip Donohue

Routledge
Taylor & Francis Group

NEW YORK AND LONDON

First published 2017
by Routledge
711 Third Avenue, New York, NY 10017

and by Routledge
2 Park Square, Milton Park, Abingdon, Oxon OX14 4RN

Routledge is an imprint of the Taylor & Francis Group, an informa business

Library of Congress Cataloging in Publication Data
Names: Donohue, Chip.
Title: Family engagement in the digital age : early childhood
educators as media mentors / edited by Chip Donohue.
Description: New York : Routledge, 2017. | Includes bibliographical
references and index.
Identifiers: LCCN 2016009935| ISBN 9781138100350 (hardback)
| ISBN 9781138100367 (pbk) | ISBN 9781315657707 (ebook)
Subjects: LCSH: Early childhood education–Computer-assisted
instruction. | Early childhood education–Parent participation. |
Computers and children. | Educational technology.
Classification: LCC LB1139.35.C64 F35 2017 | DDC 372.21--dc23
LC record available at https://lccn.loc.gov/2016009935

ISBN: 978-1-138-10035-0 (hbk)
ISBN: 978-1-138-10036-7 (pbk)
ISBN: 978-1-315-65770-7 (ebk)

Typeset in Bembo
by HWA Text and Data Management, London

Printed and bound in the United States of America by Sheridan

This is a book about family engagement and media mentors. It is about family engagement within the context and culture in which a young child grows, develops, and learns. It is about media mentors including parents, caregivers, siblings, extended family members, neighbors, and friends. And, it is about educators, librarians, child life specialists, early intervention specialists, pediatric health providers, parent educators, and so many more—anyone who works with or on behalf of young children and families in the digital age.

In these pages, we describe an ecology of family engagement that includes homes, neighborhoods, early childhood environments, school settings, early literacy initiatives, libraries and children's museums, out-of-school time programs, home-visiting projects, early intervention services, community-based efforts, and more. Along the way, we have each reflected on our own family experiences, context, and culture and on those mentors who helped to raise, guide, and engage us.

This book includes contributions from 25 authors, each with unique family histories, stories, and cultures. Woven into the chapters, case studies, and stories are helpful hints for media mentors based on what each of us has learned, reflected on, and written about families, about being in and of a family, and about creating families of our own. On our collective behalf, I dedicate this book to the families who raised and nurtured us as young children and who encourage us today as adults, and to all the mentors who helped, and continue to help, guide us on our way.

Contents

Figures and Tables

Figures

Tables

Contributors

Editor

Chip Donohue, PhD, is Dean of Distance Learning and Continuing Education, and Director of the Technology in Early Childhood (TEC) Center at Erikson Institute in Chicago. He is a senior fellow and member of the advisory board of the Fred Rogers Center for Early Learning and Children's Media at Saint Vincent College, where he co-chaired the working group that revised the 2012 NAEYC & Fred Rogers Center Joint Position Statement on *Technology and Interactive Media as Tools in Early Childhood Programs Serving Children from Birth through Age 8*. Chip is the editor of *Technology and Digital Media in the Early Years: Tools for Teaching and Learning,* co-published by Routledge/NAEYC in 2015. In 2012, he received the Bammy Award and Educators' Voice Award as *Innovator of the Year* from the Academy of Education Arts & Sciences. In 2015, he was honored as a children's media *Emerging Pioneer* at the KAPi (Kids At Play International) Awards.

Chapter Authors

Anamarie Auger, PhD, is an associate policy researcher of the RAND Corporation. Her research interests are in early childhood education, child and family policy, and educational policy. Specifically, she is interested in understanding how policy shapes the various environments children spend the majority of their time in and how environments can interact with one another to best promote positive child and family development. She is also interested in preschool classroom practices such as teacher–child interactions and the use of preschool curricula. She has co-authored papers on the association between child care quality and children's development, and the effect of a reading intervention on maternal reading practices and beliefs. She received a BA degree in psychology from the University of Texas at Austin and a PhD degree in educational policy from the University of California, Irvine.

Jeremy Boyle, MFA, received his BFA degree from the University of Illinois at Chicago and an MFA degree from The Ohio State University. He was a founding member of the Chicago group Joan of Arc and has performed music (both solo and collaborative) throughout the United States, Canada, and Japan. Jeremy has exhibited artwork, most of which is sound- and technology-based, in major cities across the United States. Jeremy currently lives in rural western Pennsylvania, and is assistant professor of art at Clarion University of Pennsylvania and resident artist at CMU's CREATE Lab. Jeremy (with Melissa Butler) speaks often and facilitates professional development workshops for groups of educators and policy makers around issues of children's innovation learning with the material of technology.

Pamela Brillante, EdD, is an assistant professor of special education at William Paterson University of New Jersey, with specialties in early childhood special education and inclusive classroom practices. A former assistive technology specialist, she has worked with children, families, and teachers to build avenues for access to general education classroom activities and curriculum for children with disabilities through the use of technology. As a professor of special education, Pam has taught classes in universal design for instruction and assistive technology as well as presented to parent and community groups on the topics of inclusive practices and home/school partnerships.

Melissa Butler, MEd, MA, is a teacher in the Pittsburgh Public Schools. She has a master's degree in curriculum theory from Penn State University and a master's degree in creative writing from the University of Cape Town. She is National Board Certified as an Early Childhood Generalist, ages 3 to 8, and is a teacher consultant with the Western Pennsylvania Writing Project and teacher in residence at CMU's CREATE Lab. Melissa co-directs the Children's Innovation Project with Jeremy Boyle. Melissa (with Jeremy Boyle) speaks often and facilitates professional development workshops for groups of educators and policy makers around issues of children's innovation learning with the material of technology.

Cen Campbell is a children's librarian, author, and founder of LittleeLit. com. She has driven a bookmobile, managed branch libraries, developed innovative programs for babies, young children, and teens, and now supports children's librarians to serve as media mentors in their communities. She was named Library Journal Mover & Shaker in 2014 for her work on LittleeLit.com. Cen is a co-author of the white paper on media mentorship by the Association for Library Service to Children, *Media Mentorship in Libraries Serving Youth.*

Margaret Caspe, PhD, is a senior research analyst at the Harvard Family Research Project (HFRP). Her research focuses on how families, early childhood programs, schools, and communities support children's learning. She develops interactive materials to prepare educators for family engagement, assists in efforts to evaluate family engagement, and has contributed to the development of resources for the Office of Head Start National Center on parent, family, and community engagement. She is co-editor of *Promising Practices for Engaging Families in Literacy* (Information Age Publishing, 2013) and author of a variety of reports and articles including "Engaging Families in the Child Assessment Process." Margaret received her PhD degree in applied psychology from the Steinhardt School of Culture, Education and Human Development at New York University and she holds an EdM degree from the Harvard Graduate School of Education.

Kevin Clark, PhD, is a professor in the division of learning technologies and the founding director of the Center for Digital Media Innovation and Diversity in the College of Education and Human Development at George Mason University. His research interests include the role of interactive and digital media in education; issues of diversity in educational media; and broadening participation in STEM careers and disciplines. Prior to becoming a professor, Kevin worked as a content designer and senior program manager for an educational software start-up company, and has more than 20 years of experience as a designer, advisor, and consultant to organizations such as National Park Service, Public Broadcasting Service (PBS), Corporation for Public Broadcasting (CPB), Common Sense Media, Fred Rogers Center, Disney Junior, Jim Henson Company, DHX Media, and Toca Boca. Kevin has been honored by the White House as a Champion of Change for his work in supporting and accelerating STEM opportunities for African American students, schools, and communities, and he was selected as a fellow for the Television Academy Foundation Faculty Seminar.

Rafiq Dossani, PhD, finance, Northwestern University, is a senior economist at the RAND Corporation, professor at the Pardee RAND Graduate School, and director of the RAND Center for Asia Pacific Policy. He has researched education issues relating to early childhood education, online education, education strategy, professional development, and technical education. In 2014, he was the principal investigator for a project sponsored by the PNC Foundation on bridging the digital divide in early childhood education. He is currently co-principal investigator of a project that is studying the impact of hybrid instruction on undergraduate student learning at the University of Texas, Tyler. Between 1998 and 2012, Rafiq worked at Stanford University's Institute for International Studies as a senior research scholar and was director of the Stanford Center for South Asia.

Amaya Garcia, MPP, MA, is a policy analyst in the education policy program at New America, where she provides research and analysis on policies related to dual language learners. Previously, she was a policy analyst at the District of Columbia State Board of Education and provided analysis on state-wide education policies and regulations, including those related to family engagement. She began her career as a research assistant at the Georgetown Early Learning Project and helped conduct multiple studies on infant learning from media and examining infant-directed media. She has a master's degree in public policy from the University of Maryland-College Park, a master's degree in cognitive studies in education from Teachers College, Columbia University, and a bachelor's degree in English and psychology from the University of Iowa.

Kristy Goodwin, PhD, is an Australian researcher, author, speaker, and consultant who explores the impact of technology on young children's health, learning, and development (and also a mum!), and founder of the Every Chance to Learn website to support parents in the digital age. She delivers evidence-based information about young children's "digitalized childhoods" drawing on research from a range of disciplines including developmental science, neuroscience, and technology research with young children. She is passionate about translating the latest research into practical and digestible information for parents and educators who are trying to navigate the digital terrain. She is an honorary associate at Macquarie University at the Institute of Early Childhood and has worked as a primary school and early childhood teacher for 14 years in a range of educational settings in Australia and Asia.

Lisa Guernsey is deputy director of the education policy program and director of the Learning Technologies Project at New America. She leads teams of writers and analysts to examine policies, tell stories, and generate ideas on new approaches to help disadvantaged students succeed. Prior to her work at New America, Lisa worked as a staff writer at the *New York Times* and the *Chronicle of Higher Education*. She has also contributed to several national publications, including *The Atlantic, The Washington Post, Newsweek, Time, Slate,* and *USA TODAY*. She is the author of *Screen Time: How Electronic Media—From Baby Videos to Educational Software—Affects Your Young Child* (Basic Books, 2012) and the co-author, with Michael H. Levine, of *Tap, Click, Read: Growing Readers in a World of Screens* (Jossey-Bass, 2015). Lisa won a 2012 gold Eddie magazine award for a *School Library Journal* article on e-books and has served on several national advisory committees on early education, including the Institute of Medicine's Committee on the Science of Children Birth to Age 8.

Devorah Heitner, PhD, is the founder of Raising Digital Natives, a source for parents and schools seeking advice on how to help children thrive in a world of digital connectedness. An experienced speaker, workshop leader, and consultant, she serves as a professional development resource for schools wishing to cultivate a culture of responsible digital citizenship. Her book, *Screenwise*, was published by Bibliomotion in 2016. After earning her PhD degree in media/technology and society from Northwestern University, she taught at DePaul University, Street Level Youth Media, and Northwestern University. She is delighted to be raising her own digital natives, too.

Kate Highfield, PhD, is a teacher educator from the Institute of Early Childhood, Macquarie University in Sydney, Australia. After teaching for more than 10 years, Kate now works with student teachers, children, and educators. Her PhD research focused on the use of simple robotics in mathematics learning and examined the key role of metacognition in problem solving. Her current research and teaching explore the use of interactive technologies for STEM learning and play, with a focus on how mobile and touch technology can be used as a tool to enhance learning. Kate is the editor of "Live Wires," a publication for Early Childhood Australia.

Sharon Thompson Hirschy has written several articles and developed a website focused on the use of technology with young children and early childhood educators. A former public school teacher, social worker, assistant director for the UNT Center for Parent Education, and private consultant, she is the author of articles, books, and curriculum for parents, child care teachers, and parent educators on child abuse, parenting skills, building parent–teacher partnerships, nutrition and fitness for families, and other topics related to early childhood educators and families.

Amy Koester, MLS, is the Youth & Family Program coordinator at the Skokie Public Library in Illinois. As a librarian serving children and their families, she has developed programming and resources that incorporate technology as a tool for building early literacy skills and learning of all kinds. She co-authored *Media Mentorship in Libraries Serving Youth*, a white paper adopted by the board of the Association for Library Service to Children (ALSC) in March 2015. Amy edited and co-authored the book *Young Children, New Media, and Libraries: A Guide for Incorporating New Media into Library Collections, Services, and Programs for Families and Children Ages 0-5* as part of her work with LittleeLit.com. She also co-authored a 2014 study and 2015 report, *Young Children, New Media, and Libraries*, a collaboration between LittleeLit.com, the iSchool at the University of Washington, and ALSC. She has written about digital media for children and other library initiatives for *Children and Libraries, School Library Journal,* and *LibrarySparks* magazine.

Kristelle Lavallee, MA, is the Content Strategist at the Center on Media and Child Health (CMCH) at Boston Children's Hospital. She holds a BA degree in psychology and communication arts from Gordon College and an MA degree in child development from Tufts University, where she based her thesis on her research for the PBS show, *WordGirl.* She manages the CMCH interactive and social media accounts and translates research into actionable advice, practical health resources, and through curricula that promote children's healthy and developmentally optimal creation and consumption of media. Her work has been presented at psychological, communications, and education conferences, and she has spoken to clinician, parent, educator, and community groups about the importance and impact of media literacy, social media, and family and child health.

Michael H. Levine is the founding executive director of the Joan Ganz Cooney Center at Sesame Workshop. The Center conducts research, builds multi-sector alliances, and catalyzes industry and policy reforms needed to advance high-quality media experiences for all children. Levine also serves on the executive team at Sesame Workshop, where he focuses on educational impact and philanthropic partnerships for the global nonprofit. Michael is a Pahara-Aspen Education Reform Fellow and a frequent advisor to the White House and the U.S. Department of Education. He writes for professional and public affairs journals, including a column for *Huffington Post,* and is a frequent keynote speaker at education and technology conferences around the world. His new book, co-authored with Lisa Guernsey of New America, is *Tap, Click, Read: Growing Readers in a World of Screens* (Jossey-Bass, 2015). He received his BS degree from Cornell University and PhD degree in social policy from the Heller School at Brandeis University.

Junlei Li, PhD, is the co-director of the Fred Rogers Center and an associate professor of psychological science at Saint Vincent College in Latrobe, Pennsylvania. In these roles, he seeks to understand and apply Fred Rogers' philosophy and approach to serve children and their helpers, and to strengthen human relationships surrounding children, promote children's "growing on the inside," and give positive meaning to the use of technology. Across all of his projects, he believes that real and lasting change starts with finding what ordinary people do extraordinarily well with children in everyday moments. Junlei has had the opportunity to learn from children's helpers across many diverse and low-resource developmental settings, including orphanages, child care, classrooms, and community programs.

M. Elena Lopez, PhD, is an associate director at Harvard Family Research Project (HFRP). Her research focuses on the relationships between families, schools, and communities as they relate to children's development and education. Additionally, she is a co-founder of the Family Involvement Network of Educators (FINE) and a regular contributor to the *FINE Newsletter*. She developed the Parent, Family, and Community Engagement framework in collaboration with the Office of Head Start and the National Center for Parent, Family, and Community Engagement. Her other professional experiences include evaluating public and philanthropic initiatives to promote children's well-being, managing education and health grants for a philanthropic foundation, and serving on national advisory and governing boards. Her recent publications include *Preparing Educators to Engage Families* (Sage, 2014) and numerous articles on family engagement in education.

Karen Nemeth, EdM, is an author, consultant, and presenter focusing on improving early childhood education for children who are dual-language learners. She is a writer and consulting editor for the NAEYC and holds leadership positions at the NABE and TESOL. She has published nine books and many articles for early childhood educators, and she provides resources for supporting diverse young learners and their families at Language Castle LLC. Karen helps Head Starts, preschools, government agencies, and organizations throughout the country to build effective systems and to put research into practice. She is a strong advocate for using digital media to help programs connect with diverse parents and support diverse young children.

Michael Rich, MD, MPH, is associate professor of pediatrics at Harvard Medical School, associate professor of social and behavioral sciences at the Harvard School of Public Health, and practices adolescent medicine at Boston Children's Hospital. He is the founder and director of the Center on Media and Child Health (CMCH) as well as a pediatrician, researcher, father, and media aficionado. As the Mediatrician, he offers research-based answers to parents', teachers', and clinicians' questions about children's media use and implications for their health and development. He provides information and strategies that are balanced, practical, and based in scientific evidence from the Database of Research (soon to be relaunched as Mediatrics), the comprehensive CMCH library of rigorous science from more than a dozen academic disciplines that address the effects of media on health and human development.

Faith Rogow, PhD, founded InsightersEducation.com in 1996 to help people learn from media and one another. She has taught thousands of teachers, students, child care professionals, media professionals, and parents to understand and harness the power of media. In ancient times, when TV ruled the media world, Dr. Rogow designed award-winning educational outreach for children's media, earning renown for her video, *Understanding Teletubbies: A Field Guide for Grown-Ups*. Her groundbreaking article, "The ABCs of Media Literacy," was one of the first to explore media literacy education methods that are developmentally appropriate for early childhood. Today she splits her time between writing discussion guides for independent documentary films and spreading the gospel of media literacy education. In her "spare time," she was the founding president of the National Association for Media Literacy Education and the co-author, with Cyndy Scheibe, of *The Teacher's Guide to Media Literacy: Critical Thinking in a Multimedia World* (Sage/Corwin, 2012).

Cyndy Scheibe, PhD, is a professor of psychology at Ithaca College where she has taught courses in developmental psychology, media research, and media literacy for more than 30 years and serves as the director of the Center for Research on the Effects of Television Lab and Archive. She is also the executive director of Project Look Sharp and co-author of *The Teacher's Guide to Media Literacy: Critical Thinking in a Multimedia World* (Sage/Corwin, 2012) with Faith Rogow. A dynamic speaker and workshop leader, she was a founding board member of the National Association for Media Literacy Education and is author of several articles on media literacy education and practice. She is a contributing editor to many of the media literacy curriculum kits developed by Project Look Sharp and co-author of the *Critical Thinking and Health Kit* series based on media literacy for elementary grades.

Fran Simon, MEd, has been an early childhood advocate and educational technologist since 1981. Fran has a BA degree and MEd degree in early childhood education. In graduate school, Fran focused on educational technology and leadership. After working as a multi-site child care administrator for 15 years, she worked in educational publishing and advocacy in marketing and interactive online system development for early childhood administrators. Fran is currently a consultant who works with nonprofit organizations and companies that serve the early childhood sector. She is co-author, with Karen Nemeth, of *Digital Decisions: Choosing the Right Technology Tools for Early Childhood Education* (Gryphon House, 2010), the author of many journal articles on educational technology, and a frequent conference presenter. She is also the producer of Early Childhood Investigations Webinars, former co-facilitator of the NAEYC

Technology and Young Children Interest Forum, and the co-founder of Early Childhood Technology Network.

Heather Weiss, PhD, is the founder and director of the Harvard Family Research Project (HFRP) and is a senior research associate and lecturer at the Harvard Graduate School of Education. She was the Project's principal investigator for the Office of Head Start's National Center for Parent, Family, and Community Engagement (2011–2015). Her recent publications focus on reframing research and evaluation to support continuous improvement and democratic decision making, examining the case for family engagement in anywhere, anytime learning from a research and policy perspective, and assessing new ways of providing and evaluating professional development. She is a consultant and advisor to numerous foundations on strategic grant making and evaluation. She received her doctorate in education and social policy from the Harvard Graduate School of Education, and she was a postdoctoral research fellow at the Yale Bush Center in Child Development and Social Policy.

Foreword

Ellen Galinsky

Author, *Mind in the Making: Seven Essential Life Skills Every Child Needs*, and executive director, *Mind in the Making*

Just say the words "children and digital media" and see what images come to mind. I suspect they are images of children, eyes transfixed on a screen, not looking up for hours on end; images of children, side by side, texting, not talking; images of adults out with their kids at a museum or restaurant, connected to their smartphones, not their kids; images of adults and children leading virtual lives, not real lives.

In response comes the admonition—"no screen time!"—especially for young children. While the research evidence is clear that very young children learn from interacting with people, not technology, what about older children? Parents who hand their child a smartphone often report feeling the harsh glares of those around, as if they are selfishly feeding their children addictive junk food in this media-saturated world.

Entering into this standoff—at just the right time—is the book that educators need: *Family Engagement in the Digital Age: Early Childhood Educators as Media Mentors,* written by an all-star cast of digital media experts and edited by the inestimable Chip Donohue. It doesn't have to be this way, they argue. In fact, they go further to say that technology is merely a tool—a powerful tool to be sure—but one that we *can* use for good.

The book goes still further by combining the critical importance of family engagement with new technology, showing that technology can become a tool for engaging children and families in learning together. And to do this, they promote a significant new role for educators: "media mentors." This is the essence of the book's brilliance.

This book backs up this new role with compelling thought leadership. For example, Jeremy Boyle, Melissa Butler, and Junlei Li challenge us to help children learn to engage meaningfully with technology, reframing the debate away from getting access to the "stuff of technology" to the "thinking behind technology." They write, "We would like to see more children engage with technology in ways similar to how they might with mud, pots and pans, puddles, or shadows"—in other words, figuring out how technology works and creating technologies and products of their own.

On these pages, you will find media mentors to help you make this transformation with what they call "helpful hints." Among my favorites is "Message From Me," a new tool for families in Pittsburgh that enables young children to document what they've done in school using digital cameras and microphones and then to send their parents a message about it via email, voice mail, or text. This tool—created by a collaboration between Carnegie Mellon University's Community Robotics, Education and Technology Empowerment Lab and the Pennsylvania Association for the Education of Young Children—prompts rich discussion between children and parents and engages families in their children's learning.

Examples from media mentors such as this one show that family engagement is *not* sending messages out from the expert educators to families; family engagement is *not* a one-way street, from educator to family. Family engagement is, as M. Elena Lopez, Margaret Caspe, and Heather Weiss write, a "shared responsibility" that is systemic, that goes beyond "random acts of technology." I see family engagement as truly engaging everyone in learning together—children, educators, and families. As Jeremy Boyle, Melissa Butler, and Junlei Li write, it is "wonderful to not know"—what is truly wonderful is figuring this new terrain out together.

Essential to this new terrain is building a cadre of media mentors, providing training and public policies to support them, and testing what works, write Lisa Guernsey and Michael H. Levine.

I can remember the advent of television for children in the 1960s. There was a similar standoff, with some experts arguing "no television," but here it is, a half a century later, completely ubiquitous, with hugely varying quality and impact. Digital media, including television, are even more ubiquitous, but with the role of media mentors, we have the genuine opportunity to figure it out together. To paraphrase the fantastic digital media message from Vroom—an initiative to share the science of early learning from the Bezos Family Foundation that I have had the honor of working on for four years— "we already have what it takes!"

Preface

Family Engagement in the Digital Age: Early Childhood Educators as Media Mentors explores the essential roles educators play in implementing technology-mediated practices that improve communication, strengthen the home–school connection, enhance parent involvement, promote family engagement, and build a sense of community for young children, parents, and families. This book explores the meaning and importance of family engagement in the digital age, the role technology can play in empowering and engaging parents, caregivers, and families, and the emerging role of media mentors to guide young children and their families in the twenty-first century.

The contributing authors have written 17 chapters that offer early childhood educators in formal and informal settings a guide for effective technology-mediated strategies to improve communication, strengthen the home–school connection, encourage parent involvement, and enhance family engagement. They offer a strengths-based approach to parent and family empowerment based on a deep understanding of child development theory, developmentally appropriate practices, best practices in parent, family, and community engagement, and the effective, appropriate, and intentional use of technology in early childhood settings to support learning, communication, and collaboration.

This book offers early childhood teacher educators; professional development providers; educators in pre-service, in-service, and continuing education in higher education and early childhood settings; and informal educators in libraries, museums; and out-of-school time programs a practical guide to using technology as a tool for parent, family, and community engagement. Spotlight on Engagement case studies, success stories, best practices, and helpful hints for educators are integrated throughout the book and woven into the chapters. The contents and approach will help educators develop the disposition, knowledge, experience, and competencies needed to reach a level of digital media literacy necessary to become media mentors for young children, parents, and families and to support parents as media mentors for their children at home.

The content is based on evidence from current research, the literature, and a set of principles and best practices in parent empowerment and family engagement based on the Head Start Parent, Family, and Community Framework; the Department of Education Dual Capacity-Building Framework for Family-School Partnerships; the work of the Harvard Family Research Project; the NAEYC Principles of Effective Practice for Family Engagement; and the Families and Media Project at the Joan Ganz Cooney Center at Sesame Workshop.

Building on these engagement principles and best practices, the book explores the uses of technology and digital media to strengthen home–school connections and enhance family engagement that are based on the NAEYC & Fred Rogers Center Joint Position Statement on *Technology and Interactive Media as Tools in Early Childhood Programs Serving Children from Birth Through Age 8*. Recent position statements and guidelines from the American Academy of Pediatrics, HighScope, RAND Corporation, and Zero to Three, and recent research from the Office of Planning, Research and Evaluation on the *Uses of Technology to Support Early Childhood Practice: Parent, Family and Community Engagement* are also integrated into the discussion.

The editor and contributing authors are all thought leaders in early childhood education, family engagement, and technology integration. They bring a range of perspectives from their work in higher education, teacher education, and professional development; consulting and training; libraries; parent education; pediatric health; policy analysis; and research. They represent a number of leading organizations including The Center on Media and Child Health at Boston Children's Hospital; Fred Rogers Center on Early Learning and Children's Media at Saint Vincent College; Harvard Family Research Project; Joan Ganz Cooney Center at Sesame Workshop; New America; RAND Corporation; and the Technology in Early Childhood (TEC) Center at Erikson Institute.

Written from their individual perspectives and presented in an engaging style, the authors have included relevant research; grounded effective teaching practices in child development theory and developmentally appropriate practice; provided examples of family engagement principles and guidelines in practice; included real-life stories and best practices shared by exemplary early childhood professionals and programs; innovative approaches to family engagement using technology tools and digital media; helpful hints for media mentors; and a collection of resources and links to learn more.

How This Book Is Organized

The book is organized into three sections: Technology, Young Children, and Family Engagement; Technology Tools and Techniques for Empowering Educators and Families; and Innovative Approaches to Technology-Enhanced

Family Engagement. Part I, Chapter 1 sets the stage for exploring the connection between family engagement and technology, beginning with three essays exploring perspectives on media mentorship, diversity, and how technology and digital media in the early years can inform our thinking about technology-mediated family engagement. Chapter 2 introduces the idea of developmentally appropriate technology integration, while Chapter 3 nudges readers to re-imagine children's engagement with technology. Chapter 4 introduces the Parents, Families and Community Engagement framework and reviews current research and best practices. Part I ends with Chapter 5 which connects the ideas of behavioral "nudges" with innovative technologies and strategies that create and sustain connections between programs and families.

Part II introduces a range of technology tools and techniques that can empower parents and families when implemented by educators as media mentors. The chapters explore lessons learned from Fred Rogers's approach to parent engagement; the metaphor of weather forecasting as a way of thinking about children's experiences in the digital age; strategies for supporting heathy media habits; what educators can do to support parents as media mentors for their children; and advice for educators as today's media mentors.

Part III explores a variety of innovative approaches to technology-enhanced family engagement including: tools and systems to facilitate family engagement; media literacy approaches; family engagement strategies for *all* languages, cultures, and abilities; the role of librarians as media mentors; and lessons learned from public media and transmedia approaches. The book ends with a call for new allies and the need to address policy and research needs.

Pedagogical Features

There are a number of recurring features that will help you consider your own role at the intersection of technology and family engagement and will provide you with additional readings, resources, and links to explore. Features include *Key Messages From the Joint Position Statement* to link principles and practices from the position statement with family engagement approaches; *Family Engagement Strategies* with practical examples and tips; *Spotlight on Engagement* case studies and stories demonstrating innovation and effective practices in technology-mediated family engagement; and *Helpful Hints for Media Mentors*, a collection of practical tips, recommendations, and action steps for applying what you've learned in your interactions with young children, parents, and families. In addition to a list of *References* that have been cited in each chapter, there is also a collection of additional *Resources*. The *Learn more…* section includes an additional collection of resources and links for those readers who want to dig deeper and explore the topics, key concepts, and big ideas presented in the chapter.

Spotlight on Engagement Profiles

Throughout this book you'll find examples, stories and case studies from exemplary family engagement programs and initiatives. The contributing authors have called out some of the best and most effective family engagement strategies to help identify the active ingredients in successful technology-mediated and enhanced parent, family, and community engagement efforts. These success stories include family engagement strategies that welcome all families; inclusive approaches to ensure every child belongs; innovations in media mentorship from children's librarians; transmedia approaches using public television; apps that enable connections between children and their families; and technology-mediated home visiting and early intervention programs that use email, text messages, apps, and video examples to empower parents and engage families. Here are brief descriptions and profiles, adapted from the websites, of the programs that were highlighted by the authors. We hope you'll take time to explore these programs and websites and learn more about these innovative approaches to family engagement.

aXcess Newark has created the Newark Family Engagement Directory, a comprehensive database with up-to-date information on sources available to Newark families and residents including child care, financial assistance, children's services, health care, employment and other services. Learn more at http://axcessnewark.com/vertex.php.

Comienza en Casa | It Starts at Home integrates technology use into a curriculum that provides parents of migrant preschool and kindergarten children with activities and information to promote their child's school readiness at home. Comienza en Casa is a program of Mano a Mano | Hand in Hand. Learn more at www.manomaine.org/programs/mep/comienzaencasa. *See the Spotlight on Engagement stories on pages 197 and 214.*

CPB/PBS Ready to Learn is a cooperative initiative funded and managed by the U.S. Department of Education's Office of Innovation and

Improvement. It supports the development of innovative educational television and digital media targeted to preschool and early elementary school children and their families. The goal is to promote early learning and school readiness, with a particular interest in reaching low-income children. In addition to creating television and other media products, the program promotes national distribution of the programming, effective educational uses, community-based outreach and research on educational effectiveness. The Ready to Learn case studies and *Spotlight on Engagement stories about KBTC and WGBH* in Chapter 16 were organized by the Corporation for Public Broadcasting www.cpb.org and PBS www.pbs.org and were contributed by EDC/SRI www.edc.org and https://www.sri.com, WestEd www.wested.org, KBTC www.kbtc.org and WGBH www.wgbh.org. Learn more at www.cpb.org/rtl/ and at the Department of Education's Ready to Learn website at http://www2.ed.gov/programs/rtltv/indev.html. *See the Spotlight on Engagement stories on pages 257 and 258.*

HITN Early Learning Collaborative Ready to Learn project, administered through the U.S. Department of Education's Office of Innovation and Improvement, encourages the development and use of video and digital programming to promote early learning and school readiness for young children and their families, and the dissemination of educational outreach programs and materials to promote school readiness. A Ready to Learn grant was awarded to HITN in 2010 to support the development and distribution of the research-based Pocoyo PlaySet, educational outreach materials and broad distribution to ensure as many young children as possible, particularly low-income children, have access to these educational materials to ensure that they start school prepared for success and at the same level as their peers. Learn more at http://earlylearningcollaborative.org.

Imajine That is an interactive children's museum, located at the Riverwalk in Lawrence, Massachusetts, which features pop up programming in various public schools and community centers. Imajinators (Imajine That staff) conduct hands on activities for children and families to engage in together in local libraries, and town events throughout the year. The focus is on family and child engagement. Learn more at www.imajinethat.com.

Kindoma makes communications tools for families around the world who are looking for better ways to communicate. Kindoma has created video calling and messaging apps specifically for young children and their loved ones that provide added interactivity, such as reading, drawing, or playing games to improve the quality of video calls. Learn more at http://kindoma.com. *See the Spotlight on Engagement story on page 133.*

Message From Me enables young children to better communicate with parents about their daytime activities at child care centers through the use of digital cameras, microphones, email, phone messaging and other technologies. The program is a collaboration between the CREATE Lab, the Children's School of Carnegie Mellon University, and the Pittsburgh Association for the Education of Young Children. Learn more at www. messagefromme.org/. *See the Spotlight on Engagement story on page 56.*

MomsRising is a network of people united by the goal of building a more family-friendly America. It is a transformative on-the-ground and online multicultural organization of more than a million members and over a hundred aligned organizations. MomsRising is also a new media outlet with over 1,000 bloggers and a combined estimated blogging and social media readership reach to over 3 million people. Learn more at www. momsrising.org/.

PACT (Parents and Children Together) is a prevention/early intervention program that provides in-home counseling, skill building, and support. The program is based on the HOMEBUILDERS' model of family preservation and operates in Washington State. The goals of the PACT program are to help families improve family functioning, increase parenting skills, improve children's behavior at home and in school, and increase family social supports and social connections. PACT collaborates with schools, public health, juvenile court, and community organizations to strengthen neighborhood and community supports, and to help families and children coordinate available resources, supports, and services. Learn more at www.institutefamily.org/programs_PACT.asp.

Parent-Child Home Program (PCHP) is a nationwide network of program sites providing low-income families with the necessary skills and tools to ensure their children achieve their greatest potential in school and in life. The National Center assists underserved communities in replicating and expanding PCHP's proven school readiness program that builds early parent–child verbal interaction and learning at home. PCHP strengthens families and communities, prepares the workforce of the future and envisions a world where every child enters school ready to succeed because every parent has the knowledge, skills, and resources to build school readiness where it starts: the home. Learn more at www.parent-child.org.

Parents as Teachers provides a proven home visiting model for organizations and professionals who meet the evolving needs of families with the goal of helping young children grow up healthy, safe and ready to learn. The Parents as Teachers network supports hundreds of thousands of families in all 50 states as well as many other countries through a proven parent education model featuring intimate, in-home visits with parents and children. Parents as Teachers equips early childhood organizations and professionals with information and tools that are relevant – and widely applicable—to today's parents, families and children. Learn more at www. parentsasteachers.org. *See the Spotlight on Engagement story on page 88.*

Parents Know (now Help Me Grow), is a program of the Minnesota Department of Education, is an online resource filled with convenient and trusted child development, health, and parenting information, founded on the belief that parents are the first and most important teacher in a child's life. The site has been developed for parents with extensive input of parents and provides up-to-date, research-based information on children from birth through grade 12, strategies to support children's learning, newsletters, expert tips, an interactive early childhood and child care search, connections to Minnesota services and resources, video clips, a parent Web literacy tutorial and a customized search function of high quality, non-commercial child development and health Websites. Learn more at http://helpmegrowmn. org/HMG/index.htm.

Raising a Reader engages caregivers in a routine of book sharing with their children from birth through age eight to foster healthy brain development, healthy relationships, a love of reading, and the literacy skills critical for school success – with special attention to children at highest-risk for educational failure. Raising a Reader reaches more than 130,000 children and families each year, nearly 80% of whom are living at or below the poverty level and more than half being English Language Learners. Learn more at www.raisingareader.org/.

Reach Out and Read is a nonprofit organization that gives young children a foundation for success by incorporating books into pediatric care and encouraging families to read aloud together. The program builds on the unique relationship between parents and medical providers to develop critical early reading skills in children, beginning in infancy. As recommended by the American Academy of Pediatrics, the program incorporates early literacy into pediatric practice, equipping parents with tools and knowledge to ensure that their children are prepared to learn when they start school. Reach Out and Read serves nearly 4.5 million children and their families annually. Learn more at www.reachoutandread.org.

ReadyRosie is an early education tool that helps schools and communities across the nation deepen and scale their parent engagement efforts by leveraging the power of video modeling and mobile technology to meet and equip parents where they are. ReadyRosie has hundreds of brief videos in English and Spanish that model everyday interactions in familiar environments with real parents. Parents and caregivers who participate are equipped to have more meaningful interactions and turn everyday situations into learning opportunities. Learn more at http://readyrosie. com/. *See the Spotlight on Engagement story on page 181.*

Ready4K is a text messaging program for parents of preschoolers designed to help them prepare their children for kindergarten. Each week during the school year, parents receive three texts about important kindergarten readiness skills. Ready4K text messages were developed at Stanford University based on child development research and linked to state educational standards. Ready4K is the first research-based text messaging program for parents of preschoolers. Learn more at https://cepa.stanford. edu/cepalabs/ready4k. *See the Spotlight on Engagement story on page 89.*

Tech Goes Home (TGH) helps to provide under-served residents the opportunity, tools, education, and access required for 21st century skills development. TGH prioritizes low-income and underserved populations, including people from challenged neighborhoods, those without technology at home, the unemployed and underemployed, people who do not speak English, and individuals with disabilities. TGH is focused on tackling the entrenched barriers to technology adoption and Internet access in Boston and across the US. Learn more at www.techgoeshome.org.

Text4baby is a free service provided by the nonprofit organization, ZERO TO THREE, and Voxiva, Inc. Women who text BABY (or BEBE for Spanish) to 511411 receive free text messages three times per week, timed to their due date or their baby's birth date, through pregnancy and up until the baby's first birthday. Text4baby sends personalized messages with trusted information developed by experts from all over the country. There is also an app that provides additional information about baby's development, pregnancy, child care tips, and more. Learn more at www.text4baby.org/.

Too Small to Fail helps parents and businesses take meaningful actions to improve the health and well-being of children ages zero to five, so that more of America's children are prepared to succeed in the 21st century. Too Small to Fail promotes new research on the science of children's brain development, early learning and early health, and helps parents, businesses and communities identify specific actions to improve the lives of young children. Too Small to Fail uses email, social media, and other technology-driven tools and innovative approaches to inform and empower parents and business leaders to track their progress and measure their success. Too Small to Fail is about parents, caregivers, other concerned individuals, and the private sector coming together to take small, research-based actions with big impacts. Learn more at http://toosmall.org.

Toyota Family Trails is a partnership between the National Center for Families Learning (NCFL) and Toyota. The partners believe that all parents – regardless of socioeconomic or educational level – can help their children succeed in school and in life. Families are the one constant across a lifetime of educational experiences, but family engagement in education doesn't happen on its own. NCFL supports families learning together, bridging the gap in education that often exists between school, home, and community. Learn more at http://familytrails.com.

Vroom is an innovative, science-based parent engagement program that turns shared moments into brain building moments. The brain develops most rapidly during the first five years of life so for everyday moments like mealtime, bathtime, or any time in between, Vroom provides resources and prompts about ways to nurture children's growing minds. Vroom offers brain building basics, daily activities, a daily Vroom video, free downloadable resources and an app. Vroom's parent empowerment message begins with, "You already have what it takes." Learn more at www.joinvroom.org and see Mind in the Making at www.mindinthemaking.org.

Acknowledgments

An edited volume such as this one takes a lot of hard work from everyone involved. Thanks to the 25 contributing authors who agreed to write the 17 chapters that make up this book, and to meet very tight writing and editing deadlines in their already busy lives. It is a privilege to bring together ideas and approaches from this collection of thought leaders, trusted sources, and innovators who are each moving the needle on family engagement in the digital age. I eagerly but humbly accepted the challenge of gathering their innovative ideas and examples into this book. Being able to learn with and from each of them has been an honor. If every child, parent, caregiver, and educator needs a media mentor to successfully navigate the digital age, then I have been most fortunate to have these 25 outstanding role models as my guides.

Thanks to all of the contributors of the *Spotlight on Engagement* case studies, stories, and profiles that have been integrated into the book between chapters and within chapters to connect research, theory, and practice with innovations in technology-mediated family engagement. I asked the contributing authors to identify and write about innovative and effective programs and initiatives in their chapters, and along the way they recommended many of the exemplary programs and practices that have been included.

Spotlight on Engagement contributors included Message From Me by Gregg Behr and Remake Learning; Parents as Teachers by Jill Saunders, Scott Hippert, and Donna Hunt O'Brien; Kindoma by Carly Shuler and the Kindoma team; ReadyRosie by Emily Roden and the ReadyRosie team; and two stories from Comienza en Casa contributed by Ana Blagojevic, Patricia Garcia, Adriana Paniagua, Juana Vazgez, Bonnie Blagojevic, and Edith Flores. Ready to Learn stories were contributed by Betsy McCarthy, Sarah Atienza, Linlin Li, Ursula Sexton, and Michelle Tiu at WestEd; Naomi Hupert, Shelley Pasnik, Savitha Moorthy, and Carlin Llorente of Education Development Center and SRI International; Dawn Cuthbertson and Ed Ulman of KBTC in Tacoma, Washington; and Mary Haggerty and Devon Smith for WGBH in Boston and the Corporation for Public Broadcasting. Thanks to Pam Johnson and my colleagues at CPB/PBS for organizing these storytellers and sharing their stories.

Thanks to Ellen Galinsky for writing the Foreword and for inspiring all of us to innovate on behalf of young children and families. There is no one who has done more to develop strategies and tools to engage and empower families through her work-life initiatives at the Families and Work Institute, her Seven Essential Life Skills Every Child Needs from Mind in the Making, and the blend of enabling technology and engagement strategies in Vroom. If there is one parent empowerment message from this work that I would like to believe captures the spirit of this book, it is the first message parents receive from Vroom that offers reassurance that, "You already have what it takes."

Thanks to my colleagues at Erikson Institute who have supported my efforts in editing two books, and the time away for professional travel that has been such a significant part of the work of the TEC Center to guide thinking and practice around intentional and appropriate use of technology and digital media in the early years. I'm inspired by their tireless efforts to improve the care and education of children age birth to eight and their commitment to understanding diversity and the complexity of family, culture, and community factors in child development. A special thanks to the Distance Learning and Continuing Education team who have remained innovative and productive despite the distractions from my travel and the demands of editing this book. In particular, thanks to Mike Paulucci, who helped me prepare the images and graphics. Our "family" includes Mike Maxse, Erin Silva, Matt Zaradich, Mike Paulucci, Gabi Frahm, Dorothy Jagonase in DLCE, and Tamara Kaldor and Katie Paciga from the TEC Center—they empower and engage me every day.

I also acknowledge my colleagues and partners at the Fred Rogers Center for Early Learning and Children's Media at Saint Vincent College where I am a senior fellow and advisor. Rick Fernandes, Junlei Li (also a contributing author), Tanya Baronti, and Karen Struble Meyers have become partners in advancing the principles and guidelines of the joint position statement and leaders in providing professional development and resources that empower early childhood educators, librarians, parents, caregivers, and others to become media mentors in the digital age.

A final thanks to my immediate family—Maria Hill, SarahMaria Donohue, and Laura Donohue—and to the extended Donohue, Belger, Hill, Vetter, and Ostermick families. You have all nurtured me and helped me better understand the meaning of family and the importance of family engagement. The support, encouragement, and love that flows to me from every member of my families can be found on the pages of this book.

Chip Donohue

Abbreviations and Acronyms

AAC Intervention	Augmentative/Alternative Communication Intervention
AAP	American Academy of Pediatrics
ACF	Administration for Children and Families
ALA	American Library Association
ALSC	Association for Library Service to Children
AT	Assistive Technology
ATL	Approaches to Learning
BCH	Boston Children's Hospital
CAST	Center for Applied Special Technology
CMCH	Center on Media and Child Health
CMHD	Center on Media and Human Development
COSN	Consortium for School Networking
CPB	Corporation for Public Broadcasting
CSM	Common Sense Media
CVS	Computer Vision Syndrome
DAP	Developmentally Appropriate Practice
DEC	Division for Early Childhood
DHHS	Department of Health and Human Services
DLL	Dual Language Learner
DML	Digital Media Literacy
DOE	Department of Education
ECLKC	Early Childhood Learning and Knowledge Center
ECRR	Every Child Ready to Read
EDC	Education Development Center
ELA	English Language Arts
ELL	English Language Learner
EMR	Electromagnetic radiation
ESL	English as a Second Language
ESSA	Every Student Succeeds Act
FINE	Family Involvement Network of Educators

Fred Rogers Center	Fred Rogers Center for Early Learning and Children's Media at Saint Vincent College
HFRP	Harvard Family Research Project
HHS	Health and Human Services
HITN ELC	Hispanic Information and Telecommunications Network Early Learning Collaborative
IARC	International Agency for Research on Cancer
IDEA	Individuals with Disabilities Education Act
IMLS	Institute of Museum and Library Services
IOM	Institute of Medicine of the National Academies
ISTE	International Society for Technology in Education
KITE	Kids Included through Technology are Enriched
NAEYC	National Association for the Education of Young Children
NAMLE	National Association for Media Literacy Education
NCFL	National Center for Families Learning
NELP	National Early Literacy Panel
NETP	National Education Technology Plan
NGSS	Next Generation Science Standards
NSF	National Science Foundation
OHS	Office of Head Start
OPRE	Office of Planning, Research & Evaluation
PACT	Parents and Children Together
PBS	Public Broadcasting Service
PECS	Picture Exchange Communication System
PFCE	Parent, Family, and Community Engagement
PLA	Public Library Association
PLN	Personal Learning Network
RAR	Raising a Reader
ROR	Reach Out and Read
RSI	Repetitive Stress Injuries
RTL	Ready to Learn
SEAT	Special Education Assistive Technology Center
SFUSD	San Francisco Unified School District
SOAR Award	Safe, On Task, Awesome Attitude, Respectful
STEAM	Science, Technology, Engineering, Art, Math
STEM	Science, Technology, Engineering, Math
TEC Center	Technology in Early Childhood Center
THA	Tacoma Housing Authority
TPS	Tacoma Public Schools
UDL	Universal Design for Learning
VOD	Video on Demand
WHO	World Health Organization

Introduction

Setting the Context: Family Engagement in the Digital Age

Chip Donohue

Family Engagement in the Digital Age: Early Childhood Educators as Media Mentors was written to provide a thought-provoking guide to using technology as a tool for parent, family, and community engagement. The intended audience is anyone who works with or on behalf of young children: early childhood teacher educators; professional development providers; educators in pre-service, in-service, and continuing education; classroom teachers and family child care providers; informal educators in libraries, museums, and out-of-school time programs; and parents and families. The intended outcome is for educators to develop the disposition, knowledge, experience, and competencies needed to achieve a level of digital media literacy necessary to become media mentors for young children, parents, and families and to support parents as media mentors for their children at home.

In these chapters, we explore the ecology of family engagement in homes, educational settings, and communities and offer a gentle nudge to early childhood educators toward effective technology-mediated strategies to engage families using a strengths-based approach to parent, caregiver, and family empowerment. Our strategies and approach are built upon a deep understanding of child development theory; developmentally appropriate practices; best practices in parent, family, and community engagement; and the effective, appropriate and intentional use of technology in early childhood settings—the active ingredients of digital-age family engagement.

Who Are Parents, Caregivers, and Families?

We recognize and celebrate the many kinds of parents and caregivers who care for, work with, and work on behalf of young children and families. Throughout this book, we use the words *parents* and *caregivers* to refer to biological and adoptive parents and other adults who are serving as children's primary caregivers, such as parents, grandparents, other adult family members, and foster parents. We also celebrate the diversity and complexity of family types and social units that young children live in. For our investigation of family engagement strategies and best practice, we use the word *family* to include two or more people related by blood, marriage, or adoption who share a mutual commitment to the relationships and well-being of the members.

We use the word *educators* to refer to adults who work with young children and families in any formal or informal early childhood setting.

We have adapted our definition of *media mentor* from our friends who are leading the charge in children's libraries (see Chapter 15, "Children's Librarians as Media Mentors" by Cen Campbell and Amy Koester). They describe media mentor as anyone who supports children and their families in their media decisions and practice around healthy media use and who has access to and shares recommendations for and research on children's media use.

As you will learn, media mentors come in all shapes and sizes and include a variety of personal roles and professional responsibilities, including but not limited to, early childhood educators, family child care providers, early intervention specialists, child life specialists, home visitors, pediatric health providers, librarians, children's museum and out-of-school time staff, parents, caregivers, and other family members. While each of these roles is distinct, the possibilities for new collaborations across settings and for engaging new allies for children, parents, families, and educators is real and compelling in the digital age of connected learning.

Family Engagement: A Working Definition

In Chapter 4, "Logging in to Family Engagement in the Digital Age," M. Elena Lopez, Margaret Caspe, and Heather Weiss from the Harvard Family Research Project (HFRP) connect the dots between the Head Start Framework for Parent, Family, and Community Engagement with effective and emerging technology-mediated approaches to digital age family engagement. HFRP was a partner in the development of the Office of Head Start, National Center on Parent, Family, and Community Engagement and the PFCE framework that will be introduced below.

To set the stage for all that follows, here is a primer on big ideas and key concepts in family engagement that have guided our work. I begin with some operating assumptions we made about the goals and outcomes for family engagement. We connect family engagement with active, respectful, and effective efforts focused on positive relationships, child health, and school readiness. When done well and intentionally, family engagement relationships are reciprocal—part of an ongoing partnership dedicated to family well-being, children's learning, and healthy growth and development. Family engagement is linked to and supports children's development, learning, and success in school. We believe in a strength-based approach to parent empowerment that recognizes, respects, and supports families as connected members of their communities, as advocates and leaders, and as lifelong teachers and learners who strive for success for their children and for their families.

We have based our definition of family engagement on recent frameworks, research, and reports from the Office of Head Start, the Department of Education, NAEYC, and the Harvard Family Research Project.

Essential Family Engagement Frameworks

- Head Start Parent Family and Community Engagement (PFCE) Framework http://eclkc.ohs.acf.hhs.gov/hslc/standards/im/2011/pfce-framework.pdf
- Department of Education Dual Capacity-Building Framework www.ed.gov/family-and-community-engagement
- NAEYC Principles of Effective Practice for Family Engagement, Engaging Diverse Families Project www.naeyc.org/familyengagement/principles
- Harvard Family Research Project www.hfrp.org

In an integrated review of the literature (Halgunseth, Peterson, Stark, & Moodie, 2009), the authors articulated a definition of family engagement that included six essential factors.

1 **Early childhood education programs encourage and validate family participation in decision making related to their children's education.** Families should act as advocates for their children and early childhood education program by actively taking part in decision making opportunities.
2 **Consistent, two-way communication is facilitated through multiple forms and is responsive to the linguistic preference of the family.** Communication should be both school and family initiated and should be timely and continuous, inviting conversations about both the child's educational experience as well as the larger program.
3 **Families and early childhood education programs collaborate and exchange knowledge.** Family members share their unique knowledge and skills through volunteering and actively engaging in events and activities at schools. Teachers seek out information about their students' lives, families, and communities and integrate this information into their curriculum and instructional practices.
4 **Early childhood education programs and families place an emphasis on creating and sustaining learning activities at home** and in the community that extend the teachings of the program so as to enhance each child's early learning.

5 **Families create a home environment that values learning and supports programs.** Programs and families collaborate in establishing goals for children both at home and at school.

6 **Early childhood education programs create an ongoing and comprehensive system for promoting family engagement** by ensuring that program leadership and teachers are dedicated and trained and receive the supports they need to fully engage families.

> From *Family Engagement, Diverse Families, and Early Childhood Programs: An Integrated Review of the Literature* (2009), pp. 3–4
> http://naeyc.org/files/naeyc/file/research/FamEngage.pdf

On NAEYC's Engaging Diverse Families Project website, six related principles of effective family engagement to look for in action are identified:

1 programs invite families to participate in decision making and goal setting for their child;
2 teachers and programs engage families in two-way communication;
3 programs and teachers engage families in ways that are truly reciprocal;
4 programs provide learning activities for the home and in the community;
5 programs invite families to participate in program-level decisions and wider advocacy efforts; and
6 programs implement a comprehensive program-level system of family engagement.

> Developed by NAEYC's Engaging Diverse Families Project,
> www.naeyc.org/familyengagement

The Head Start Parent, Family, and Community Engagement Framework, Promoting Family Engagement and School Readiness from Prenatal to Age 8 (2011) identifies seven outcomes for parent and family engagement.

1 **Family well-being**: Parents and families are safe and healthy and have increased financial security.
2 **Positive parent–child relationships**: Beginning with transitions to parenthood, parents and families develop warm relationships that nurture their child's learning and development.
3 **Families as lifelong educators**: Parents and families observe, guide, promote, and participate in the everyday learning of their children at home and school and in their communities.
4 **Families as learners**: Parents and families advance their own learning interests through education, training, and other experiences that support their parenting, careers, and life goals.
5 **Family engagement in transitions**: Parents and families support and advocate for their child's learning and development as they transition to

new learning environments, including Early Head Start to Head Start, Early Head Start/Head Start to other early learning environments, and Head Start to kindergarten through elementary school.

6 **Family connections to peers and community**: Parents and families form connections with peers and mentors in formal or informal social networks that are supportive and/or educational and that enhance social well-being and community life.

7 **Families as advocates and leaders**: Parents and families participate in leadership development, decision making, program policy development, or community and state organizing activities to improve children's development and learning experiences.

From *The Head Start Parent, Family, and Community Engagement Framework* (2011), p. 6

Finally, the Department of Education (DOE) has added the Dual Capacity-Building Framework for Family–School Partnerships to the conversations around family and community engagement and family-school partnerships. The capacity-building framework honors and recognizes families' existing knowledge, skill, and preferred forms of engagement; creates welcoming, inviting school cultures that promote family engagement and development; and connects family engagement initiatives to student learning and outcomes.

The DOE seeks to empower educators and mentors who can empower children and families to be:

- *supporters* of their children's learning and development;
- *encouragers* of an achievement identity, a positive self image, and a "can do" spirit in their children;
- *monitors* of their children's time, behavior, boundaries, and resources;
- *models* of lifelong learning and enthusiasm for education;
- *advocates/activists* for improved learning opportunities for their children
- and at their schools;
- *decision makers/choosers* of educational options for their children, the school, and community; and
- *collaborators* with school staff and members of the community on issues of school improvement and reform.

From the *Dual Capacity-Building Framework for Family–School Partnerships*, pp. 2–3, www2.ed.gov/documents/family-community/partnership-frameworks.pdf

Family Engagement Meets Twenty-First-Century Technology

This book is about blending what we know about family engagement with what we know about effective technology-mediated and technology-enhanced approaches that leverage digital technology and new media to strengthen family engagement efforts and improve outcomes for children, parents, and families—and what we are learning about the role of media mentors in connecting the dots.

Key Message from the Joint Position Statement

With technology becoming more prevalent as a means of sharing information and communicating with one another, early childhood educators have an opportunity to build stronger relationships with parents and enhance family engagement. Early childhood educators always have had a responsibility to support parents and families by sharing knowledge about child development and learning.

Technology tools offer new opportunities for educators to build relationships, maintain ongoing communication, and exchange information and share online resources with parents and families. Likewise, parents and families can use technology to ask questions, seek advice, share information about their child, and feel more engaged in the program and their child's experiences there.

NAEYC & Fred Rogers Center (2012), p. 7

Our thinking about technology and digital media in the early years and new tools for family engagement has been informed by a number of position statements and guidelines issued by leading early childhood organizations recently and over the past few years. The guidance and recommendations from these technology frameworks are woven throughout the book, and Key Messages from the NAEYC and Fred Rogers Center joint position statement (2012) are highlighted in many of the chapters.

Essential Technology Frameworks, Guidelines, and Resources

- National Association for the Education of Young Children, & Fred Rogers Center for Early Learning and Children's Media at Saint Vincent College. (2012). *Technology and Interactive Media as Tools in Early Childhood Programs Serving Children from Birth through Age 8* www.naeyc.org/content/technology-and-young-children
- Department of Education, *National Education Technology Plan, Future Ready Learning: Reimagining the Role of Technology in Education* http://tech.ed.gov/netp/
- Institute of Medicine and the National Research Council, *Transforming the Workforce for Children From Birth through Age 8: A Unifying Foundation* http://iom.nationalacademies.org/Reports/2015/Birth-To-Eight.aspx
- Office of Planning, Research & Evaluation, *Uses of Technology to Support Early Childhood Practice* www.acf.hhs.gov/opre

- American Academy of Pediatrics, *Beyond 'Turn it Off': How to Advise Families on Media Use* www.aappublications.org/content/36/10/54
- Association for Library Service to Children, *Media Mentorship in Libraries Serving Youth* www.ala.org/alsc/mediamentorship
- RAND Corporation, *Using Early Childhood to Bridge the Digital Divide* http://www.rand.org/pubs/perspectives/PE119.html
- HighScope, *Using Technology Appropriately in the Preschool Classroom* www.highscope.org/file/NewsandInformation/Extensions/ExtVol28No1_highres.pdf
- Joan Ganz Cooney Center at Sesame Workshop, Families and Media Project www.joanganzcooneycenter.org/initiative/the-families-and-media-project/
- Zero to Three, *Screen Sense: Setting the Record Straight* www.zerotothree.org/parenting-resources/screen-sense/

Starting Points and Unifying Foundations

The frameworks and guidelines are an important place to start your investigation of the issues and opportunities related to technology and digital media in the early years. In the spring of 2015, the Department of Education Office of Early Learning and Office of Educational Technology convened a symposium with invited experts from across the country to explore how best to integrate technology into early childhood settings. Lisa Guernsey (who has contributed an essay about media mentors in Chapter 1 and Chapter 17 with Michael H. Levine about supporting media mentorship thought research and policy) posted a blog, Tech and Young Children: U.S. Dept. of Ed Elevates Need for Guidance and PD (Guernsey, 2015). In her blog, Lisa called out three key issues that had emerged during the Symposium:

1 educators and parents need succinct, research-based messages about what works best;
2 teachers and leaders need professional development on how to skillfully integrate technology into their teaching; and
3 the app marketplace needs markers of quality informed by the science of child development.

Guernsey (2015)

These three needs serve as a taking-off point for all that follows. The need for research-based guidance and professional guidance echo the recommendations related to technology, teaching, and learning found in the Institute of Medicine (IOM) and National Research Council (NRC) report, *Transforming the Workforce for Children From Birth Through Age 8: A Unifying Foundation* (2015). The report addresses topics related to educational practices, child assessment, working with special populations, engaging with families, and using technology effectively. Effective use of technology was addressed in three ways: technology use, technology in teacher preparation, and technology for family engagement.

According to the IOM and NRC report, issued related to using technology effectively to foster early learning include:

> The use of technology in educational settings can take two major forms, both of which have implications for the competencies needed by professionals. The first is use of technology as a tool for directly facilitating children's learning. In terms of professional competency, educators must have proficiency in technology as a set of tools that can enhance pedagogy, knowledge of how and when children learn through what kinds of technology and the ability to integrate that knowledge into their pedagogy and lessons, and proficiency in teaching children how to use technology and acquire digital literacy skills. The second entails the use of technology to facilitate other aspects of professional practice, such as assessment of children, creation and management of the learning environment, documentation, information sharing, and communication with families and with other practitioners.
>
> Institute of Medicine and the National Research Council (2015),
> p. 275

IOM on Technology Competencies and Professional Development

> Educators across professional roles and age ranges are expected to have competency in the use of technology for learning. This competency includes knowing how children learn through technology and having the ability to integrate that knowledge into practices that support development and learning. These professionals need better support than in the use of technology and more opportunities to learn how to use technology appropriately, effectively, and to its fullest potential to foster early learning for children aged 0–8.
>
> Institute of Medicine and the National Research Council (2015),
> p. 283

IOM on Technology for Family Engagement

Care and education professionals need skills in communicating, working collaboratively, and developing partnerships with families. They have an important role in preparing families to engage in behaviors and activities that enhance development and early learning, and to maintain continuity and consistency across home and out-of-home settings and learning environments for young children. Even with few resources, there are actions care and education can encourage parents can take to improve their children's school readiness.

Institute of Medicine and the National Research Council (2015), p. 291

Finally, a report from the Office of Planning, Research & Evaluation (OPRE), Administration for Children and Families (ACF), and U.S. Department of Health and Human Services (DHHS) explores the ways educators are using technology to support early childhood practice. The report, *Uses of Technology to Support Early Childhood Practice* (2015), reviews what is known about how early childhood professionals who work directly with children and families are using technology to support teaching and family engagement. The review of the literature connected training, intentional use, well-designed technologies, and evidenced-based programs; OPRE found that technology use can improve outcomes for children and their families, increase family engagement, and provide more effective and efficient methods to engage professionals in training. (OPRE, 2015). On the topic of parent, family, and community engagement, OPRE (2015) found evidence of technology use to support parent involvement in children's learning and development, parent–child relationships, and partnerships between families and early childhood practitioners.

Moving on: Family Engagement in the Digital Age

You have been introduced to many of the big ideas and key concepts that have informed our thinking and the writing in this book. You have learned about frameworks for parent, family, and community engagement; frameworks and guidelines for intentional and appropriate use of technology and digital media in the early years; and begun to consider the intersection of family engagement and technology with new ideas from recent reports. The intent of this Introduction was to begin to build your foundational knowledge of family engagement and technology—the ecology of family engagement in the digital age—and to suggest a "unifying foundation" of essential frameworks, guidelines, and reports to guide your next steps as you move on in this book and on to becoming a media mentor.

About the Book

Family Engagement in the Digital Age: Early Childhood Educators as Media Mentors is divided into three parts:

i   Technology, Young Children, and Family Engagement;
ii Technology Tools and Techniques for Empowering Educators and Families; and
iii Innovative Approaches to Technology-Enhanced Family Engagement.

The book describes the essential roles educators play in implementing technology-mediated practices that improve communication, strengthen the home–school connection, increase parent involvement, enhance family engagement, and build a sense of community for young children, parents, and families. In these pages, you will explore the meaning and importance of family engagement in the digital age, how technology can empower and engage parents, caregivers and families, and the emerging role of media mentors to guide young children and their families in the twenty-first century.

Part I focuses on broad issues and opportunities with technology and young children including: why media mentorship matters; the role of diversity in media and family engagement; how technology and digital media can be tools for teaching and learning and the implications for technology-mediated family engagement; a new framework for developmentally appropriate technology integration; the importance of re-imagining children's engagement with technology, frameworks for parent, family, and community engagement; the power of nudges; and examples of effective and innovative approaches to improving communication, strengthening the home–school connection, increasing parent involvement, and enhancing family engagement to support young children, parents, and families in the digital age.

Part II presents a rationale and strategies for empowering educators and families using technology and technology-enhanced approaches to family engagement with chapters that focus on Fred Rogers' approach to parent engagement; the implications of the fast-paced digital age for childhood and child development; strategies for developing healthy media habits; supporting parents as media mentors; and advice for today's media mentors from a noted pediatrician and children's media expert.

Part III offers innovative approaches to: technology-enhanced family engagement in early childhood program administration; media literacy education; supporting dual language learners; providing an inclusive environment where every child belongs; the role of librarians as media mentors; public media strategies for engaging families; and the need to identify and mobilize new allies in support of media mentorship.

Throughout the book, you will find *Spotlight on Engagement* case studies, success stories, best practices, helpful hints from and for media mentors and *Learn More* resources woven into the chapters to connect the dots between child development, early learning, developmentally appropriate practice, family engagement, and digital age technology. These real-life examples and stories provide evidence of innovation and put the spotlight on effective models for family engagement and technology in the twenty-first century.

The organizations of the sections, chapters, and topics allows you to read through from front to back or to select specific topics of interest to you to read first. Wherever you begin, the topics and key concepts will help deepen your understanding of digital age family engagement opportunities and strengthen your role as a media mentor to the young children, parents, and families in your care.

Writing from their individual perspectives and presented in an engaging style, the authors have included relevant research; grounded family engagement strategies and technology use in child development theory and developmentally appropriate practice; provided examples of family engagement principles and guidelines in practice; included real-life stories and best practices shared by exemplary early childhood professionals and programs; highlighted innovative approaches to family engagement using technology tools and digital media; offered helpful hints for media mentors; and curated a collection of resources and links to encourage you to learn more.

About the Authors

The authors invited to contribute chapters to this book are all thought leaders in early childhood education, family engagement, and technology integration. They bring years of experience, and expertise to their writing and offer a range of perspectives from their work in higher education, teacher education and professional development, consulting, media literacy, libraries, parent education, pediatric health, policy analysis, and research. They come from as far as Australia and from across the United States, and they work in leading organizations including the Center for Digital Media Innovation and Diversity at George Mason University; Center on Media and Child Health at Boston Children's Hospital; Children's Innovation Project in Pittsburgh; Fred Rogers Center for Early Learning and Children's Media at Saint Vincent College in Latrobe, PA; Harvard Family Research Project in Boston; Joan Ganz Cooney Center at Sesame Workshop in New York City; New America in Washington, DC; RAND Corporation in California; and the Technology in Early Childhood (TEC) Center at Erikson Institute in Chicago.

A Final Word

Fred Rogers said the words below frequently to remind us of why family engagement strategies and the effective use of technology are so important and to gift us with his well-known gentle nudge toward understanding that respecting and empowering parents need to come ahead of strategies, technologies, education and advice—in the digital age and in any age.

We invite you to explore the frameworks, position statement, and guidelines that have been included in the chapter, along with the resources and links below, and then turn the page to begin your exploration of technology-mediated and enhanced family engagement strategies that support, children, parents, and families in the digital age. We believe you will find it all very engaging and empowering.

"Strengthen a parent ... and you strengthen a child."

Fred Rogers, *You Are Special* (1995), p. 197

References

Department of Education. (2014). *Dual Capacity-Building Framework for Family–School Partnerships*. Washington, DC: DOE.

Guernsey, L. (2015, September 14). Tech and Young Children: U.S. Department of Ed Elevates Need for Guidance and PD, New America, Ed Central blog. Retrieved from www.edcentral.org/tech-young-children-u-s-dept-ed-elevates-need-guidance-pd/

Halgunseth, L. C., Peterson, A., Stark, D., & Moodie, S. (2009). *Family Engagement, Diverse Families, and Early Childhood Programs: An Integrated Review of the Literature*. Washington, DC: NAYEC and pre[k]now.

Institute of Medicine and National Research Council. (2015). *Transforming the Workforce for Children from Birth through Age 8: A unifying foundation*. Washington, DC: National Academies Press.

National Association for the Education of Young Children, & Fred Rogers Center for Early Learning and Children's Media at Saint Vincent College. (2012). *Technology and interactive media as tools in early childhood programs serving children from birth through age 8*. Washington, DC: NAEYC; Latrobe, PA: Fred Rogers Center for Early Learning and Children's Media at Saint Vincent College. www.naeyc.org/content/technology-and-young-children

Office of Head Start. (2011). *Head Start Parent, Family, and Community Engagement Framework: Promoting Family Engagement and School Readiness, from prenatal to age 8*. Washington, DC: U.S. Department of Health and Human Services, Administration for Children and Families, Office of Head Start.

Office of Planning, Research & Evaluation. (2015). *Uses of Technology to Support Early Childhood Practice*. Washington, DC: U.S. Department of Health and Human Services, Administration for Children and Families, Office of Head Start.

Rogers, F. (1995). *You Are Special: Words of Wisdom for All Ages from a Beloved Neighbor*. New York: Penguin Books.

Resources for Media Mentors

- *Key Messages of the NAEYC/Fred Rogers Center Position Statement on Technology and Interactive Media in Early Childhood Programs.* www.naeyc.org/files/naeyc/12_KeyMessages_Technology.pdf
- *Beyond Random Acts: Family, School, and Community Engagement as an Integral Part of Education Reform.* Harvard Family Research Project and SEDL www.hfrp.org/publications-resources/browse-our-publications/beyond-random-acts-family-school-and-community-engagement-as-an-integral-part-of-education-reform
- *Envisioning a Digital Age Architecture for Early Education*, New America Policy Brief, Lisa Guernsey www.newamerica.org/downloads/DigitalArchitecture-20140326.pdf
- *Families Powered On: Improving Family Engagement in Early Childhood Through Technology* www.rand.org/pubs/research_reports/RR673z5.html
- *Family Engagement, Diverse Families, and Early Childhood Education Programs: An Integrated Review of the Literature*, NAEYC www.naeyc.org/files/naeyc/file/research/FamEngage.pdf
- *Partners in Education: A Dual Capacity-Building Framework for Family School Partnerships*, U.S. Department of Education http://www2.ed.gov/documents/family-community/partners-education.pdf
- *Research News You Can Use: Family Engagement and Early Childhood Education*, NAEYC, Kyle Snow www.naeyc.org/content/research-news-family-engagement
- *Tap, Click, Read: Growing Readers in a World of Screen*, Lisa Guernsey and Michael H. Levine www.tapclickread.org
- *Technology and Digital Media in the Early Years: Tools for Teaching and Learning*, Chip Donohue (Ed.) www.routledge.com/products/9780415725828
- *You Are Special: Words of Wisdom for All Ages from a Beloved Neighbor*, Fred Rogers, Penguin Books, 1995.

Learn More...

- *Ask the Mediatrician*, Dr. Michael Rich http://cmch.tv/parents/askthemediatrician/
- Campaign for Grade Level Reading, *Technology for Successful Parenting* http://gradelevelreading.net/resources/technology-for-successful-parenting
- Center on Media and Child Health at Boston Children's Hospital http://cmch.tv
- Center on Media and Human Development, Northwestern University www.cmhd.northwestern.edu
- Common Sense Media www.commonsensemedia.org/

- Children's Technology Review http://childrenstech.com/
- Every Chance to Learn, Dr. Kristy Goodwin http://everychancetolearn.com.au
- Family and Community Engagement, DOE www.ed.gov/parent-and-family-engagement
- Family Engagement Resource List, NAEYC www.naeyc.org/familyengagement/resources/resource-list
- FINE Network, Family Involvement Network of Educators, HFRP www.hfrp.org/family-involvement/fine-family-involvement-network-of-educators
- Fred Rogers Center for Early Learning and Children's Media at Saint Vincent College www.fredrogerscenter.org
- HITN Early Learning Collaborative http://earlylearningcollaborative.org
- NAEYC Diverse Families Project www.naeyc.org/familyengagement
- New America www.newamerica.org
- Parent, Family, and Community Engagement, Head Start https://eclkc.ohs.acf.hhs.gov/hslc/tta-system/family
- Raising Digital Natives http://raisingdigitalnatives.com
- Remake Learning http://remakelearning.org
- Seeding Reading www.edcentral.org/learningtech/seedingreading/
- TEC Center at Erikson Institute www.teccenter.erikson.edu

Part I

Technology, Young Children, and Family Engagement

Editor's Introduction

This book, and the chapters in Part I, set the stage for all that will follow. You are introduced to the concept of media mentors and the role of diversity and will begin to identify the active ingredients in technology-mediated family engagement. You will explore the connections between what we know about the effective, appropriate, and intentional use of technology and digital media in the early years and the role of technology innovation in digital age family engagement.

Part I begins with three short essays. In the first, **Lisa Guernsey** writes about who media mentors are, why they are essential in the digital age, and what it will take to prepare early childhood educators for media mentorship. Next, **Kevin Clark** explores issues of diversity in media and why educators need to be mindful of diversity when designing and delivering technology-mediated approaches to family engagement. I briefly step outside of my role as editor for the third essay that connects the dots between family engagement and technology and creates a context for the discussion of innovative and effective technology-mediated strategies to engage families based on what we know about technology and digital media in the early years.

In Chapter 2, **Sharon Thompson Hirschy** introduces her framework for developmentally appropriate technology integration—a new way of thinking that connects the developmentally appropriate practices framework to the section, use, integration, and evaluation of technology in early childhood classrooms and other settings. She discusses why technology integration in early childhood environments is essential to effective, appropriate, and intentional use of technology and digital media with young children. The role of media mentors, implications for teacher preparation and professional development, and strategies for using the framework to develop and deliver technology-mediated family engagement approaches that facilitate communication and interaction are presented.

Jeremy Boyle, **Melissa Butler**, and **Junlei Li** share new ways of thinking about children's experiences with technology and explore why children need to engage more deeply with technology in Chapter 3. They offer an approach to technology use in the early years that enables young children to experience technology and innovation by moving children from being users and consumers of technology to being creators. They provide gentle but persuasive nudges to early childhood educators about re-imagining children's engagement with technology and offer strategies for media mentors including rethinking materials; providing access to thinking; growing habits that make thinking possible; and slowing down.

Chapter 4 introduces the work of the Harvard Family Research Project (HFRP) as a partner in the development of the Head Start National Center on Parent, Family, and Community Engagement (PFCE). **M. Elena Lopez**, **Margaret Caspe**, and **Heather Weiss** present a systems approach to family engagement, introduce the elements of the PFCE Framework, and identify promising practices and innovative approach to technology-mediated family engagement. They connect the Framework with the potential of digital media to support positive family outcomes in a strengths-based, parent empowerment approach. They encourage media mentors to draw on digital media assets to provide families with clear and actionable ideas and tools, and they create a context for all that follows about what family engagement is and why it matters in the digital age

Part I closes with strategies for empowering parents and families from **Rafiq Dossani** and **Anamarie Auger** of the RAND Corporation. They introduce the concept of behavioral "nudges" and describe the power of a nudge to influence behavior and the potential of technology tools to provide empowering messages, information, and encouragement to parents and families when and where they need it. They review research on interactions between educators and parents as a key dimension of parental involvement, and the impact of parent engagement programs on children's achievement and parenting practices, and they identify innovative programs that use technology-mediated nudges. The chapter, and Part I, end with tips for media mentors about leveraging technology tools to provide nudges as effective strategies for strengthening home–school communication and connections and deepening family engagement.

Chapter 1

Three Perspectives on Family Engagement

Why Media Mentorship Matters: Equity in the Twenty-First Century

Lisa Guernsey

Technology Tools for Family Engagement: The Role of Diversity

Kevin Clark

Why Family Engagement, and Media Mentors Matter

Chip Donohue

WHY MEDIA MENTORSHIP MATTERS: EQUITY IN THE TWENTY-FIRST CENTURY

Lisa Guernsey

It's a Saturday morning in March, and the room at the government center in Fairfax, Virginia, is packed but quiet. Rachel C. Martin, a child care specialist, is standing at the front. Behind her is a large screen that projects images of children's books and games. The images emanate from a touchscreen tablet balanced on the podium. The title of her workshop? *Emerging Literacy: Digital Storytime.*

In front of her are dozens of child care providers and early educators, many of whom manage very small programs in their homes. They serve low-income families across northern Virginia, an area that, like much of the United States, has a teeming population of immigrants from all over the globe and struggles with vast disparities in income levels. Many of their families qualify for subsidized housing and nutrition assistance. At least half the women here this morning are immigrants themselves, hailing from Latin America, Asia, and the Middle East.

These faces reflect an untapped opportunity to embrace, teach, and lift up America's next generation. In a country with more than 20 percent of U.S. children in poverty, with the same percentage of children being raised by parents who speak non-English languages, and with technological advances reshaping the lives of families and kids every day, the work of these child care providers matters immensely. Exactly how these adults interact with the children in their care, the way they advise the children's parents and family members, and their ability to mold new mindsets around learning and literacy will have cascading effects that set the course for the America of the twenty-first century.

But at this moment—at 10:37 a.m., as a few people are still straggling in to grab plastic chairs in the back of the room—the long-term significance of their work takes a backseat to day-to-day struggles in running a child care program, not to mention scarcity of tools and training in general. To many, digital technology feels like a pipe dream or, worse, a distraction. Before the session started, a few participants leaned into whispered conversations about the challenges of using touchscreens with kids. As Martin speaks, some still have eyebrows raised in skepticism.

"Don't worry," Martin says as she welcomes her audience, "I was nervous about using technology at first too." But she invites everyone to explore: How might electronic books spark a range of early literacy activities with young children? Could they prompt new ways of reaching the preschoolers in your care?

Martin opens up a website called Unite for Literacy. Let's look at this, she says. Here are books in multiple languages.

The child care providers suddenly perk up. Multiple languages? Really? Which ones?

Soon, several members of the audience are raising their hands, asking questions about the e-book app and what it can do. Martin flips through a book on owls, which is narrated in Farsi. Here's one about insects, in Vietnamese. And it's free, Martin tells them. The founders of Unite for Literacy are funding this through donations. But Martin is not here to pitch apps; instead, she wants her audience to review and think critically about different types of media. For example, with Unite for Literacy, she says, the print on the pages is not in the same language as the narrated language. When you are showing kids these books, she counsels, you'll want to be thoughtful about the ages of the children and how they are learning print.

Scenes like this one are starting to play out in a few spots around the country. The Association for Library Services to Children has encouraged librarians who work in youth services to rise to the challenge and provide workshops on new media and technology for parents and early educators. As this book in your hands makes clear, an impassioned cadre of thought leaders—from the National Association for the Education of Young Children to the TEC Center at Erikson Institute and more—are calling for people across the early childhood landscape to recognize the need for media mentors for parents and families as well as for members of the early childhood profession themselves, whether they be teacher-education faculty or social workers in home-visiting programs.

Yet so far, people such as Rachel C. Martin are rare. Consider her hybrid credentials: Martin has a bachelor's degree in child development, a master's degree in children's literature, and is now studying for a master's degree in library science, a combination that has helped her make new relationships with the Fairfax County Public Libraries as well as bridge the work of the public libraries with that of the early childhood division of the public schools.

One of her recent endeavors is to show public school teachers and leaders how to use Skype to conduct virtual field trips to places such as Yellowstone National Park, enabling children to talk with park rangers and ask questions about sites they may not otherwise have a chance to visit. For children in preschool environments, she has encouraged the use of remote video technology to engage children in nursery rhymes or songs performed by "special guests," such as parents who call in from their workplace or relatives who live far away.

In short, her role is not to work directly with families or children but instead to bring tools and strategies to early childhood professionals who may use new literacy and language-development tools in their classrooms and who want to relay the information to families through parenting workshops or other events.

"The idea," Martin says, "is that we can facilitate events through their center, helping them to plan." Ultimately, she said, this can "help parents to understand how teachers use technology with their children and also how to use it at home."

Most American children and their families are now consuming and playing with digital media and video stories (think TV) for several hours every day. Hundreds of thousands of children's apps are in the marketplace. New online software and electronic books come online every month. Figuring out how to manage, curate, and smartly use all of these materials is a huge challenge for today's educators and parents. Adults who work with children will increasingly need moments to talk with experts, examine and reflect upon new tools, and figure out how to customize their use of different kinds of media (print included) to help those children develop.

As Michael H. Levine and I write in *Tap, Click, Read*:

> We cannot afford to ignore the affordances of technology, especially for disadvantaged children and families of many different backgrounds who may not otherwise have access to information and learning opportunities. And yet to leave the fate of these children to technology alone would be a big mistake.

Studies conducted in libraries, in schools, and in homes show just how much of a difference an adult can make for a child when that adult engages with kids around technology and media in ways that scaffold learning. Today's young children who are using technology to learn and create *while working with adults who can set good examples and guide them to new heights* are receiving tremendous advantages. If only the privileged few have the opportunity for that kind of tech-assisted but human-powered learning, divides will only grow wider.

As Martin's session ends on that morning in Fairfax, many early educators are lingering over e-book devices that Martin has passed around for demonstrations. Others chat about downloading apps to their smartphones without having to purchase expensive equipment. Instead of being expressionless, they are now teeming with questions. For sure, many are still wary of technological snafus and unsure they could manage technology among many children at one time. But now they know who to reach out to, who can help them make choices that make sense for their particular children. They have a media mentor in their midst.

Which brings us to the next burning question for the field—and the reason for this book—Where do we get more of them?

Learn More...

- *Tap, Click, Read: Growing Readers in a World of Screens*, Lisa Guernsey and Michael H. Levine www.tapclickread.org
- More than Ebooks vs. Print: The Concept of "Media Mentors", *EdCentral*, 9/4/14 https://www.newamerica.org/education-policy/edcentral/beyond-ebook-vs-print-book-concept-media-mentors/
- A Media Mentor for Every Child, *Connect Safely*, 5/19/14 www.connectsafely.org/media-mentor-every-child/
- *How the iPad Affects Young Children and What We Can Do About It*, Lisa Guernsey at TEDxMidAtlantic, 4/27/14 www.youtube.com/watch?v=P41_nyYY3Zg
- The Smart Way to Use iPads in the Classroom, *Slate*, 4/15/13 www.slate.com/articles/technology/future_tense/2013/04/ipads_in_the_classroom_the_right_way_to_use_them_demonstrated_by_a_swiss.html

TECHNOLOGY TOOLS FOR FAMILY ENGAGEMENT: THE ROLE OF DIVERSITY

Kevin Clark

The word *diversity* conjures up attributes such as race, ethnicity, gender, income, education, geography, language, and the like. Even when we examine these attributes individually, we should keep in mind that there is diversity within groups. For example, not all members of a particular race have the same skin tone, income, or level of education. As educators think about and use technology tools to communicate and connect with parents, strengthen the home–school connection, and enhance family engagement, no one product or tool can effectively address all of these attributes. Instead of trying to address each attribute individually, there should be a holistic approach to diversity.

Diversity can be displayed through the distribution and/or embodiment of different characteristics and traits as well as through the portrayal and representation of particular people and characters. According to Dale's Cone of Learning (1969), people retain 10 percent of what they read, 20 percent of what they hear, and 30 percent of what they see. Additionally, people retain 50 percent of what they see and hear, 70 percent of what they say, and 90 percent of what they say and do. Media can be used to facilitate and support learning by supporting knowledge construction, acting as a vehicle for the exploration and access to information, supporting contextual and real-life learning situations, acting as a medium for collaboration and dialogue, and providing a mechanism to reflect on and represent their knowledge (Roschelle et al., 2000).

Because media help to create cognitive and affective environments that describe and portray people, places, and things that influence how and what young people learn, educators need to think about what children hear, see, and do in the media tools they use and in their everyday lives. Do children see different types of people, characteristics, and attributes? Do children hear a variety of sounds, voices, and music? And last, are a variety of situations being depicted (e.g., family structure, lifestyles, power/working relationships)? Not only should educators be concerned about what is heard, seen, and done in particular media tools and/or products, they should also think about these attributes across the entire collection of media tools and products. Not in one book but throughout a library of books. Not in one type of media or tool but throughout multiple media and tools.

Because children primarily reside in three environments—home, school, and community—educators should also be concerned about diversity in those environments. When thinking about creating, selecting, and utilizing effective media throughout these settings, it is helpful to examine whether the media meet the needs of diverse audiences. The concept of personas can be used to more clearly define and appropriately address the needs of the target audience. Personas are abstract representations of users that include diverse characteristics, uses, and approaches to the media.

Particularly effective in designing educational media, personas are developed to determine and provide the most effective environments and situations that allow the learner to be successful in the acquisition of content knowledge (Pulsinelli & Roubie, 2001). Personas help to better define the target audience by describing them based on their interests, needs, skills, values, and demographic attributes (Dickelman, 1997). Designers and creators benefit from the use of personas because it allows them to create a concrete user, which helps them focus specifically on the needs, interests, expectations, prior knowledge, and behavior patterns of their target audience (Cooper, 1999).

Personas can be given complete identities that include personal characteristics, a name, a photograph, and a narrative description of their skills, motivations, and goals as well as a quotation that exemplifies what they represent. The information needed to construct personas is collected by interviewing a wide range of people from the target audience as well as by observing and documenting their responses during usability testing. It is important to note that the persona is not a real person or group of people but rather an abstract representation of the relationship between the user and the media or system (Constantine & Lockwood, 1999). Just as designers and creators use personas to help them view media design and development from different perspectives, educators and media mentors can use personas to help them more effectively select and utilize media with and for diverse communities.

As educators think about and use technology tools to communicate and connect with parents, strengthen the home–school connection, and enhance family engagement, no one product or tool can effectively address all of these attributes. Instead of trying to address each attribute individually, there should be a holistic approach to diversity.

References

Constantine, L. L. & Lockwood, L. A. D. (1999). *Software for use: Practical guide to the models and methods of usage-centered design*. New York: ACM Press.

Cooper, A. (1999). *The inmates are running the asylum: Why high-tech products drive us crazy and how to restore the sanity*. Indianapolis, IN: SAMS.

Dale, E. (1969). Audio-visual methods in teaching. (3rd Edition). New York: Holt, Rinhart, and Winston.

Dickelman, G. J. (1997, September/October). Gershom's Law. *CBT Solutions Magazine* [Online]. http://www.pcd-innovations.com/law/cbt_art.htm

Pulsinelli, A., & Roubie, C. (2001). Using diversity modeling for instructional design. *Performance Improvement, 40*(7), pp. 20–27.

Roschelle, J. M., Pea, R. D., Hoadley, C. M., Gordin, D. N., & Means, B. M. (2000). Changing how and what children learn in school with computer-based technologies. *Children and Computer Technology, 10*(2), pp. 76–101.

WHY FAMILY ENGAGEMENT, TECHNOLOGY, AND MEDIA MENTORS MATTER

Chip Donohue

In these pages, we describe an ecology of family engagement that includes homes, neighborhoods, early childhood environments, school settings, early literacy initiatives, libraries and children's museums, out-of-school time programs, home visiting projects, early intervention services, community-based efforts, and more. As I have learned more about family engagement strategies while writing and editing this book, I have thought a lot about my own lifetime of family experiences: the family I was born into, the family I married into, and the family I helped create with my wife and two daughters. All of these families and their many extensions have nurtured me, raised me, guided me, engaged me, and mentored me. As I have reflected on my own family history, culture, and context, I have been reminded of why the topics of family engagement, technology, and mentorship matter so much in the digital age.

Family Engagement, Technology, and Media Mentors

In her opening essay, Lisa Guernsey made the case for media mentors to guide young children, parents, and families through the digital age. In a TEDx Atlantic talk from April, 27, 2014, she offered this nudge to all who care for and care about young children and families: *"What if we were to commit to ensure that every family with young children had access to a media mentor?"*

I agree with Lisa. Every child needs a media mentor. Every parent needs a media mentor. Media mentors matter. And that means that early childhood educators across settings and roles need to gain the digital media literacy needed to become effective media mentors for children, parents, and families in the twenty-first century.

Young children and their families need relationships with mindful media mentors who are positive, enthusiastic tour guides and curious co-explorers in the digital age. We all need media innovators to address access and equity issues; promote early learning, language, and literacy; open new doors for engaging families; and create new opportunities for technology-mediated professional learning—and you will meet many in the pages that follow.

Media mentorship has at its heart a fundamental element of quality early childhood education and family engagement: relationships. When the selection, use, integration, and evaluation of technology and digital media begin with relationships, opportunities increase for learning, joint engagement, and deeply engaging family engagement that matters.

I have been watching the emergence of media mentors for children and parents across many roles and in many settings including libraries, children's museums, out-of-school-time programs, early childhood programs, schools, home visiting programs, public media initiatives, and so many more that you'll be introduced to in this book. I have met early childhood educators, family child care providers, early intervention specialists, child life specialists, home visitors, pediatric health providers, librarians, children's museum and out-of-school time staff, parents, caregivers, and other family members who have embraced media mentorship. Potential media mentors are everywhere—they just need a gentle nudge.

The challenge is to find trusted tour guides and role models who are well prepared for the role of media mentor.

Key Messages from the Joint Position Statement

Early childhood educators are the decision makers in whether, how, what, when, and why technology and media are implemented through applying their expertise and knowledge of child development and learning, individual children's interests and readiness, and the social and cultural contexts in which children live.

NAEYC & Fred Rogers Center (2012), p. 6

Media Mentors as Digital Decision Makers

Early childhood educators are not un-equipped to be digital decision makers but often feel ill-equipped. While we all have much to learn in the fast-paced digital age, educators bring to the classroom—and to their interactions with parents and families—knowledge of child development, early learning, the influence of family, culture and community, and strategies for creating learner-centered experiences that are appropriate for each child. The decisions they make every day about the tools for learning and the experiences they offer children to support healthy development should inform their technology choices, modeling for children and parents, and understanding of what matters most. Start with all you know about how children grow, develop, and learn; add what we know and what we are learning about young children and technology; and build increasing levels of digital media literacy on top.

Based on more than 40 years of research on television and young children and the emerging research on children's use of digital tools, we know that there are essential principles and active ingredients that matter for young children:

- **Digital media literacy matters,** so media mentors need a positive disposition toward technology and the knowledge, experience, and competencies to support digital age children and families.

- **Whole-child development matters,** so educators should base technology use and integration on what they know about the individual needs of each child and how children develop physically, cognitively, linguistically, socially, and emotionally.
- In early childhood, **relationships matter most.** We know that young children learn best in the context of interactions and relationships with attentive, responsive, and caring adults, so technology should be used to support and strengthen adult/child relationships and promote joint engagement with media—using media together supports learning.
- **Content matters:** both the quality of the content and the level of engagement can help children engage, express, explore, and connect with others.
- **Context matters** so decisions about when, where, and how technology is used need to complement and extend children's play and interactions.
- **Creating media matters** in the digital age, so help young children express themselves through media and progress from media consumer to creator.

If all of this matters, then media mentors really matter. Young children, parents, and families need help to safely navigate the digital age. As you explore the ideas of family engagement, technology, and media mentorship, start with what you know, understand what matters most, and embrace your role as a media mentor in the twenty-first century. In this book, you will explore the evidence from current research and the principles and best practices in parent empowerment and family engagement drawn from foundational family engagement and technology frameworks and guidelines that have informed the work of the contributing authors in the chapters that follow.

Are you a media mentor?

Reference

Guernsey, L. (2014). "How the iPad Affects Young Children, and What We Can Do about It." *TEDxMidAtlantic* video, 13:14. Posted April 27, 2014. Retrieved from www.youtube.com/watch?v=P41_nyYY3Zg

Resources

- Center for Digital Media Innovation and Diversity https://cdmid.gmu.edu
- Diversity In APPs http://diversityinapps.com
- Joan Ganz Cooney Center at Sesame Workshop www.joanganzcooneycenter.org/
- New America www.newamerica.org

- *Tap, Click, Read: Growing Readers in a World of Screens*, Lisa Guernsey and Michael H. Levine www.tapclickread.org
- TEC Center at Erikson Institute http://teccenter.erikson.edu
- *Technology and Digital Media in the Early Years: Tools for Teaching and Learning*, Chip Donohue, Editor www.routledge.com/products/9780415725828
- Unite for Literacy www.uniteforliteracy.com

Learn More...

- Fred Rogers Center for Early Learning and Children's Media at Saint Vincent College www.fredrogerscenter.org
- *Media Mentorship in Libraries Serving Youth*, ALSC www.ala.org/alsc/mediamentorship
- NAEYC, National Association for the Education of Young Children www.naeyc.org

Chapter 2

Developmentally Appropriate Technology Integration

Sharon Thompson Hirschy

Introduction

Technology in early childhood classrooms? It is no longer a question but a statement of current practice. Yet research and comments from early childhood educators indicate a lack of understanding regarding appropriate ways to manage and integrate technology in the classroom. In the digital age, early childhood educators can be media mentors for young children, caregivers, and families, but they need adequate knowledge, skills, and experience with technology and digital media to utilize technology appropriately in classrooms and in mentoring others.

Technology integration, the process of infusing the technology into teacher pedagogical practices, is dominating early childhood, public school, and higher education discussions today. What does it mean? How can technology in the classroom be integrated in appropriate ways? Most of all, how do we help teachers find their way through the maze of mandates, instructions, and differing technologies to incorporate digital media and hardware into the learning environment and to enhance family engagement?

In the digital age, early childhood educators can be media mentors for young children, caregivers and families, but they need adequate knowledge, skills and experience with technology and digital media to utilize technology appropriately in classrooms and in mentoring others.

Technology is one of many tools for facilitating growth, learning, and communication in classrooms. Technology integration involves "thinking about technology across the curriculum, throughout the day—not technology as a separate activity" (Donohue, 2015, p. 24). Some question whether the term *technology integration* is developmentally appropriate (Brantley-Dias & Ertmer, 2013; Ertmer & Ottenbreit-Leftwich, 2013; Sutherland, Eagle, & Joubert, 2012). They suggest another term is needed that underscores technology as only one of many effective pedagogical practices that enable educators to plan and provide appropriate learning experiences and environments.

Early childhood educators recognize the term *developmentally appropriate* to include practices that exemplify good teaching and that provide children with support and instruction that will result in optimal growth and development. *Developmentally appropriate technology integration* entails skill development in the use of technology *and* in the use of developmentally appropriate practices in the integration of technology into curriculum development and implementation. Developmentally appropriate technology integration implies an understanding of different technologies and their use, digital media literacy, and the ability to assimilate technology as one of many curricular tools.

Developmentally appropriate technology integration entails skill development in the use of technology and in the use of developmentally appropriate practices in the integration of technology into curriculum development and implementation.

Technology as a "Third Space" for School and Family

Technology today is an important factor in engaging families and creating partnerships. There is often a disconnect between what is happening at home and at school as well as a lack of information sharing. Parents can feel powerless to understand and affect their children's education and care. The term *third space* has been adopted into the education field to identify informal and formal methods and places where the learning and development of children occur between two entities in their ecological system. Third space can refer to informal settings for learning, such as libraries or programs. One example is literacy programs that encourage and promote learning between home and school. Third space can also be methods of sharing and transferring knowledge that serve as a bridge between two systems to increase understanding, learning, and communication (Moje et al., 2004; Pahl & Kelly, 2005). Technology as a third space between school and home can provide opportunities for teachers and families to share and expand learning opportunities, provide and receive information about a child's growth and development, create partnerships, and strengthen family engagement.

Spotlight on Technology as a Third Space

Anna is four years old and came to school one day very excited about watching her mother make tortillas. She tells Mrs. James, her teacher, about it, and Mrs. James sends Anna's mother an email (using technology as the third space to promote communication) asking for a picture of her tortillas and the recipe. Mrs. James then posts them on her classroom blog for all of the families in her classroom. Learning is also extended as a tortilla press is introduced into the dramatic play center. White, red, and brown play dough, pictures, and tortilla recipes are placed in the art center after a group discussion and watching a short video clip about tortillas.

As you can see, technology gives teachers and families a third space in which communication and sharing become part of the curriculum and home environment and build home-school connections that bridge the child's experience in the classroom and at home.

Digital media can increase children's learning and family engagement when used appropriately. Technology is unique as a teaching methodology, and that can make its appropriate use problematic. It includes hundreds of devices and media. Technology is constantly changing, and teachers have to continually assess and build their abilities and understanding of new technologies. Teachers must not only learn to use an overwhelming variety of hardware, software, apps, and other media but to use them in ways that are appropriate to the classroom.

Spotlight on New Tools

Rella uses Facebook daily at home. She is building a Facebook page for her classroom as most of her parents have told her they use it daily. But building a page for her classroom requires a set of skills different from those in regular Facebook use. She will need to set privacy settings so that she can invite only parents in her class and will need to develop a forssm so parents can give permission to post pictures and classroom information there. A flyer will explain what type of privacy settings she will use and how to access the page and create an account if they do not have one. Rella's page is for educational purposes, so page design and exactly what is appropriate to include in the page, as well as how often she will update it, must be considered.

Another example is creating a newsletter. Most teachers can use basic word processing software, but a newsletter requires a higher level of knowledge in design. An understanding of what information is appropriate for newsletters and how the information should be worded to appropriately engage, empower, and communicate with families is critical.

Implementing Developmentally Appropriate Technology Integration

How can teachers implement developmentally appropriate technology integration in their classrooms? *Technology and Interactive Media as Tools in Early Childhood Programs Serving Children from Birth through Age 8,* the position statement developed by the NAEYC and the Fred Rogers Center for Early Learning and Children's Media at Saint Vincent College (2012), conceptualizes the use of technology and interactive media in early childhood. When used as a foundation, the position statement helps teachers begin to recognize what is developmentally appropriate.

The position statement indicates that effective teachers are intentional, appropriate, effective, and able to integrate and balance their use of technology with other educational resources. They make sure the technology used with children is interactive and engaging, accessible, and equitable and facilitates joint engagement of children's activities with adults and peers (NAEYC & Fred Rogers Center, 2012).

Educators select, use, integrate, and evaluate technology as they build learning experiences in the classroom and are continually involved in professional development in response to the fluid and dynamic nature of technology in early childhood education (Donohue, 2015). Educators incorporate these key words not only in their practice with children but in their role as media mentors for families.

Measuring Progress: Stages of Teacher Growth Toward Developmentally Appropriate Technology Integration

How do teachers measure their proficiency and progress in the integration of technology in the classroom? How do teachers identify skills and knowledge needed? A continuum of skills and knowledge needed to embed developmentally appropriate technology integration in teaching practice can provide a blueprint. The framework in Figure 2.1 (Hirschy, 2015) divides this process into stages and identifies knowledge and skills that demonstrate understanding and ability.

Recognition Stage

Learn Developmentally Appropriate Practices When Using Technology in Early Childhood Education

Reading the NAEYC/Fred Rogers Position Statement (2012) and more about Developmentally Appropriate Practices on both the NAEYC website and in the Copple and Bredekamp (2009) book creates a firm foundation. Most educators use a variety of technology in their personal lives, But how and why technology is used in the early childhood classroom requires different understanding and skills.

Key Messages from the Joint Position Statement

When the integration of technology and interactive media in early childhood programs is built upon solid developmental foundations and early childhood professionals are aware of both the challenges and the opportunities, educators are positioned to improve program quality by intentionally leveraging the potential of technology and media for the benefit of every child.

NAEYC & Fred Rogers Center (2012), p. 1

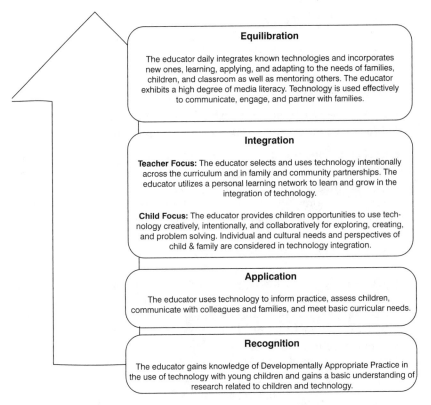

Equilibration

The educator daily integrates known technologies and incorporates new ones, learning, applying, and adapting to the needs of families, children, and classroom as well as mentoring others. The educator exhibits a high degree of media literacy. Technology is used effectively to communicate, engage, and partner with families.

Integration

Teacher Focus: The educator selects and uses technology intentionally across the curriculum and in family and community partnerships. The educator utilizes a personal learning network to learn and grow in the integration of technology.

Child Focus: The educator provides children opportunities to use technology creatively, intentionally, and collaboratively for exploring, creating, and problem solving. Individual and cultural needs and perspectives of child & family are considered in technology integration.

Application

The educator uses technology to inform practice, assess children, communicate with colleagues and families, and meet basic curricular needs.

Recognition

The educator gains knowledge of Developmentally Appropriate Practice in the use of technology with young children and gains a basic understanding of research related to children and technology.

Figure 2.1 Developmentally Appropriate Technology Integration

Application Stage

Identify and Learn Technologies to Use in the Classroom and with Families

Building on the basic foundation of developmentally appropriate practice, the educator identifies basic technology that can be used to develop curricula, find help, communicate with families and colleagues, and assess children in their classroom.

Basic knowledge, tools and skills include:

- ability to use word processing software or apps;
- effective searching and locating answers to questions on the Internet;
- access to a few basic websites and Web tools for developing curricula, such as virtual field trip sites, templates for creating folder games, or tutorials on creating newsletters;

- use of email and other methods of communication in appropriate ways with families and colleagues; and
- how and where to find and/or develop basic checklists and forms to assess children as well as to share information with families.

Integration Stage

Teacher Focus—Select and Use Technology in Planning, Assessment, and Using Personal Learning Networks (PLNs) for Professional Growth

The teacher is intentional in incorporating technology in the classroom environment and in family engagement, focusing on learning objectives when considering any type of technology. The teacher uses technology for planning and assessing. PLNs, an organized process and format for learning using social media, Web tools, and other technology, are actively used for professional development.

Basic knowledge, tools, and skills include:

- identification of technology that will meet learning objectives for the classroom and use digital media as one of many teaching tools;
- developing lesson plans and a learning environment that is flexible and able to meet the needs of all children when using technology;
- proficiency in using technology to create and locate assessment tools and to assess children's growth and development appropriately; and
- creation of a PLN whereby resources such as bookmarks of URLs and tutorials are collected and stored; resources from professional organizations are identified and used; and social media are employed to connect with colleagues. The ability to find information related to new technologies and pedagogical practices becomes simplified as the teacher reaches out to other professionals for guidance and ideas.

Spotlight on Documentation

Jonathan often uses a digital camera in his classroom of three-year-olds. He takes pictures of their work, including artwork and block structures they have built. He videotapes examples of their running, jumping, and skipping. He records verbal interactions with other children. These short clips and pictures are included in the online portfolio Jonathan has developed for each child and shared privately with parents using Google Drive, a free application. He uses the digital media for parent conferences. Jonathan does his curriculum planning after reviewing portfolios to identify individual children's abilities and needs.

Integration Stage

Child Focus—Identify and Incorporate in Classroom Learning Experiences Technology That Meets Planned Goals and Objectives

The teacher identifies appropriate apps, sites, media, and hardware for children to use in the classroom that meet identified learning objectives and are incorporated with other learning tools and experiences. The children's use of technology in the classroom is intentional and collaborative and encourages creativity and problem solving. Technology in the classroom encourages learning that takes into account the individual needs of the child and family, special needs, language differences, and cultural considerations.

Basic knowledge, tools, and skills include:

- effective assessment of media and hardware using rubrics, evaluation checklists, and trusted websites that evaluate technology for children;
- creating a learning environment that fosters creation, social interaction, and problem solving, such as establishing centers that have open-ended projects and experiences, rather than worksheets or single-focus games; and
- communicating with families about the technology used in classrooms, acting as a media mentor to educate parents on how technology can be used in developmentally appropriate interactions with their children.

The children's use of technology in the classroom is intentional and collaborative and encourages creativity and problem solving… and takes into account the individual needs of the child and family, special needs, language differences, and cultural considerations.

Equilibration Stage

Create a Learning Environment where Developmentally Appropriate Technology is Fully Integrated and Balanced with other Pedagogical Tools

The teacher uses known technologies as part of her or his daily pedagogical toolkit. New technology is incorporated by learning, applying, and adapting them to the classroom and individual children's needs. The teacher is proficient in assimilating technologies and accommodating teaching practices and knowledge as new technology is encountered. Offering support and mentoring peers and other professionals is a regular part of the week. Technology is used to mentor, partner with, and engage families in their child's learning and development. The teacher has a high level of media literacy—understanding, awareness, and ability to analyze, access, and create media messages (Rogow, 2015).

Basic knowledge, tools, and skills include:

- establishing learning networks and posting information through social media and/or mentoring colleagues on what the educator has learned;
- adapting technology to teaching rather than adapting teaching to the technology; and
- understanding, creating, and using media messages as a media mentor for peers and families, to teach children and partner with families and advocate on their behalf.

This framework and others can help teachers focus first on children and promote and enhance learning and development by using all of the learning tools in the pedagogical toolkit—including technology.

Influences on Developmentally Appropriate Integration of Technology in the Classroom

Outside influences, attitudes, and emotions play a central role in a teacher's ability to effectively integrate technology in classrooms. The ability of a teacher to create a developmentally appropriate learning environment where technology is fully integrated is often dependent on these factors.

Research in all levels of education identifies factors that impact teachers' use and integration of technology. Decisions and abilities to integrate technology in developmentally appropriate ways are influenced by age, family, culture, peers, efficacy, motivation, attitudes, time, access to technology, and administrators.

Self-efficacy, the belief in one's ability to accomplish a task with and become proficient in the use of technology, is a primary influence on an educator's effective integration of technology. When teachers' belief in their ability with technology is low, they are less likely to attempt to learn and integrate technology as a teaching tool (Ajjan & Hartshorne, 2008). When belief in ability is high, teachers seek out new information and technologies and incorporate them. Administrators, families, and peers can assist teachers by commenting positively on what they have already done, providing information and workshops to build confidence, and offering simple and quick ideas on how to implement technology. Positive attitudes toward technology integration play a dominant role in a teacher's willingness to try new things and self-efficacy.

Time is a mitigating factor in learning about and using technology. Having time during the week to play with and plan using technology and the ability to take technology home for practice increases the likelihood that technology will be integrated. When teachers have opportunities to play and explore technology, they grow more confident and experience active learning—something we know is important for adults as well as children.

Administrators play a critical role in the adoption of technology by teachers. Teachers feel motivated by their administrators' encouragement and praise for use of technology but can be discouraged by attitudes of disapproval or mistrust. They often lack motivation to incorporate technology in their classrooms and at times feel penalized by administrators and peers for their efforts when they are not supported and encouraged.

Allie wanted to take pictures of the children and their work to send home to parents and asked for a digital camera for her classroom. She was told the director would not buy one. She tried to use her phone to take pictures but was told that was not allowed and was reprimanded.

Some administrators offer small awards such as "techie of the month" certificates or other tangible motivators. One administrator offered a free "Jeans Day" coupon to teachers who participated in technology training sessions and implemented one idea they received.

Teachers who are pressured by administrators to put too much into their curriculum and to overemphasize academics have little time and motivation to integrate technology (Ajjan & Hartshorne, 2008). It is critical that programs examine their learning goals, objectives, and practices to be sure they are developmentally appropriate.

Culture, age, and family influence how educators approach and use technology (Nistor, Lerche, Weinberger, Ceobanu, & Heymann, 2014). While older teachers are less likely to embrace the use of technology in classrooms, this is not a mandate to lower expectations nor is it a universal truth. Many older teachers exhibit more patience in learning technology skills and may have a greater understanding of developmentally appropriate practices. Their years of experience make them comfortable enough with their teaching to tackle new and challenging technologies.

Teachers who are reticent to incorporate technology but are given mentors, time, and support often find that technology becomes an exciting part of their classroom practices. An older teacher taking a technology integration course with me a couple of years ago threw her laptop on the floor in frustration when asked to create a Facebook page for parents. That same teacher today has a Facebook page for her parents created during the class that she uses weekly (and sometimes daily) to share information!

Cultural and family attitudes and views create perceptions not only of one's abilities but of the appropriateness of technology. Knowledge of research and ideas on how technology can support cultural and family values often reassure those who have concerns.

Peers are an important factor in teacher success with digital media. Peers encourage other teachers to incorporate technology in their classrooms (and sometimes discourage them). Supportive peers who are proficient with technology become media mentors for others and can give suggestions and share ideas they have used. Some programs have each teacher learn one type of technology and practice in the classroom, such as how to take and import pictures from a digital camera into portfolios or how to use a Web tool to create books with and for children. The teacher then shares with the other teachers what she or he has learned and helps them to incorporate the technology. Peer sharing and mentoring is often much more effective than workshops or other forms of instruction in the integration of technology in classrooms (Fulford, Main-Anakalea, & Boulay, 2008; Kukulska-Hulme, 2012). Workshops may improve skills but do not necessarily assist teachers in integration (Figg & Jamani, 2013).

Many influences impact a teacher's successful incorporation of technology in the classroom. Figure 2.2 outlines factors that impact the integration of technology into developmentally appropriate practices and how technology can be an essential part of good teaching practice. Due to the focus of this book on family engagement and the role of media mentors, one of these practices is explored here.

Developing Relationships With Families

Developmentally Appropriate Technology Integration Facilitates Communication and Interaction With Families

This practice illustrates a critical role that technology can play today in engaging families and in creating that third space in which parent and teachers can find common ground and communication opportunities.

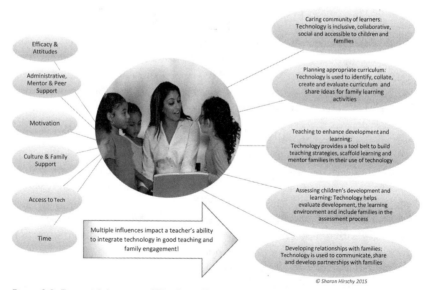

Figure 2.2 Essential Aspects of Teaching, Engagement and Integration

Using technology, we can:

- empower family members to participate in the day-to-day care and teaching of their child and use family knowledge of the child as an ongoing, critical source of information;
- involve the family in joint goal setting and decision making regarding their child's growth and learning;
- encourage families to participate in administrative decisions and community advocacy;
- provide learning activities for families to do together;
- provide opportunities via technology for families to participate in administrative decision making and involvement in programs; and
- link families to needed services and resources.

Perhaps nowhere do developmentally appropriate use and integration of technology impact children more than in our work with families. Providing and receiving information; creating partnerships that involve families in children's learning, assessment and development; and linking families to resources and opportunities for advocacy are now possible in ways that were not even recognized prior to the advent of our current technology age!

Perhaps nowhere does developmentally appropriate use and integration of technology impact children more than in our work with families.

Conclusion

Developmentally appropriate technology integration is much more than using or providing technology in classrooms. Integration implies enhancing learning and development by using technology as an effective and integral tool in pedagogical practices. The use of the NAEYC position statement on technology (NAEYC & Fred Rogers Center, 2012); the developmentally appropriate practice framework (Copple & Bredekamp, 2009); the stages mentioned here; this book; and many other current publications and online resources can create a roadmap to guide the development and use of technology in classrooms. Technology as the "third space" provides one of the best vehicles for communication and partnerships with families. Keeping the focus on developmentally appropriate technology integration and not on the technology itself provides teachers with a construct that focuses on building essential skills and knowledge in the classroom. Digital media become one of the many tools in a teacher's toolkit used to create a developmentally appropriate learning environment.

Helpful Hints for Media Mentors

- Further explore the meaning of developmentally appropriate technology integration—go to the interactive position statement at www.naeyc.org.

- Learn one or two new types of technology a month. Learn a new app or work with a new Web tool by first practicing with it for fun, then applying it in the classroom.
- Evaluate all new digital media for your classroom, and identify whether they are appropriate for each individual child and family, your learning environment, and your objectives.
- Develop a plan and PLN (personal learning network) to help you learn more about technology.
- Share what you learn with others in your program.
- Focus on the idea of using technology as a "third space" in your classroom. Consider ways technology can help you communicate with families, build relationships, share children's work and learning, collaborate on assessment, and bring children's family experiences into the classroom as learning activities
- Share a new technology with families each month. Send links to forms you create, an email or text to which they can reply, a website with a virtual trip to the zoo, or a link to a YouTube video or playlist that the children have used in class to sing and dance.

Digital media become one of the many tools in a teacher's toolkit used to create a developmentally appropriate learning environment.

References

Ajjan, H., & Hartshorne, R. (2008). Investigating faculty decisions to adopt web 2.0 technologies: Theory and empirical tests. *The Internet and Higher Education, 11*(2), 71–80.

Brantley-Dias, L., & Ertmer, P. A. (2013). Goldilocks and TPACK. *Journal of Research on Technology in Education, 46*(2), 103–128.

Copple, C., & Bredekamp, S. (Eds.). (2009). *Developmentally appropriate practice in early childhood programs serving children from birth through age 8.* 3rd ed. Washington, DC: NAEYC.

Donohue, Chip. (Ed.). (2015). *Technology and digital media in the early years: Tools for teaching and learning.* New York: Routledge; Washington, DC: NAEYC.

Ertmer, P. A., & Ottenbreit-Leftwich, A. (2013). Removing obstacles to the pedagogical changes required by Jonassen's vision of authentic technology-assisted learning. *Computers & Education, 64,* 175–182.

Figg, C., & Jamani, K. (2013). Transforming classroom practice: Technology professional development that works! *Teaching & Learning, 8*(1), 87–98.

Fulford, C., Main-Anakalea, C., & Boulay, R. (2008). Sabbaticals for technology integration. In *World Conference on Educational Multimedia, Hypermedia and Telecommunications* (Vol. 2008, pp. 660–669).

Hirschy, S. (2015). *Effective technology integration in early childhood education.* Retrieved from https://sites.google.com/site/ecetechintegration/

Kukulska-Hulme, A. (2012). How should the higher education workforce adapt to advancements in technology for teaching and learning? *The Internet and Higher Education, 15*(4), 247–254.

Moje, E. B., Ciechanowski, K. M., Kramer, K., Ellis, L., Carrillo, R., & Collazo, T. (2004). Working toward third space in content area literacy: An examination of everyday funds of knowledge and discourse. *Reading Research Quarterly, 39*(1), 38–70.

National Association for the Education of Young Children & Fred Rogers Center for Early Learning and Children's Media at Saint Vincent College. (2012). *Technology and interactive media as tools in early childhood programs serving children from birth through age 8.* Joint position statement. Washington, DC: NAEYC; Latrobe, PA: Fred Rogers Center for Early Learning and Children's Media at Saint Vincent College.

Nistor, N., Lerche, T., Weinberger, A., Ceobanu, C., & Heymann, O. (2014). Towards the integration of culture into the unified theory of acceptance and use of technology. *British Journal of Educational Technology, 45*(1), 36–55.

Pahl, K., & Kelly, S. (2005). Family literacy as a third space between home and school: some case studies of practice. *Literacy, 39*(2), 91–96.

Rogow, F. (2015). Media literacy in early childhood education: Inquiry-based technology integration. In C. Donohue (Ed.), *Technology and digital media in the early years: Tools for teaching and learning* (91–103). New York, NY: Routledge; Washington, DC: NAEYC.

Sutherland, R., Eagle, S., & Joubert, M. (2012). A vision and strategy for technology enhanced learning: Report from the STELLAR Network of Excellence. Retrieved from http://www.teleurope.eu/pg/file/read/152343/a-vision-and-strategy-for-technology-enhanced-learningreport-from-the-stellar-network-of-excellence

Resources

Evaluating Apps and Websites

- Children's Technology Review http://childrenstech.com/
- Common Sense Media www.commonsensemedia.org/
- Tap, Click, Read www.tapclickread.org

Family Communication and Involvement With Technology

- Families, Powered On! www.rand.org/pubs/research_reports/RR673z5.html
- Ten Tips for Involving Families through Internet-Based Communication www.naeyc.org/files/yc/file/200909/Ten%20Tips%20for%20Involving%20Families.pdf

General Resources

- Selected Resources on Technology in Early Childhood Education, NAEYC www.naeyc.org/content/technology-and-young-children/resources
- Resources for Supporting Appropriate Technology Integration, Illinois State Board of Education www.isbe.net/earlychi/preschool/preschool_tech.htm

Personal Learning Networks and Mentoring

- 10 Great Guides for Better Professional Learning Networks www.educatorstechnology.com/2013/01/10-great-guides-for-better-professional.html
- Stages of Personal Learning Network Adoption www.thethinkingstick.com/stages-of-pln-adoption/
- Teacher's Guide on Creating Personal Learning Networks www.educatorstechnology.com/2012/11/teacher-tutorial-on-creating-personal.html

Professional Development, Organizations, and Research

- Center on Media and Child Health Database of Research http://cmch.tv/
- Fred Rogers Center www.fredrogerscenter.org/blog/
- International Society of Technology in Education www.iste.org/

Skill Building and Tools for Teachers

- The 20 Digital Skills Every 21st Century Teacher Should Have www.educatorstechnology.com/2012/06/33-digital-skills-every-21st-century.html
- Edutopia www.edutopia.org/
- Pinterest (www.pinterest.com) Search topics "Early Childhood Curriculum" and "Early Childhood and Technology"
- Tech for a Global Early Childhood Education https://globalearlyed.wordpress.com/

Learn More...

- Daugherty, L., Dossani, R., Johnson, E., & Wright, C. (2014). *Getting early childhood educators up and running.* Rand Corporation, (Research Report RR-673/4-PNC). www.rand.org/pubs/research_reports/RR673z4.html
- Hirschy, S. (2015). Effective Technology Integration in Early Childhood Education website. https://sites.google.com/site/ecetechintegration/
- Hirschy, S. (2015). Developmentally appropriate technology in my classroom—But how? *Texas Child Care Quarterly, 39*(1). www.childcarequarterly.com/pdf/summer15_technology.pdf
- Mishra, P., & Koehler, M. (2006). Technological pedagogical content knowledge: A framework for teacher knowledge. http://punya.educ.msu.edu/publications/journal_articles/mishra-koehler-tcr2006.pdf
- Technology and Young Children Interest Forum, NAEYC. http://techandyoungchildren.com/home/
- Uses of Technology to Support Early Childhood Practice, OPRE. www.acf.hhs.gov/programs/opre/resource/uses-of-technology-to-support-early-childhood-practice-full-report

Chapter 3

Thinking, not Stuff

Re-imagining Young Children's Engagement With Technology and Innovation

Jeremy Boyle, Melissa Butler, and Junlei Li

Introduction

For many milestones in a young child's development, there seems to be a natural progression of learning and doing. For walking, an infant first learns to flip over onto his or her belly, then crawls, then stands up holding on to the railings on a crib, and eventually tumbles a few steps into an adult's open arms. For talking, a toddler starts by noticing and imitating sounds, then he or she connects the sounds with meaning and uses simple words, then two or more words are strung together into simple sentences and sentences into bigger ideas. For socialization and interaction, young children begin by smiling and receiving smiles back, looking and pointing when someone else looks and points, and eventually to tireless repetitions of give and take. Because such progressions seem so logical and natural, parents can almost intuitively grow to know how to support their children's development. After all, we were all children once—we went through the same progressions, we observed other children going through these same phases, and we learned how to learn.

This is not the case with children's use of technology in our digital age. Unlike walking, talking, and interacting, where we adults are clearly more "expert" than a developing child, technology in our age seems as new to us as it is to children. With each marketing season, technology is only getting newer and more unknown. This unfamiliarity gives rise to the often-repeated cliché of hapless grandparents or parents who need their grandchildren or children to figure out how to use their own "smart" devices or teachers who need their students to troubleshoot the classroom smart board, computer, or printer. Whereas we were all *learners* in the natural progressions of our own development, most of us are now relegated to be *users* and *consumers* in the rapidly evolving world of digital technology (Nourbakhsh, 2015). As technology becomes smaller, thinner, and more beautiful in its form, we are ever more distanced from how and why it works. We become consumers and want digital devices that make our lives easier, where the nuts and bolts and gears and parts we cannot name are all hidden inside a small, elegant, beautiful form that we hold in our pocket. We are taught to expect our digital devices to be beautifully formed and work by click and by touch, and we are not invited to ask why or how.

Here lies a great challenge for parents and educators: How do we help children learn to engage meaningfully with technology—*in ways deeper than just using and consuming*—when we ourselves have not gone through a learning progression with such technology?

In this way, educators and parents are in a similar predicament. A parent might ask a teacher for a recommendation for the latest educational app, but neither the parent nor the teacher can begin to understand or explain how the app was made, how it was delivered onto the screen in your hands, and how the digital images and sounds respond to touching and swiping on a rigid glass surface. As adults, we seem to (in the absence of alternatives) accept our detachment from the workings of technology. Smartphones and touch screen devices are made for us to use, not to understand, tinker, or fix. Most devices do not even afford us an opportunity to change their batteries. Our state of unfamiliarity with the inner workings of our most-used technology might be visible to our children as well. Whereas our children used to be able to take a broken toy to us with the expectation that we the adults could somehow fix it, today if a child takes a broken smartphone to a parent, the parent is often as helpless as the child. It is difficult for us to engage deeply with technology when we can barely keep up with understanding how to use it in our daily lives.

But do we want our children to experience technology only in this way? What do these fully formed devices teach children about the possibilities (or the lack of possibilities) for their engagement with technology? Is it possible for children to have deeper and more meaningful engagement with technology besides using and consuming? What does deep engagement mean, and what might it look like in our homes, child development centers, and school classrooms?

The three of us who are writing this chapter do not have answers, but we want to share what we wonder and notice about these questions in our work with children and teachers. None of us is remotely "expert" on the topic of technology in the digital age. Each of us approaches this subject from a different perspective. Jeremy is an artist, musician, and professor of art, and Melissa is a public school teacher. Together they created *Children's Innovation Project* to grow ideas for children and teachers to re-imagine technology and innovation in support of children's thinking and approach to learning. Junlei is a developmental psychologist who observes and thinks about how adults and children interact with one another and wonders what Fred Rogers's ideas and words mean for today's world. For the last three years, the three of us have been working together to support teachers to learn and grow, as teachers create spaces in their classrooms to help children learn and grow. We draw ideas from our own questions and explorations in the hope that some of these may connect with parents and educators and that we can grow a space for more noticing and wondering about the kinds of relationships and engagement our children ought to have with technology.

Why Is It Important for Children to Engage Deeply With Technology?

Children need to explore materials deeply in order to be able to create with them. We are reminded of Fred Rogers's reflection in the parenting resource book he compiled after he retired from television:

> The very best kinds of playthings are open-ended, those that a child can make conform to his or her own unique fantasies and feelings. If most of their playthings are "single-action" toys, their play tends to be limited, as if they're following the "formula" of what the manufacturer determined.
>
> Fred Rogers (2005)

How do we create opportunities for such open-ended play with technology? For children to be empowered to innovate and create, we believe that technology needs to be explored deeply by children in ways beyond using it as a tool (or worse, as mere products to buy, consume, discard, and upgrade). Children need to be afforded opportunities to dig into the material of what technology is, play with and talk about its logic, use their own thinking to gain access inside technology, and develop a sense of agency—"I can choose to make and re-make my world"—amid the technological systems that surround us.

We would not ask children to innovate using masking tape without first allowing ample opportunities for them to play with tape and understand its qualities, possibilities, and limits. We would not ask children to talk about what makes the writing of a book good without giving them the time to know and love a book, to listen to the book, read it themselves, look and wonder about the illustrations, linger in an image or idea, and think about the characters or stories. To play with any material, whether it is tape, clay, ideas in a book, soil in a garden, or numbers, children need opportunities for multiple experiences to delve deeply into the materials.

For teachers and parents, this seems intuitive. After all, that is how we learned most things ourselves. But, how do we do that with modern technology? Although there are numerous and increasingly more examples of innovative technology available for use in our schools and homes, there seem to be fewer everyday examples of children actually engaging directly with the material of technology. We want children to innovate with technology, to find or create something new, but in most educational contexts, children are kept as far from the material—what it is made of, how it is designed, how it works—of technology as possible. And as children (and most of us adults) become further removed from the material of technology, technology becomes that much more difficult for children to understand, talk about, and explore with the intention of innovation. This resignation of using technology while being distanced from the thinking of technology is so ubiquitous that we might imagine such a relationship as "the way it always was with technology," although this is not so even within our own lifetime. Most of us can recall that as children, we ourselves knew how to put a fallen chain back onto the gears of our bicycles, we watched records spin on a turntable and could see where one song ended and another began, and we had parents or grandparents who knew how to change the oil or spark plugs in their automobiles, and some of us, hopefully, still knew how to read a map to find our way on hiking trails or highways. To be alienated from the workings of the technology in our daily lives has never before been the default human phenomena until the current age of consumer and digital electronics.

…as children (and most of us adults) become further removed from the material of technology, technology becomes that much more difficult for children to understand, talk about, and explore with the intention of innovation.

When the focus of children's technological engagement is limited to giving them access to the *stuff* of technology rather than to the *thinking* of technology, children's capacity to learn and to wonder are neither respected nor served. With more *stuff*, children might learn how to use the tools as defined, but this can hardly empower them to have the abilities to invent their own tools, ideas, or expressions. Innovative technological gadgetry, rather than innovative thinking, may give children the illusion that they are innovators and inventors through their use of over-scaffolded and prepackaged products. Such experiences may engineer away possible opportunities to encounter real and sustained failures and the need to endure and persist through necessary struggles within the process of learning. The false sense of confidence and success that may come with technology use, without the necessary struggles and the desirable experience of difficulty, may do more to set children up for failure in real-world situations and prepare them poorly to be successful in the actual fields of science, technology, engineering, arts, and mathematics.

When the focus of children's technological engagement is limited to giving them access to the stuff of technology rather than to the thinking of technology, children's capacity to learn and to wonder are neither respected nor served.

What Is the Material of Technology?

In order to think about what it might mean for children to engage deeply with the material of technology, we need to think about what we mean by technology. What sorts of things might we consider to be technology? Why? Are there things we consider to be technology that other people might not define as technology? As time passes, more of what used to be considered technology seems to be excluded from many people's lists of what constitutes technology. For example, is a pencil technology? A screw? A doorknob? And as technology becomes more ubiquitous, there are fewer spaces and opportunities for us to stop to consider definitions of technology. Even more glaringly, there are fewer opportunities for us to reflect on our thinking and assumptions about technology and how these might matter to not only how we experience the world but to how we as teachers and parents are teaching children to experience technology in the world. Teachers want iPads in their classrooms and want to use technology in ways that support student learning, but the options for how technology is used seem somehow underwhelming compared to other engaging activities where children are actively playing with and exploring materials. We think this is similar to how parents feel about technology at home. We know many children are attracted or "glued" to technology, but we would like to see more children engage with technology in ways similar to how they might with mud, pots and pans, puddles, or shadows.

If we want children to innovate with technology, they need to explore its material in meaningful, slow, and deep ways. So what does this mean? What is the material of technology? So much new technology seems to have attractive "wow" factors that create the appearance that children can create previously unimaginable marvels using technology tools (3D printing a necklace, instantly creating a movie trailer using automated templates, turning an ordinary snapshot into a gorgeous professional photograph with the touch of a filter). We keep getting more projects that look good and appear as if children are using technology in innovative ways. But more often than not, it is the technology that is doing the innovation, not the children themselves. There is very little learning that supports deep understanding of the material of technology so children have opportunities to create new ideas and new forms with the material.

...we would like to see more children engage with technology in ways similar to how they might with mud, pots and pans, puddles, or shadows.

In contrast, we can imagine different possibilities for children's exploration with technology in ways similar to how we might have children explore with paint, clay, or paper. When we say this, we mean that we want children to work with technology in a way that allows them to touch its raw parts and talk about and understand its raw logic. We believe it is important for children to work at the grain of technology so they can more deeply explore it, so they can move things around, play with combinations of things, so they can talk to describe colors, shapes, textures, what feels heavy, squishy, what makes noise.

This might seem difficult to imagine because we do not often see this approach with new technology in classrooms. If we want children to explore the raw material of technology, we need to flip our thinking in two ways. One, instead of focusing on ways for children to create a *product*, we need to focus on children's learning of *process*. Two, instead of viewing the complexities of the material as something to avoid (to hide or work around, or eliminate by encasing in tidy, un-open-able shells), we need to embrace complexity as opportunity. There is an infinite space for meaningful student engagement with the actual material of technology if we can allow ourselves to think differently.

…innovation is reframed as finding something new inside something known…

We have found that it is possible to help children explore the raw material of technology when innovation is reframed as *finding something new* inside something known, shifting away from a focus on making some *thing*. Children need to have opportunities to dig deeper into materials they think they already know, in order to discover for themselves what is new and unexpected—rather than merely relying on yet another new gadget or app to "wow" them. We cannot expect this to happen if children work at a distance from the grain of the material. We cannot task children with "inventing" or "making" something way beyond their capacity to understand the *thinking* inside the creative process. We need to honor the small spaces where children are engaged in learning, where they are noticing and wondering about materials, where they are noticing and wondering about their own thinking even as they learn to develop such thinking. We need to support children as innovators by encouraging a creative process that helps them think about themselves in relation to the materials they explore.

How Might We Support Children's Development of Process and Habits of Mind?

By positioning technology as a raw material to explore while practicing innovator habits, instead of as a tool to use, we cannot only shift children's relationship with technology in their world (from consumptive use to productive discovery) but allow children to deeply engage with technological thinking in ways that empower them to carry this confidence and understanding with them into other areas of their world.

One way to think about this is to think about how we teach children in a writing workshop. As teachers, we know to teach the writer, not the writing. We know to let children explore and play with various crafts that other authors use in their books: repetition, interesting beginnings, thoughtful dedications, movement and perspective in illustrations, provoking back covers, beautiful images that make a reader feel things. Instead of rushing to correct children's writing or teach them to improve the actual book in which they are working, we listen to what children are doing, help them name the things they are doing as writers, and nudge them a little bit further in their thinking as a writer to support their growing confidence and creativity.

This is how we can approach our work with technology material and innovation, too. We can work and wonder alongside young innovators in our classrooms and children in our homes. We can support their noticing about materials, their play and exploration of how things work and don't work, their approach to wondering and imagining, and their process of staying with a struggle when things get difficult. We need to teach the innovator, not the innovation. We need to focus on process of thinking, not the use of or making of a specific *thing*.

When children are given opportunities to play with objects that are unknown to them and also to look more closely at objects that they know a little bit about but have never been allowed to play with before (such as a screw), they are excited. A single little screw opens so much potential for children's noticing and wondering about how it looks, how it feels, how it moves, where they have seen it before, what tool might work with it. A pile of hinges, doorknobs, springs, plastic brackets, pieces of foam, old circuit boards, conductive rubber panels, metal hooks, old thermostat controls, toggle switches—these all open up new worlds for children. Children not only get excited to talk about and describe such parts of things, they also start to wonder what things are part of and how things fit together in the world. They begin to look more closely at doors, cupboards, refrigerators, school light fixtures, their appliances at home, and also at a classroom set of electronic and mechanical toys.

If children can have access to this raw material of technology, then they can begin to notice it more closely, wonder about it in relation to things that interest them, move things around, manipulate various combinations, and invent new connections and understandings of systems (parts in relation to whole; cause–effect). These understandings grow alongside language to describe them and, in this way, such logic understandings (and approaches) may then be carried with children into other learning contexts when they attempt to understand more abstract and conceptual systems.

And, through opportunities to slow down and play with parts of things— such as raw pieces of technology—children start to find connections between objects, and they start to think about systems and how things matter in relationship to other things, people, ideas. This is significant. This is what allows children to begin to have words to wonder inside the things they cannot see. They begin to know they have the language, logic, confidence, and persistence to keep wondering and know that there is always more to see (whether they can actually see something or cannot).

What Does Deep Engagement With Technology Look Like?

Making connections, growing curiosities, asking questions, and imagining are all components of deep engagement. It is important to reflect on our own engagements with media and technology and to examine closely the interactions we facilitate or provide for our children. What opportunities are being provided for deep engagement? Is the technology necessary, or does it merely mediate an experience that could be more direct? How can we help to guide the interaction so that children are able to find these opportunities within their experiences? There are plenty of examples of engagement with technology and media that are far from deep. We are familiar with many examples of shallow engagement, staring passively into or swiping and tapping mindlessly on a screen. Often these engagements occur for long increments of time, but time alone does not make for deep engagement. Some modes of current educational technology use (in the best-case scenarios) do enable rich engagement with other subject matters, but the relationship between children and technology itself is almost always one of shallow engagement. Children use technology in one way and use it quickly and efficiently. If children are manipulating parts of technology, the focus is usually to make a product or to complete a design challenge with a desired outcome. The overall uses tend to be much more individual than social, more consumptive than inventive, and focus typically on questions to be answered rather than on questions that grow new questions and new paths of inquiry.

Here is a snapshot of what we see as deep engagement from a third-grade classroom in the Pittsburgh Public Schools. Listen in on this conversation and notice when the teachers nudge children to reflect back on their exploration with various electronic toys (opened for noticing and wondering).

Spotlight on Deep Engagement

Teacher: Whenever I was talking to K and C, they found the rotary switch and they made the connection back to their air conditioner that we talked about and then there was another switch that you also had to rotate but it was different. I thought it was another kind of rotary switch, but they didn't. And whenever I left, they didn't stop there. They kept looking and thinking more and more about it and exploring. So even though I thought that was a rotary switch too, they didn't just take that, they kept working. And at the end, K had a question of: "Is that it?" We realized it wasn't a rotary switch. We looked underneath it, and there was a lever and a push button switch. So then K had a question that was: "Is it a lever or a push button switch or is it both?"

Student 1: We were talking about…can I show you?

Teacher: We already put it away, you'll have to describe it with very precise language.

Student 1: There was a yellow-looking motor where I thought it was, I'm not sure but I thought, so we were looking at it really carefully and trying to figure out. While we were thinking about the motor, we were also thinking about which path the electricity went. There was all these wires. So A thought it took a longer way, and I thought it took a shorter way because before, I think in second grade, we talked about electricity is lazy and that's why I thought it was the shorter way. But, I was also thinking about what A said about this little bump. There was a bump on top of a bump, it was a smaller bump and a bigger bump. Yeah the metal-looking thing, there was actually a cover for that that we took off, and it's in our bag, where the push buttons were.

Student 2: I still got this thing, there was no wires connected to it there. The wires were connected from the motor to um…

Student 1: To the spring thing? And then it pushed over the block thing, and that's what I was talking about…

Student 2: It traveled through. It probably went in a circle and then went back.

Student 3: But we have to remember that electricity wants to go the easier way. There might be an easier way than both of our ideas.

Teacher: So what I hear is that no one in here is trying to be right. Mr. J's not trying to be right. He doesn't know everything. You're not trying to be right. You're listening and considering everything, always kind of wondering, right? And you're trying to find more questions.

Student 4: Here's a question for you, C: "What's a spring thing?"

Student 1: Okay, the spring thing was the spring, it was a spring. The black button.

Student 4: Was it the conductive rubber?

Student 1: No, it was nothing like that, no. The push button, you pushed it. And somehow the motor would spin, well, I thought it was the motor. And there was this metal, almost stick, a really skinny cylinder and it went in the little hole. So I thought that you pushed the button, the motor spins because I think I remember that toy has a speaker and LED lights when it is on.

Teacher: I literally would be happy to just stay here all night and just sit in this chair and listen to you because you're really, really brilliant. And when you're going back and forth. And what I like is over there, you weren't talking. And a lot of you we didn't even get to talk about the wonderful conversations at your table and you're fine with that. You don't care that we didn't get to talk about your toy or you, it's not about you. It seemed like you were enjoying listening, just like the teachers were, is that true? And were you learning from your listening? It seemed like that.

Student 5: It's like a story.

There are many things worth noticing about this snippet of classroom conversation. How are children engaging with technology? What is being valued by the teachers in the classroom? What processes are children learning? How are children engaged in thinking and thinking about thinking? For us, more than anything else, this scene shows that children are highly capable of engaging with the material of technology, its language, and its logic, and are eager to do so.

Deep engagement in this manner is slow, layered, complex, and full of questions and wonderings (Richhart, Church, & Morrison, 2011). It invites noticing, grows lots of language, and creates lots of conversation between children about small discoveries and new ways of playing or working with the materials. We see many opportunities for children's deep engagement in thinking, and we see a particular opportunity for this deep engagement in thinking when children are allowed to work with the material of technology.

Deep engagement with technology allows children to grow their own sense of agency with and in relation to the material. Engagement with technology allows children to think of what technology means differently, to be confident that they have the ability to create new ideas and expressions using the material, and to see themselves differently in relation to the technological world.

Deep engagement with technology supports access to the *thinking* behind technology, not just getting access to *stuff* of technology. More than using devices and consuming applications to learn and drill discrete skills, we believe children can and need to talk with one another, think, and *think about their thinking*.

Deep engagement with technology supports access to the thinking behind technology, not just getting access to stuff of technology.

Helpful Hints for Media Mentors

We are simultaneously eager to share our explorations with media mentors, educators, and parents and hesitant to offer "how-to" tips. What we do in our classrooms and with our teacher colleagues has grown from our particular context, our interests and strengths, and the particular interactions with the children we teach. We believe that educators and parents need to support their children's engagement with technology in ways grown from their own contexts and interactions and in ways responsive to children's interests and needs. What we have to offer here, perhaps, are four of the more enduring ideas that have guided, nudged, and pushed us to continue our exploration.

1 Re-think materials: Use what you have.
2 Provide access to thinking, not stuff.
3 Grow habits that make thinking possible.
4 Slow down: Don't be scared children will be bored.

Re-think Materials: Use What You Have

There is not a direct relationship between the newest, fastest, most powerful technology and innovative and deep learning experiences. In our observation, these experiences are often less likely to come through the newest examples of technology than through discarded or commonplace technology. An experience with an old rotary telephone is more likely to generate layered conversations about how technology actually worked to support human communication than the latest smartphone. Something as small and ordinary as a gear or a bolt or a spring is more likely to spark insightful connections within a child's thinking of technology. Meaningful learning experiences often do not require us to purchase and upgrade to the latest technological innovations. More important are the sensibilities through which we as teachers and parents engage children with technology. And to do this, the found materials around your home or unnoticed in a classroom are often best. Don't underestimate the learning potential from pieces of cardboard, a collection of old keys, a used doorknob, a piece of packing foam, the slant of light pushing its way onto your kitchen floor in the morning.

Another question for educators and parents to consider when thinking about materials is: Are they not in a form that most supports children's imagination? Take a look around our classroom or home play environment. How many materials for children's play prescribe a formula for what they are expected to play? Does the housekeeping area have materials that are all recognizable in children's lives, or are there materials that are unknown and open to varied interpretation? Is the block area full of cars, trains, people, and other objects that encourage specific kinds of talk and understanding, or are there plain blocks that children can pretend are anything they want?

Many, many play products—and especially apps and new STEM-focused educational toys—pre-set a narrative for children's play and specifies what they will talk about and think about with the material. One significant shift we can make in support of children's innovative thinking is to insert more raw materials into children's opportunities for play. A set of unrecognizable raw recycled materials, a clump of yarn, pieces of cut cardboard, scraps of different dimensions and thicknesses of plastic—these materials are more apt to allow children to find their own sustained attention with their own imaginative thinking and daydreaming.

Provide Access to Thinking, Not Stuff

In all experiences with technology, we might ask ourselves (as teachers and as parents): Does this technology experience allow children access to the thinking of technology or does it focus on access to the stuff of technology? How might we support all children to access innovative thinking with the material of technology (Richhart, 2015)? We believe this happens through children's engagement with the raw component materials of technology in slow, deliberate ways and also through children's engagement with the language of the logic systems of technology. If we want all children to have access to the thinking of technology, we need to focus on the relationship between language and logic as children work with materials. A focus on language and its relationship to logic allows children to be able to imagine how things work and feel confident in talking about what they know about how things work.

For example, at home or in the classroom, we can have "do-happen" and "same-different" conversations: What might you *do* to make *happen*? What makes some things work the same way and some things work differently? These are language and logic constructs we use in *Children's Innovation Project* that allow all children to access the thinking of why things happen ("I push this button and the light goes on." "I pull this lever and the small cylinder pops out.") and discuss relationships between things and ideas ("The carrot is like the wood because they both have a grain." "That device has something that spins, but this device goes back and forth and makes more noise.") These are only two examples of the kind of conversations adults have had with children—long before the availability of digital devices—that are important logic and language frames to engage with modern technology. We believe these conversations are significant for children to play with and practice alongside their play with materials they can touch. It is through these experiences with language that children learn to express and create their own logic and grow access and agency to their own creative thinking.

Grow Habits That Make Thinking Possible

When we talk about children engaging deeply, we are interested in their engaging deeply with material in order to dig deeply into learning about the material, learning about a process of innovation and creativity, and learning about themselves. Our thinking work is primarily focused on children's development of what we call habits of mind: to notice, wonder, and persist. We want all children to grow internalized sensibilities to slow down and appreciate that there is always more to see and more to wonder (Langer, 2014). We want to help them follow questions to find new questions, to embrace struggle in a way that they learn to appreciate it, and want to continuously find new challenges for themselves (Dweck, 2008). Fred Rogers—whose children's program "Mister Rogers' Neighborhood" is both beloved and occasionally parodied by comedians for being so deliberately slow—wrote:

> Sustained attention to things tends to foster deliberate thought. Readiness to develop the capacity for deliberate thought begins very early as children engage in their own kind of thinking—daydreaming, fantasizing, and making up all kinds of activities that we call play.
>
> Fred Rogers (1994), p.91

One of the things we can do to support children to have more space to engage with their own thinking and daydreaming is to be thoughtful about the language we use around children while they are playing and talking with us. As much as possible, we feel it is important to use conditional language—words such as "might" or "maybe" or phrases such as "that could be…" or "I wonder what else you'll find." This language supports children to continue with their thinking and imagining and not stop with one way of thinking (or knowing). It encourages children's sustained attention with their own imagining (Langer, 2014).

We want all children to grow internalized sensibilities, to slow down and appreciate that there is always more to see and more to wonder. We want to help them follow questions to find new questions, to embrace struggle in a way that they learn to appreciate it, and want to continuously find new challenges for themselves.

Another method for engaging children in thinking about their own thinking, and a primary method of classroom practice in *Children's Innovation Project*, is a process of observational drawing focused on seeing in order to find more to see. We believe that a quiet space of observational drawing is important for children's development as noticers about their environment, as well as noticers about the process of their own thinking and perspectives of seeing. As children draw, we as adults can notice more about children's thinking and find new questions to ask them in order for them to see more and wonder more and grow their own interest in sustained attention to things.

Slow Down: Don't Be Scared Children Will Be Bored

In order for children to innovate with technology, they need to explore it deeply. In order to explore technology deeply, children need to slow down and notice. This requires a sensibility of caring about small things and knowing that there is always more to see. We believe this sensibility can be taught (or in the case of children who have this sensibility already, we believe it can be nurtured and named so children learn to keep it as part of their ongoing sensibilities and not lose it).

For example, in our classrooms, we find that there is so much possibility in a single screw, so much for children to notice and wonder, so many opportunities for rich vocabulary and language expression, so many possibilities for connections to other things about which children are thinking. Children arrange screws by length, sort screws by size and patterns on the heads, use a piece of yarn wrapped around the shaft to notice more about the thread, its grooves and how it allows movement for the screw. Children do not bore from a screw. In fact, we have found that the longer children stay with their noticing of a single screw, the more interested they become in noticing further. We appreciate this quotation from the American avant-garde composer, John Cage:

> If something is boring after two minutes, try it for four. If still boring, then eight. Then sixteen. Then thirty-two. Eventually one discovers that it is not boring at all.
>
> John Cage, *Silence: Lectures and Writing* (1961), p. 93

This is one of the core assumptions we bring with us as we engage children with a single piece of technology material. Teachers and parents can take on this approach with technology: it is as much about the materials you provide for children to explore as it is about the assumptions you bring about how they might engage with such materials. In *Creating Cultures of Thinking*, Ron Ritchhart talks about the importance of modeling as one of the important cultural forces that matter in learning (2015). We cannot decide to model or not to; we are always modeling. We model by being who we are. Fred Rogers often liked to say, "Attitudes are caught, not taught." If we get bored or we think we know something for sure or we like things that are easy or we are not interested in a small crack in a tea cup or a spider at the bus stop, then our children will probably embrace this thinking, too. If we want our children to slow down and notice to wonder, if we want them to love and stay with the challenges that they find for themselves in the smallest of things, then we need to do this, too.

Conclusion

Blind Leading the Blind—and It's a Good Thing

If we believe that technology matters and we want to make sure children are engaging with technology in ways that empower them as thinkers in the world, what materials might we select that will allow students to dig deeply into their learning with technology? What lessons might we design to allow children opportunities to practice innovator habits they will internalize and carry with them in the world? What might our homes or classrooms look like—and, more important, feel like—to children? These are not easily answerable questions for us (the three authors), for our colleagues who explore and experiment in classrooms, for educators across the country, and for parents of all backgrounds.

A significant mantra for our teacher colleagues—and for the children they teach—is that it is wonderful to *not know*. It is not necessary for any "media mentor" to know answers to any questions we have posed here in this chapter. In fact, it is better if this chapter has caused you to find more questions and be less certain about your knowing. We think it is important for educators and parents to ask more questions and share these questions with other educators and parents. It is often not helpful for others to hear someone else's answers. But, if they can hear that someone else is struggling with questions too, this might invite them into thinking. What we ultimately share as teachers and parents is our noticing and wondering about how children might learn and grow in the current landscape of ubiquitous and overwhelming technology. We hope that educators, parents, and community members can grow more opportunities for conversations, more opportunities to come together to notice, to wonder, and to persist in this struggle around what it might mean, for ourselves and for our children, to engage meaningfully with technology.

*It is wonderful to **not know**.*

References

Cage, J. (1961). *Silence: Lectures and writings.* Hanover, NH: Wesleyan University Press.

Dweck, C. S. (2008). *Mindset: The new psychology of success.* New York: Ballantine Books.

Langer, E. (2014). *Mindfulness.* Boston, MA: Da Capo Press.

Nourbakhsh, I. (2015). *Parenting for technology futures.* Amazon Digital Services Inc.

Richhart, R. (2015). *Creating cultures of thinking.* San Francisco, CA: Jossey-Bass.

Richhart, R., Church, M., & Morrison, K. (2011). *Making thinking visible.* San Francisco, CA: Jossey-Bass.

Rogers, F. (1994). *You are special: Words of wisdom from America's most beloved neighbor.* New York: Penguin Books.

Rogers, F. (2005). *The Mister Rogers' parenting resource book.* Philadelphia, PA: Running Press.

Resources

- Children's Innovation Project www.cippgh.org
- Fred Rogers Center for Early Learning and Children's Media www.fredrogerscenter.org
- Fred Rogers Center's Blog page www.fredrogerscenter.org/news–events/blog/
- Project Zero—children "making," not just "consuming" technology www.agencybydesign.org/
- Remake Learning http://remakelearning.org
- Remake Learning Playbook http://remakelearning.org/playbook/

Learn More...

- *The Simple Human Interactions That Make Learning Possible*, Remake Learning Blog, Junlei Li, January 6, 2016 http://remakelearning.org/blog/2016/01/06/the-simple-human-interactions-that-make-learning-possible/
- *The Simple Human Interactions That Make Learning Possible (Part Two: People Who Help Us Try)*, Remake Learning Blog, Junlei Li, January 8, 2016 http://remakelearning.org/blog/2016/01/08/the-simple-human-interactions-that-make-learning-possible-part-two-3/
- *The Simple Human Interactions That Make Learning Possible (Part Three: Technology that enriches, rather than replaces, human interactions)*, Remake Learning Blog, Junlei Li, January 12, 2016 http://remakelearning.org/blog/2016/01/12/the-simple-interactions-that-make-learning-possible-part-three/
- *The Teachers' Innovation Project*, Fred Rogers Center Blog, Sarah Jackson, September 16, 2014 www.fredrogerscenter.org/2014/09/16/the-teachers-innovation-project/
- *Helping Children Find Something New Inside Something Known*, Fred Rogers Center Blog, Jeremy Boyle, October 27, 2014 www.fredrogerscenter.org/2014/10/27/helping-children-find-something-new-inside-something-known/

Spotlight on Engagement

Message From Me—Message From Pittsburgh

When Renee Hughes asks her preschool-aged daughter, Olivia, about what she did at school, she gets replies that all parents get.

Nothing. I don't know. I played. These ubiquitous, time-honored non-answers are especially common among young children such as Olivia, whose brains are still developing the ability to converse about past events. For many families, this is the extent of school-focused discussions. Children may truly not remember what they did or what they learned, or they may be unable to express it in conversation. Adults, then, are left to devise their own ways of keeping up with their child's learning, whether by chatting with teachers or poring over assessments.

But Hughes has a new tool at her disposal, one that's gaining popularity among Pittsburgh's parents and educators. She pulls out her cell phone and opens a text message that she received earlier in the day. It's a photo of Olivia drawing, along with a voiceover that Olivia herself recorded.

"Hi, mom," Olivia says in the message, "I'm drawing a picture of our family!" Olivia's eyes light up as she watches her mother's screen. Suddenly, she's able to tell Hughes about what she did that day—in this case, her class learned about families and then drew family portraits. Equipped with this information, Hughes is able to ask her daughter specific questions and lead a productive, insightful conversation about Olivia's learning. "I point to people in her drawings and ask, 'Who is that? What does that person do?'" says Hughes. "I can ask her about her work and give her real, targeted praise. I can expand on what she learned at school, get her to use her higher-level thinking skills, and have healthy conversations about learning with her."

This is the promise of Message From Me, an iPad app that lets preschoolers such as Olivia take pictures, record voice messages, and send them home as an electronic package during class time. Developed as a collaboration between Carnegie Mellon University's Community Robotics, Education and Technology Empowerment (CREATE) Lab and the Pennsylvania Association for the Education of Young Children (PAEYC), Message From Me enables children to better communicate their learning with adults back home. The app is an initiative of Remake Learning, a network of 250 multi-sector organizations—including the CREATE Lab and PAEYC—that work collaboratively to accelerate learning innovation in southwest Pennsylvania. "Remake Learning fosters a spirit of connectedness," says PAEYC's Sue Polojac, one of the app's original developers. "It's about collaboration instead of competition. The network provides the table for all of to sit at and talk about how to take projects like Message From Me to the next level."

Polojac and other members of Remake Learning have continuously refined and expanded the ways in which Message From Me is used to engage families. "Feedback from parents and teachers really drives those changes," says Polojac. She recalls one meeting in which a tearful mother described how Message From Me changed her family's dynamic. "Her husband worked a lot, and didn't have a lot of interaction with their son. But the first time he received a message via Message From Me, he couldn't wait to come home and ask their child about what he'd learned in school that day. It became a regular thing. Their son's grades improved, and they became closer as a family."

Hughes has had a similar experience. "As a parent, you're constantly busy," she says. "Message From Me helps you find out what your child is proud of, and that builds a relationship. My daughter and I have really bonded over it." And Hughes knows as well as anybody what it's like to be a busy parent: When she's not home with her daughter, she's hard at work as a preschool teacher. In her classroom, she sees Message From Me doing for other families what it has done for her own. "Families love it," she says. "They absolutely love it. It's easy to use: My students are between three and five years old, and they've picked it up with no problem. They use it during center time, or I'll make it part of our lessons. Parents are always better able to engage with what their children are learning when they can see it for themselves. It's also great because as a teacher, I can go into the system and look at what my students have been sending. It's another tool for assessing progress, and it's fun."

Contributed by Gregg Behr, Grable Foundation and Remake Learning, Pittsburgh, PA

Learn More...

- Message from Me http://remakelearning.org/project/message-from-me/
- CREATE LAB, The Children's School of Carnegie Mellon University http://cmucreatelab.org
- PAEYC http://paeyc.org
- Remake Learning http://remakelearning.org/
- Grable Foundation http://grable.org

Chapter 4

Logging in to Family Engagement in the Digital Age

M. Elena Lopez, Margaret Caspe, and Heather Weiss

Introduction

Digital media and technology are part of young children's learning landscape. Research shows that children from birth to age 8 spend an average of 3 hours a day engaging with various forms of media, including television, computers, mobile devices, and gaming consoles. Surprising, perhaps, is the finding that children younger than age 2 spend twice as much time watching television and videos as they do reading books or being read to (Rideout, 2013). With the flood of digital products to entice young children, parents are seeking advice on where to find the best resources to boost their children's learning. They are turning to family, libraries, schools, peer networks, and, especially, early childhood providers for this guidance. Early childhood providers today are taking new roles as mediators between new technologies and families. Many are already using digital media not only to direct families in children's use of apps, e-books, and the like but also to enhance parenting skills, home–school communication, and family health and well-being.

Family engagement is a shared responsibility of families and educators for children's learning.

Early childhood providers need to be intentional about how and why they are using digital media with families and the promise digital media hold for impacting families themselves. This is the goal of our chapter—to help early childhood educators as media mentors adopt a systems framework for understanding the role of digital media within a larger early-education program that includes its leadership and management, staff development, and teaching and learning activities with children and their families. In the first section, we introduce a family engagement framework to guide programs in the use of digital media while maintaining a focus on advancing family outcomes. In the second section, we show how by providing families with information, equipping families with understanding and skills, and helping families take action, digital media have the power to positively influence a wide variety of family outcomes.

Key Messages from the Joint Position Statement

Technology tools offer new opportunities for educators to build relationships, maintain ongoing communication, and exchange information and share online resources with parents and families. Likewise, parents and families can use technology to ask questions, seek advice, share information about their child, and feel more engaged in the program and their child's experiences there.

NAEYC & Fred Rogers Center (2012), p. 7

By family engagement, we mean a shared responsibility of families and educators for children's learning. We focus on family engagement because it makes a difference for children's success *and* is a matter of equity. Studies have shown that upon kindergarten entry, there are vast differences in children's average educational achievement by socioeconomic background (Lee & Burkam, 2002). Differences also exist in young children's access to the adult guidance that can help them acquire "information capital" for success in school and in life (Neuman and Celano, 2012). These gaps can be explained, in part, by families from low-income households having fewer resources, less access to high-quality preschools and social supports, and reduced opportunities to give children the full benefits of digital media for learning that high-income households do. Effectively tackling early inequalities means that we must broaden our understanding of how families and schools can work together to optimize digital media use so that children have full and equal access to and participation with it (Harvard Family Research Project, 2014a). Even more, tackling inequality means thinking broadly about how digital media can enrich the lives of families themselves.

The Parent, Family, and Community Engagement Framework: Beyond Random Acts of Technology

Research shows that family engagement efforts are most effective when they are systemic. This means they go beyond random isolated acts of engaging families and instead weave family engagement practices throughout the entire program (Weiss, Lopez, & Rosenberg, 2010). In a systems approach, family engagement is a key strategy—alongside leadership, curriculum and instruction, and teacher professional development—to achieve the goal of children's school readiness. From 2011 to 2015, Harvard Family Research Project partnered with the Brazelton Touchpoints Center to operate the Office of Head Start's National Center on Parent, Family, and Community Engagement. The Center developed a Parent, Family, and Community Engagement Framework (known as the PFCE Framework) to guide a systems approach to family engagement (U.S. Department of Health and Human Services, 2011; Figure 4.1).

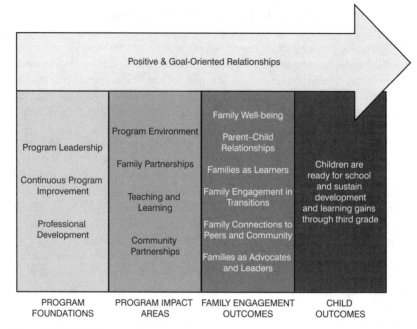

Figure 4.1 PFCE Framework
(Courtesy of Harvard Family Research Project)

In a systems approach, family engagement is a key strategy—alongside leadership, curriculum and instruction, and teacher professional development—to achieve the goal of children's school readiness.

The PFCE Framework anchors family engagement in an organizational system and directs relationships and activities toward seven family outcomes that are linked to children's healthy development and school readiness. Beyond Head Start, the systemic approach is relevant for early childhood programs as they embark on a pathway of media mentorship in a digital age. A systems approach keeps programs from slipping into isolated, random acts of technology use and maintains a focus on adopting digital media to advance family outcomes.

Elements of the Framework

The PFCE Framework emphasizes three key elements: leadership (program foundations), practices (program impact areas), and family outcomes that support children's school readiness. Embedded across these elements is the commitment to build trusting relationships with families. Effective engagement depends on respectful relationships with families and valuing the diverse ways in which they promote their children's outcomes. Program

Table 4.1 Family Engagement and Digital Media—Program Foundations
(Courtesy of Harvard Family Research Project)

Program Foundations	Examples of What Programs Can Do
Leadership	Develop, in partnership with families, clear and specific policies and expectations regarding the uses of digital media for children and families.
Continuous Improvement	Establish processes for families to provide input and feedback on the program's use of digital media—e.g. to communicate with families; to offer children and families content that reflects their language and culture; to ensure access and equity as children use digital media for learning.
Professional Development	Hold regular dialogues with staff and families about developmentally appropriate practices in the use of technology and interactive media (e.g. dialogues about joint position statement of NAEYC and Fred Rogers Center for Early Learning and Children's Media, 2012). Moreover, use digital media as one tool in combination with others for professional development opportunities.

leadership is about making family engagement a priority and embedding it in all activities that link to children's learning and development. It is what drives the foundational work for using digital media for family engagement, including setting policies, aiming for continuous improvement of practices, and building capacity through professional development (see Table 4.1).

Effective engagement depends on respectful relationships with families and valuing the diverse ways in which they promote their children's outcomes.

The PFCE Framework offers four types of practices or impact areas that influence family engagement:

1 program environment
2 teaching and learning activities
3 family partnerships, and
4 community partnerships.

Table 4.2 Family Engagement and Digital Media—Program Impact Areas

Program Impact Areas	Examples of What Programs Can Do
Program Environment	Create safe and welcoming physical spaces that invite family participation in various forms of media—books, crafting materials, computers, 3D printers, tablets etc.—with their children, individually, or with other families.
Teaching and Learning	Provide opportunities—such as conferences, meetings and video clips—for families and staff to share their observations and practices about children's use of digital media.
Family Partnership	Learn how families use—and want to use—digital media for communication, connection, and participation in the early childhood program.
Community Partnership	Invite community agencies to share information, fun activities, and workshops that use digital media for learning and skill development for adults and young children alike.

Today, digital media, not just in terms of the technology but in terms of the thinking underlying it, are reinventing these practices. For example, the digital age has made us more keenly aware that we are all learners. A climate conducive to learning is, above all else, an environment in which everyone thinks about him- or herself as a learner (Caspe & Lopez, 2014). A learning climate creates a safe space wherein both children and adults, all with different learning styles and expertise, can explore, take risks, and co-construct knowledge together. For example, program staff members learn how to improve outreach and communication with families through text messaging, Facebook, and YouTube. And, in fact, a growing body of research shows that these new modes of digital communication have the potential to change the nature of parent–teacher communication and increase family engagement in schools (Blair, Mazer, & Grady, 2015). Table 4.2 provides examples of how program settings, activities, and partnerships can be harnessed for family engagement within the context of a climate that values learning at all ages.

A learning climate creates a safe space wherein both children and adults, all with different learning styles and expertise, can explore, take risks, and co-construct knowledge together.

Table 4.3 Seven PFCE Framework Family Outcomes

7 Family Outcomes	Definitions
Family Well-being	Families are safe, healthy, and financially secure.
Parent–Child Relationships	Families maintain warm relationships with their children that nurture their child's learning and development.
Families Lifelong Educators	Families are a child's first teacher.
Families as Learners	Families advance their own learning interests through education, training, and other experiences that support careers, parenting, and life goals.
Family Engagement in Transitions	Families support and advocate for their child's learning and development as they transition to new learning environments.
Family Connections to Peers and Community	Families connect with peers and family members.
Families as Advocates and Leaders	Families participate in leadership development, decision making, program policy development, and community and state organizing activities.

The PFCE Framework also offers clear and specific family engagement outcomes that research has shown to be important contributors to children's successful outcomes. The seven family outcomes acknowledge the different roles families play in children's development in the home, early childhood program, and community (Table 4.3). In the next section we explore these family outcomes more deeply and the role of digital media in promoting them.

The Potential of Digital Media to Support Family Outcomes

Below, we describe what we know from research and evaluation about the potential for digital media to promote the seven PFCE Framework family outcomes. Specifically, we show that digital media can promote family outcomes when used to provide families information, equip families with understanding and skills, and help families take action. Embedded throughout each section, we provide promising program practices, even in cases where the evidence-base for these practices might not yet be robust, simply because the rapidly evolving use of digital media has far outpaced the research that can shed light on its value or its potential shortcomings. We are caught, as the saying goes, "building the plane while learning how to fly it."

Use Digital Media to Provide Families With Information

Many different characteristics of children, parents, families, and the communities in which they live affect *family well-being*. Digital media have the power to promote and improve families' circumstances by providing families with access to resources in quick and convenient ways. For example, Text4baby is a text messaging service designed to promote maternal and child health. Expectant mothers who sign up for the service—the majority of whom are from low-income households—receive free text messages throughout the week addressing topics such as labor signs, pre- and post-natal care, and developmental milestones. Mothers who use the service have been found to demonstrate higher levels of health knowledge, feel more prepared to be new mothers, and be more connected to health services than those who do not (Text4baby, n.d.).

Low-income families often hold multiple jobs, work nontraditional hours, and must juggle the competing demands of work and engagement in children's learning (Chin & Newman, 2002). Digital media have the potential to ease the stresses of this situation in small but important ways by providing families with access to online, on-demand resources that can be accessed anywhere, anytime (Patton & Caspe, 2014). For example, aXcess Newark is an app that offers timely information about available social services and resources in the city. Family members can find agencies that will help them find employment, housing, domestic violence shelters, early child care providers, health clinics, and other services whenever is convenient for them. Importantly, Newark parents had a voice in the app's design, contents, and marketing in the community (Callaghan, 2014).

Digital media can also support *family engagement in transitions*. It is during transition points that families are most in need of information as they must choose providers and schools that are right for their child. The Parents Know website, hosted by the Minnesota Department of Education, is an online resource developed with parent input whereby parents can access information on child development, consumer safety, and health and nutrition. To support transitions, the website includes a "Getting School Ready" video and monthly activities for parents to do with their children to prepare for kindergarten. Parents expressed that they wanted information available in their first language and preferred to access the information digitally rather than receive it on paper, so all of the information on the website is presented in multiple languages and is available in multiple formats including text, interactive tools, webinars, videos, and audio podcasts. The website is promoted through social media and advertising on billboards and public transportation (Patton and Wang, 2012).

Spotlight on Libraries Addressing Families' Digital Learning Needs

Today's library is a modern and trusted space that supports digital learning needs for the entire family. Libraries provide families and children access to an array of high-quality digital resources, such as e-books, apps, and public-access computers. And, through their role as "digital navigators," librarians give families and children guidance on how to use these ever-evolving resources (Semmel, 2014). Increasingly, libraries, early childhood programs, and families are teaming up to align learning opportunities across communities, with a strong focus on digital use and production.

Leverage Digital Media to Equip Families With Understanding and Skills

Digital media can be used not only to provide families with information but also to increase their understanding to use that information effectively and creatively. By doing so, families take on the roles as *lifelong educators* and *learners*: They become powerful teachers for their own children who also gain new skills themselves (Harvard Family Research Project, 2014a). For example, Iridescent is a science education nonprofit that engages underserved children and families in science, technology, engineering, and math (STEM) project-based learning. Iridescent teaches parents about STEM concepts but also provides training on how to engage children with these concepts at home and in the community through in-person workshops and online videos and mentorship. Families who participate in the trainings and completed design experiments with their children increased the extent to which they discuss science and actively engage in science activities, such as building, designing, and creating things together with their children (Chivloski, 2015).

Key Messages from the Joint Position Statement

Modeling the effective use of technology and interactive media for parent communication and family engagement also creates opportunities to help parents themselves become better informed, empowers them to make responsible choices about technology use and screen time at home, engages them as teachers who can extend classroom learning activities into the home, and encourages co-viewing, co-participation, and joint media engagement between parents and their children.

NAEYC & Fred Rogers Center (2012), p. 8

Family learning is most beneficial when families clearly understand their children's interests and opportunities for growth. Early childhood professionals have a responsibility to communicate with families about what children are doing in school and the progress they are making, and digital media can play an important and innovative role in this process. For example, Message from Me a is a digital kiosk placed in early learning classrooms that allows young children to document what they've done in school using digital cameras and microphones and then send their parents a message about it via email, voice mail, or text (Message From Me, n.d.). This fluidity of communication between home and school supports parent–child conversations about children's work and creates real-time authentic portfolios.

Spotlight on Parents

It's one thing to hear about and discuss what your child is learning in school with teachers and staff, but it's another to actually see it and hear it yourself. It helps bridge a gap between home and school. What is taught in class can be observed and repeated at home.

Message from Me Parent

Message from Me has changed how my husband talks with our child. My husband was too busy before, but with the MFM message, he connects—gets more involved in the conversation. My son drags him to see the messages, and he makes all his brothers see the messages, too. It makes them have a REAL conversation, rather than just, "How was your day?" "Good." Message from Me makes them more involved together.

Message from Me Parent

And, programs are starting to offer parent workshops on choosing educational apps for their children. Guided by developmentally appropriate principles, Imajine That in Lawrence, Massachusetts, simultaneously shows adults the apps, demonstrates and models their use, and organizes literacy and science spaces where families and children enjoy the use of tablets, games, and apps together (Harvard Family Research Project, 2014c). To ensure quality in these types of experiences, programs are beginning to develop assessment tools to understand what quality programming of this nature involves, what adult–child interactions might look like, and the outcomes for children.

Figure 4.2 Imajine That Provides a Space for Families and Their Young Children to Engage in Hands-on Digital and Real-world Projects Together
(Courtesy of Krysta O'Neill, Imajine That)

Draw on Digital Media to Help Families Take Action

Families benefit when digital media provide clear and actionable ideas and tools that families can use on behalf of their children's learning, their family, and community. One of the key roles of early childhood programs is to serve as gatekeepers and to share with families digital tools that are grounded in the research based on early childhood development. For example, apps such as Vroom and Let's Play from Zero to Three (Harvard Family Research Project, 2014b) give parents specific suggestions and ideas for games they can play with their children while they are at home or out in the community that build *parent–child relationships* and help support children's learning. In fact, research shows that text messaging and voice mail reminders of newly learned parenting strategies in addition to in-person home visits improve responsive parenting and reduce maternal depression and stress, even more than just home visits alone (Bigelow, Carta, & Lefever, 2008; Carta, Lefever, Bigelow, Borkowski, & Warren, 2013). Even more, when early childhood programs text parents on a consistent basis with facts about children's development, ideas for parent–child activities to do at home, and general words of parenting encouragement, parents increase their engagement with their children around home literacy activities that can lead to improvements in children's learning (Hurwitz, Lauricella, Hanson, Raden, & Wartella, 2015; York & Loeb, 2014).

Digital media can also be used so that families can actively *connect to peers* in their community. Research shows that mothers of young children with wider social networks are less likely to feel depressed and isolated and more likely to have access to material resources, in turn improving parental warmth and feelings of efficacy (Small, 2009). There are many simple things that programs can do involving digital media to support connective relationships among families in a program. For example, providers can email directories at the beginning of the year that include families' cell phone and email information to facilitate connections. And digital platforms and apps such as Toyota Family Trails create online social communities where families can share videos and pictures of family moments captured at home or in the community and spark ideas for other families on places to explore and learn together.

Digital media have the power to support *families as advocates and leaders.* They offer a platform for families to voice their interests and concerns for their children and for children's issues. For example, MomsRising is an advocacy group that focuses on issues such as early care and education, maternity and paternity leave, and healthy eating. Through online letter-writing campaigns, active Twitter chats, online petitions, and on-the-ground organizing efforts, the organization has successfully influenced policy efforts at the national and local level (MomsRising.org, n.d.).

TATUM FAMILY: PICKING STRAWBERRIES

Written by Sheena Tatum

June 30th, 2015

I'll admit it. I have high and sometimes unrealistic expectations for summer vacations and activities. Having lived in the Midwest my entire life, I'm conditioned to want to bust out of the joint every summer. This year, I let go of my grand plans of a long-distance vacation to focus on the bigger picture. The more I planned, the more draining it became trying make sure every single variable was taken care of. And the more pregnant I grew, the more I simply wanted to stay close to home.

Figure 4.3 Family Activities with Toyota Family Trails
(Courtesy of Emily Kirkpatrick, National Center for Families Learning)

Logging in and Opening Opportunities

As the digital movement sweeps across the country, it is important to remember that digital media are tools rather than ends. As tools, they must be viewed in the wider context of an early childhood program's family engagement goals and organizational capacities to achieve them. We used the Head Start Parent, Family, and Community Engagement Framework to identify a systems approach to family engagement. In this approach, digital media are mobilized to promote family outcomes and to ensure that families can use digital media to become better informed decision makers and partners in their children's learning.

Digital media open many possibilities for family engagement. Families are logging in to access information, learn what their child is doing in preschool, avail themselves of community resources, communicate with home visitors and teachers, connect with other families, and make decisions about children's transition to school. Far from being a passive medium, we are coming across examples of families using digital media to produce content. They are logging in to provide input for app design, make STEM projects with their child, create content about outdoor activities to share with other families, and write blogs to advocate for children's education and well-being. With these trends growing and new possibilities yet to come, digital media are likely to become an indispensable asset to promote meaningful family engagement.

Digital media are tools rather than ends. As tools, they must be viewed in the wider context of an early childhood program's family engagement goals and organizational capacities to achieve them.

References

Bigelow, K. M., Carta, J., & Lefever, J. B. (2008). Txt u ltr: Using cellular phone technology to enhance a parenting intervention for families at risk for neglect. *Child Maltreatment, 13*(4), 362–367. Doi:10.1177/1077559508320060

Blair, C. T., Mazer, J. P., & Grady, E. F. (2015). The changing nature of parent–teacher communication: Mode selection in the smartphone era. *Communication Education, 64*(2), 187–207. Doi:10.1080/03634523.2015.1014382

Carta, J. J., Lefever, J. B., Bigelow, K., Borkowski, J., & Warren, S. F. (2013). Randomized trial of a cellular phone-enhanced home visitation parenting intervention. *Pediatrics, 132*(S 2), 167–173. DOI:10.1542/peds.2013-1021Q

Caspe, M., & Lopez, M. E. (2014). How organizations provide learning opportunities for children and families. *Family Involvement Network of Educators (FINE) Newsletter, 6*(5). Retrieved from www.hfrp.org/publications-resources/browse-our-publications/how-organizations-provide-learning-opportunities-for-children-and-families

Chin, M. M., & Newman, K. S. (2002). *High stakes: Time, poverty, testing, and the children of the working poor.* New York: Foundation for Child Development.

Chivloski, T. (2015). Engaging families in science, technology, engineering, and math (STEM) project-based learning. *Family Involvement Network of Educators (FINE) Newsletter,* 7(1). Retrieved from www.hfrp.org/publications-resources/browse-our-publications/engaging-families-in-science-technology-engineering-and-math-stem-project-based-learning

Harvard Family Research Project. (2014a). April *FINE Newsletter:* Making it Real—Connected Learning in the Digital Age. *Family Involvement Network of Educators (FINE) Newsletter,* 6(2). Retrieved from www.hfrp.org/family-involvement/fine-family-involvement-network-of-educators/fine-newsletter-archive/april-fine-newsletter-making-it-real-connected-learning-in-the-digital-age

Harvard Family Research Project. (2014b). Q&A with Rebecca Parlakian: Learn anytime with the Let's Play App. *Family Involvement Network of Educators (FINE) Newsletter,* 6(4). Retrieved from www.hfrp.org/publications-resources/browse-our-publications/q-a-with-rebecca-parlakian-learn-anytime-with-the-let-s-play-app

Harvard Family Research Project. (2014c). Q&A With Susan Leger Ferraro and Fran Hurley: Learning through technology-infused play. *Family Involvement Network of Educators (FINE) Newsletter,* 6(3). Retrieved from www.hfrp.org/publications-resources/browse-our-publications/q-a-with-susan-leger-ferraro-and-fran-hurley-learning-through-technology-infused-play

Hurwitz, L. B., Lauricella, A. R., Hanson, A., Raden, A., & Wartella, E. (2015). Supporting Head Start parents: Impact of a text message intervention on parent-child activity engagement. *Early Childhood Development and Care, 185*(9), 1373–1389. Doi:10.1080/03004430.2014.996217

Lee, V. E., & Burkam, D. T. (2002). *Inequality at the starting gate: Social background differences in achievement as children begin school.* Washington, DC: Economic Policy Institute.

Message from Me. (n.d.). Message from me: Welcome. Retrieved from www.messagefromme.org/

MomsRising.org, (n.d.). MomsRising.org wins. Retrieved from www.momsrising.org/issues_and_resources/wins

National Association for the Education of Young Children, & Fred Rogers Center for Early Learning and Children's Media at Saint Vincent College. (2012). *Technology and interactive media as tools in early childhood programs serving children from birth through age 8.* Washington, DC: NAEYC; Latrobe, PA: Fred Rogers Center for Early Learning and Children's Media at Saint Vincent College.

Neuman, S. B., & Celano, D. C. (2012). *Giving children a fighting chance: Poverty, literacy, and the development of information capital.* New York: Teachers College Press.

Patton, C., & Caspe, M. (2014). Finding time together: Families, schools, and communities supporting anywhere, anytime learning. *Family Involvement Network of Educators (FINE) Newsletter,* 6(4). Retrieved from www.hfrp.org/publications-resources/browse-our-publications/finding-time-together-families-schools-and-communities-supporting-anywhere-anytime-learning

Patton, C., & Wang, J. (2012). *Ready for success: Creating collaborative and thoughtful and transitions into kindergarten.* Cambridge, MA: Harvard Family Research Project.

Programs for Parents (n.d.). Mayor Baraka, Programs for Parents, Foundation for Newark's Future launch new mobile app for parents. Retrieved from http://www.programsforparents.net/component/content/article/81

Rideout, V. (2013). *Zero to eight: Children's media use in America 2013*. San Francisco, CA: Common Sense Media. www.commonsensemedia.org/research/zero-to-eight-childrens-media-use-in-america-2013

Semmel, M. (2014). Lessons from museums and libraries: Five ways to address families' digital learning needs. April FINE Newsletter: Making it Real—Connected Learning in the Digital Age. *Family Involvement Network of Educators (FINE) Newsletter, 6*(2). Retrieved from www.hfrp.org/publications-resources/browse-our-publications/lessons-from-museums-and-libraries-five-ways-to-address-families-digital-learning-needs

Small, M. (2009). *Unanticipated gains: Origins of network inequality in everyday life*. New York: Oxford University Press.

Text4baby. (n.d.). *Understanding the impact of Text4baby*. Retrieved from https://partners.text4baby.org/templates/beez_20/images/HMHB/t4b%20impact%20factsheet%205.20.13.final.pdf

U. S. Department of Health and Human Services. (2011). *The Head Start parent, family, and community engagement framework promoting family engagement and school readiness, from prenatal to age 8*. Retrieved from http://eclkc.ohs.acf.hhs.gov/hslc/standards/im/2011/pfce-framework.pdf

Weiss, H. B., Lopez, M. E., & Rosenberg, H. (2010). *Beyond random acts: Family, school, and community engagement as an integral part of education reform*. Cambridge, MA: Harvard Family Research Project. Retrieved from www.hfrp.org/publications-resources/browse-our-publications/beyond-random-acts-family-school-and-community-engagement-as-an-integral-part-of-education-reform

York, B. N., & Loeb, S. (2014). *One step at a time: The effects of an early literacy text messaging program for parents of preschoolers*. Working Paper 20659. National Bureau of Economic Research.

Resources

- aXcess Newark http://axcessnewark.com/vertex.php
- Imajine That www.imajinethat.com
- Iridescent http://iridescentlearning.org
- Let's Play app, Zero to Three https://itunes.apple.com/us/app/zero-to-three-lets-play/id807952060?mt=8
- Message from Me www.messagefromme.org/
- MomsRising.org www.momsrising.org/
- Parents Know, Minnesota Department of Education www.parentsknow.state.mn.us/parentsknow/index.html
- Text4baby www.text4baby.org/
- Toyota Family Trails http://familytrails.com
- VROOM app www.joinvroom.org

Learn More...

- Department of Education, Family, and Community Engagement Framework www.ed.gov/family-and-community-engagement
- Families and Media Project, Joan Ganz Cooney Center www.joanganzcooneycenter.org/initiative/the-families-and-media-project/
- HFRP, Harvard Family Research Project www.hfrp.org
  - o *Family Engagement in Anywhere, Anytime Learning* www.hfrp.org/publications-resources/browse-our-publications/family-engagement-in-anywhere-anytime-learning
  - o FINE Network, Family Involvement Network of Educators www.hfrp.org/family-involvement/fine-family-involvement-network-of-educators
  - o *Finding Time Together: Families, Schools, and Communities Supporting Anywhere, Anytime Learning* www.hfrp.org/publications-resources/browse-our-publications/finding-time-together-families-schools-and-communities-supporting-anywhere-anytime-learning
  - o *Social Media—Engaging Families in Children's Learning and Use of Digital Media* www.hfrp.org/publications-resources/browse-our-publications/social-media-engaging-families-in-children-s-learning-and-use-of-digital-media
  - o *Strengthening Family Engagement Through Teacher Preparation and Professional Development* www.hfrp.org/publications-resources/browse-our-publications/strengthening-family-engagement-through-teacher-preparation-and-professional-development
- Office of Head Start, Parent, Family, and Community Engagement http://eclkc.ohs.acf.hhs.gov/hslc/tta-system/family
- Office of Head Start PFCE Framework http://eclkc.ohs.acf.hhs.gov/hslc/tta-system/family/framework/interactive.html

Chapter 5

Families, Powered on

The Power of Nudges

Rafiq Dossani and Anamarie Auger

Introduction

The power of a "nudge" to influence behavior is shown to be effective in many areas of social development, such as civic engagement, education, and health care. A nudge—a brief suggestion or reminder of a positive behavior—is a small step that is typically inexpensive and a non-intrusive means of promoting behavioral changes. Nudges include actions that might subconsciously change behavior, such as displaying healthy food options more prominently than less healthy options in a convenience store or school cafeteria, as well as more overt actions, such as text messages recommending a book to read with one's child. In education, nudges have been used in several ways, including increasing college attendance and encouraging parental involvement in children's early learning.

A nudge—a brief suggestion or reminder of a positive behavior—is a small step that is typically inexpensive and a non-intrusive means of promoting behavioral changes.

Traditionally, early childhood educators have used non-technological nudges via signs on the classroom door or fliers sent home with a child to engage parents in their child's learning or provide pertinent information. Although this type of low-tech communication continues to be effective for some, technology provides educators with potentially more effective communication platforms. Recent findings relating to the use of technological nudges in preschool settings are encouraging for changing parent behaviors and children's development. For example, text messaging parents about the importance of reading has led to an increase in the time parents spend reading to their child, and parents who received phone texts about ways to promote children's early literacy interacted more intensively with their child on literacy activities (Dynarski, 2015: Mayer, Kalil, Oreopulos, & Gallegos; 2015; York & Loeb, 2014). Children whose parents participated in the intervention showed higher early literacy skills in some areas compared with children whose parents didn't participate in the study (York & Loeb, 2014).

This chapter explores how nudges have been used in early childhood education and their potential for greater effect as technology becomes more sophisticated. We begin by providing an overview of nudges and a summary of early childhood education and family engagement research, focusing on findings about the importance of family engagement for children's academic and social development. We present research on educational nudges, focusing on early childhood education (preschool years), and the power of technology to facilitate and improve the effectiveness of nudges. We also highlight recent successful interventions that utilize text messaging and other nudges to promote parent engagement in children's early learning. Finally, we suggest ways in which educators can leverage technology to promote family engagement, including ways technology can be used to establish and encourage a dialogue about children's learning between families and early childhood educators.

What Nudges Achieve and Why They Work

As a matter of public policy, it is important that nudges fulfill two criteria: preserve options and direct toward "better for everyone" options. Additionally these two criteria must be compatible with each other. First, nudges should preserve options, not reduce them. For example, the authors of *Nudge* (Thaler & Sunstein, 2009) point to research studies in which patients' medical decisions can be influenced by the framing of success rates or high schools can increase college enrollment by providing financial aid information and weekend tax consultation sessions for parents. Both of these examples preserve options but alter the presentation of options available to "nudge" a specific behavior (e.g., opting in for a procedure or attending college).

A second criterion is that the nudge should also seek to direct consumers toward choices that are "better for all" and away from choices that are "bad for all." For example, health warning labels on tobacco products and calories provided on restaurant menus. Both examples promote well-being and health of consumers (while also preserving options). However, sometimes, the two criteria may not be compatible, in which case we would not consider the proposed change to be a nudge. For instance, suppose that a school district wants to determine whether high schools should introduce the use of wireless clickers to answer multiple-choice questions. To find out whether it helps learning, the school district randomly equips half the district's schools with clickers while the other half continue as before. Suppose it is found that clickers dramatically improve learning for all students and, after considering the costs and other options, suppose that the district decides to introduce the compulsory use of wireless clickers in all high schools. Although we may be able to argue that the action of compulsorily introducing clickers is good for learning and should be done, it is not a nudge. It fulfills the criterion of improving learning but, being compulsory, fails the criterion of choice preservation.

The theory of why nudges work is still nascent. Thaler and Sunstein (2009) argue that nudges are important because human beings are not always consciously rational about their choices. For instance, obesity afflicts two-thirds of Americans, yet the obese find it difficult to stop overeating. Such persons may find nudges (of both the implicit and explicit kinds) to be a useful reinforcement to positive behavior. For instance, experiments have shown that serving food in smaller plates leads to less overeating (Thaler and Sunstein, 2009, p. 44). The converse is also possible. For instance, corporate marketing research has demonstrated the importance of product placement to encourage impulse purchases (i.e., to increase irrational behavior; Mattila and Wirtz, 2008).

Another reason why nudges may work is that they may help overcome some significant informational barriers. Consider, for instance, that a child's teacher might share information with the parents of her or his students about a new reading app that, in her or his experience, makes it more enjoyable for the child to read. A parent may not have known about the app ("too little information"), or might have been overwhelmed by the number of choices of reading apps available ("information overload"). Receiving an app from a trusted source—the teacher, in this case—is valued by parents, leading the nudge to have an effect.

Receiving an app from a trusted source—the teacher, in this case—is valued by parents, leading the nudge to have an effect.

Sometimes, the informational barrier may instead have to do with complexity. Parents may want to ensure that a book that they would like to read with their child is appropriate in a number of respects: age-appropriate in its content, gender-sensitive, relates to a theme, contains lively multimedia content that could be appropriately enjoyed in a range of technology settings (from cut-outs in a book to multimedia digital images on a laptop), and so on. Choosing the right book can be a daunting task in the face of such a complex set of attributes. A nudge from a teacher suggesting a book, or an app that helps with this process, that she feels meets these tests of appropriateness helps overcome the information complexity barrier.

Early Childhood Education and Parent Engagement

Research has acknowledged the interaction between parents and teachers as a key dimension of parental involvement (e.g., Fan & Chen, 2001; Hoover-Dempsey & Sandler, 1997). Parent involvement or family engagement has many definitions and theories on what approach is most effective. In a recent publication commissioned by the Office of Planning, Research, and Evaluation, the authors present several definitions of parent engagement but note that work by the Harvard Family Research Project and others is finding a shift in the definition of parent engagement or involvement "towards a more reciprocal and responsive family involvement and family engagement framework across K–12 and early care and education programs (Gonzalez-Mena, 2006; Halgunseth et al., 2009; McWilliam, Maxwell, & Sloper, 1999; Weiss, Bouffard, Bridgall, & Gordon, 2009; Weiss et al., 2010)" (Forry et al., 2012, p. 10). Additionally, the authors note that these perspectives of family involvement emphasize "programs and schools play an important role in supporting and strengthening families in their childrearing as well as encouraging families to become actively involved in school events and programs" (Forry et al., 2012, p. 10).

Parents who participate in activities such as school events, programs, and home-based activities are more likely to display positive parenting behaviors, and their children have higher academic and social skills compared with children whose parents do not engage in their education in similar ways (Miedel & Reynolds, 2000; El Nokali, Bachman, & Votruba-Drzal, 2010; McWayne, Fantuzzo, Cohen, & Sekino, 2004). However, firm conclusions from these studies are limited in that a majority of the studies did not use random assignment and thus biases (e.g., parents who participate in the family engagement activities were already more likely to participate in home activities with their child even without the family engagement activities from the preschool) in the results may exist. In addition, few studies measured the value or cost of time. Increased parental engagement with school activities comes at a cost of time that could be used elsewhere, such as for earning income. Low-income parents, for instance, might prefer engagement activities that are less demanding of time during regular working hours. Nudges may be an alternative method to achieve similar increases in parent engagement.

Formal Evaluations of Parent Engagement and Early Learning Programs

Random assignment studies, widely considered the "gold standard," whereby one group is assigned to receive a parent or family engagement intervention (or early care program with parent engagement component) and the other group does not receive the intervention, demonstrate positive effects of parent engagement on parenting behaviors and child outcomes (e.g., Anthony, Williams, Zhang, Landry, & Dunkelberger, 2014; Love et al., 2005; Puma, Bell, Cook, & Heid, 2010; Walker, Gooze, & Torres, 2014). For example, a family engagement program, Raising a Reader (RAR), involves parents in their children's education by providing the family with books and information for teachers on how to promote "shared reading practices, classroom instructional strategies, and take-home activities" (Anthony et al., 2014, p. 497). The program also includes a parent meeting where parents are provided information on the program, including strategies on how to read to and engage with their child, even including information on how to read picture-only books for parents who are struggling readers. Additionally, the program aims to connect families with libraries by providing information on what programs are offered at the library and how to utilize the library services, and to provide parents with a library card to promote reading at home. Currently RAR operates in 34 states and in 2013 served more than 100,000 children and their families (Walker et al., 2014). An augmented version of the program includes five parent engagement workshops, and findings suggest it is effective in enhancing children's oral language skills compared with families that did not receive the enhanced version of RAR (Anthony et al., 2014). In addition, the non-enhanced original version of RAR did not lead to positive changes in children's language skills.

Two national early childhood programs for low-income families, Early Head Start and Head Start, require parent participation either through home visits, volunteering in a classroom, or other activities. The two programs were evaluated, independently, using a random assignment design: A family was either assigned to participate in Head Start or Early Head Start or was assigned not to participate in the program. The National Evaluation of Early Head Start (Love et al., 2005) demonstrated positive effects on children's language and cognitive development and on positive parenting behaviors such as the type of discipline used and being more emotionally supportive. Similarly, a national evaluation of Head Start indicated that at the end of the programming year, 3-year-olds who participated in Head Start had higher academic skills including vocabulary, math, emergent literacy skills, and social skills compared with children who did not participate, and their parents reported reading more to their child and providing more cultural enrichment opportunities (Puma et al., 2010). The 4-year-old cohort demonstrated few positive outcomes at the end of the Head Start program year but still displayed more advanced literacy skills as compared with children who were not in Head Start. Although these studies indicate that early education programs that include a parent engagement component have an impact on children's achievement and parenting practices, it is not clear exactly how or why parenting behaviors are affected, and more research is needed to disentangle the effects of the parent engagement element from the early education or center-based care components.

Long-Term Impacts of Family Engagement Programs

A few studies have examined the long-term impact of parent engagement programs on children's development and parenting behaviors. In one such study, Miedel and Reynolds (2000) examined whether children whose parents had participated in family engagement activities in a school setting, such as attending school meetings, going on class trips, and volunteering in the classroom during preschool and kindergarten, had better academic outcomes later in life as compared with children whose parents did not participate. The authors used data from the Chicago Longitudinal Study, which was funded to determine the effects of a preschool and kindergarten program (Chicago Parent–Child Centers) that provides educational activities and family support services to central-city families in Chicago (Reynolds, 2000). The authors found that children did in fact have better literacy outcomes and on-time grade promotion than did children whose parents did not participate in multiple family engagement activities during preschool and kindergarten (Miedel & Reynolds, 2000). Other evaluations of early education programs with a parent engagement component (e.g., Early Head Start and Head Start national evaluations) have found similar long-term impacts on parenting behaviors and parent engagement in school such as time spent reading and whether the parent attends school meetings or open houses during preschool (Gelber & Isen, 2013; Vogel, Brooks-Gunn, Martin, & Klute, 2013).

Although these studies demonstrate the long-term effects of parent engagement and early learning programs, the mechanism through which the effects are sustained is not known, and more research in this area is needed. Additionally, many of these programs are expensive, and as funding for programs comes under scrutiny and is harder to receive, low-cost interventions are needed to promote family engagement in children's early schooling. In the next section, we describe early childhood educational interventions that are relatively inexpensive and utilize "nudge theory."

Early Childhood "Nudge" Interventions

Several effective early childhood interventions have relied on nudges. One of the most notable parent education interventions is Reach Out and Read (ROR), an intervention aimed at parents of infants through preschoolers that provides parents with information on how to read to their child and promote school readiness skills and provides free children's books during pediatric visits (Zuckerman, 2009). ROR began in a Boston clinic in 1989 and is now a nationwide program operating in more than 5,000 sites and will have served approximately 4.5 million children and families since the program's inception (Klass, 2015). ROR is relatively inexpensive: approximately $8 per child per year, or $40 for the program from birth to age 5, assuming a total of 10 pediatric visits during that age range (Zuckerman, 2009). ROR has been evaluated multiple times using random assignment methods, and results from evaluations demonstrate that the program had a positive impact on children's expressive and receptive language skills (e.g., High, LaGasse, Becker, Ahlgren, & Gardner, 2000; Mendelsohn et al., 2001; Zuckerman, 2009) and parent literacy practices in the home (Diener, Hobson-Rohrer, & Byington, 2012; Sharif, Rieber, & Ozuah, 2002).

Another early childhood intervention "nudged" parents to practice positive parenting practices, home safety, and proper nutrition and provided parents with developmentally appropriate child development knowledge embedded in children's baby books (Reich, Bickman, Saville, & Alvarez, 2010). The intervention provided baby books at obstetrician clinics in a southern U.S. state to low-income first-time mothers randomly assigned to the treatment group during their third trimester of pregnancy and when the child was 2, 4, 6, 9, and 12 months of age. The books were written at first-grade reading level so mothers with low literacy levels could still participate in the intervention. Mothers in the intervention not assigned to the treatment group either received traditional baby books with no educational content or did not receive any baby books. The educational nudges embedded in the children's baby books proved to be effective at positively altering home safety practices (Reich, Penner, & Duncan, 2011), maternal perceptions about the importance reading to their child (Auger, Reich, & Penner, 2014), improving self-efficacy (Albarran & Reich, 2014), and reducing support for corporal punishment (Reich, Penner, Duncan, & Auger, 2012).

The two interventions included in this section are both low-cost interventions that provide parents with information on child development and parenting practices and provide tips on how to promote positive development, including promoting children's school readiness. In the next section, we examine ways in which educational researchers have utilized technology to provide nudges to parents and youths to promote positive parenting practices and child development.

Electronic Nudges

Nudges are found in everyday life and, as discussed previously, are commonly used in educational interventions. Nudges are no more apparent than when they are used in combination with technology. For example, emails can be used to alert or "nudge" shoppers of a sale at one of their favorite stores or to remind customers to pay a credit card bill. Phone or tablet applications routinely send notifications about weather updates, sports scores, and calendar events. Educators can leverage technology to reach parents and provide important information about upcoming school events, a child's progress in class, or tips for home activities parents can participate in with their child. One such promising technology to reach parents is by text messages.

Given the large increase in cellular (cell) phone use and ownership (PEW Research Center, 2015), text messages have been shown to be an effective medium for nudges, and these interventions have been utilized in numerous fields, including health and education (Castleman & Page, 2015; Malhotra, Michelson, Rogers, & Valenzuela, 2011; Shapiro et al., 2008; Thaler & Sunstein, 2009). The adoption of mobile phones that are capable of sending texts is nearly ubiquitous, meaning that texts are effective even for low-income families that can prove difficult to reach via other means (MarketingCharts, 2015; see Resources). Text messages are simple and fast ways to communicate and may be particularly useful ways for educators to communicate with youth or parents. Additionally, the increase in cell phone use and in social media platforms provides rich opportunities for educators to promote dialogue with parents and facilitate parent–parent connections to engage parents in children's early learning.

In a recent *New York Times* article, Susan Dynarski (2015) details how nudges can be and are currently being used in education to help low-income children and families succeed. The article covers electronic nudges used in education, mainly focusing on text messaging interventions. Dynarski highlights seminal educational interventions using nudges, such as Benjamin Castleman and Lindsey Page's work helping high school students overcome the "summer melt"—high school seniors who are enrolled in college but do not attend college in the fall (Castleman & Page, 2015; Dynarski, 2015). The article also highlights how successful interventions in early childhood can be used to influence parental behavior in the home and how those changes in the home environment lead to improvements in children's academic skills.

One such promising school readiness intervention in northern California, READY4K!, utilized text messaging to send parents of preschoolers information about ways they can engage with their child to promote school readiness skills (York & Loeb, 2014). READY4K! sends parents three texts per week over an 8-month time period. The text message intervention is sent to parents in the intervention conditions 3 text messages per week; a fact about reading/early literacy skills, a tip on how to engage with children to promote children's skill development in relation to the fact text, and a growth text that provided parents with words of encouragement and an additional tip (York & Loeb, 2014).

Examples of the texts include

> *FACT: Beginning word sounds are essential for reading. You can help your child learn to read by saying the beginning of words. "Read" starts w/"rrr."*

> *TIP: Say two words to your child that start with the same sound, like happy & healthy. Ask: can you hear the "hhh" sound in happy & healthy?*

> *GROWTH: By saying beginning word sounds like "ttt" in taco & tomato, you're preparing your child 4K. Now have your child make the "ttt" sound.*

> (p. 13)

Additionally, the authors note that the text messages were aligned with California's Preschool Learning Foundations, which provides potential for other states to adopt the text messaging intervention and align the messages with their state's early learning guidelines. The intervention was very low-cost (approximately $1 per family). Results from the study, where one group of parents was randomly chosen to receive the informational texts and another group of parents received "placebo" texts (e.g., texts with information about mandatory school vaccinations) are striking. Parents who received the informational texts participated in more literacy activities with their child, were more involved in school, and their children demonstrated significant gains in several early literacy skills. The results of the study are extremely promising given the extensive use of text messaging (PEW Research Center, 2015), the low-cost, and the gains associated with the READY4K! program.

Another early childhood parent engagement intervention, Parents and Children Together (PACT), which uses simple reminders to encourage parents to read to their children, also demonstrates noteworthy results. Mayer and colleagues (2015) designed a 6-week intervention using "behavioral tools" including weekly reading goal setting, text message reminders, and small social rewards to promote reading on e-book tablet application. Families in Head Start centers in Chicago who agreed to participate in the study were provided with tablets loaded with an application "A Story Before Bed" that contains more than 500 children's books. The application records the amount of time parents spend reading books from the application. Half of the families were also given the behavioral tools, including informational text messages, opportunities to set reading goals each week, and receiving small social rewards, such as celebratory weekly texts for the parent who logs the most time reading, to remind parents or "nudge" them to read more to their child. Parents in the control group did not receive these behavioral tools and reminders.

Results from the study indicate that parents who received behavioral tools and reminders read to their child more than double the time spent by parents who did not receive any of the behavioral tools. Similar to the READY4K! intervention the PACT intervention demonstrates an encouraging way in which behavioral nudges can be used to promote reading practices in the home environment. Additionally, this intervention takes a step further and provides parents with an e-book tablet application that provides a library of children's books and allows parents to view real-time results of the time spent reading. The pairing of the behavioral tools and e-book application demonstrates how technology can be used to successfully encourage and promote parents' reading to their preschool-age child.

The READY4K! (York & Loeb, 2014) and PACT (Mayer et al., 2015) interventions demonstrate how successful simple electronic nudges can be in encouraging parent–child interactions and, in the case of the READY4K! intervention, how nudges can translate into early literacy gains for preschool children. In the concluding section, we discuss other technological platforms that can be used to encourage parent engagement and how early childhood educators can leverage the different technologies to promote parent involvement and positive child development.

Concluding Discussion

The "holy grail" for nudges in education is a low-cost intervention that preserves options and is "better for all," all while helping parents overcome barriers such as information access and management. An area to explore further is how alternative technologies (e.g., apps and social media) might make nudges more effective than the one-way interactions that text messages represent. One key for success is for nudges to be simple enough so that they do not overwhelm the recipient. For instance, we earlier discussed the case where a teacher suggests a new reading game (app) to a parent. To make the choice richer, the teacher might include a link to a demonstration of a number of apps that she has found useful, so that the parent could try these easily on his or her smartphone before deciding on whether to buy the app. However, such richness comes at the price of time: The parent has to decide whether to invest time in testing the different apps and may well decide not to do so in many cases for various reasons, including work demands.

A similar situation may apply when parents use social media. For instance, a group of parents may set up a site on social media to exchange information about books to read to children. To be useful, such a group needs to invest time in sharing the books, assessing them, and sharing recommendations. Further, in the absence of expert opinion, the participants may not trust recommendations from such a group.

The lack of time and expertise may be why, even in the world of nearly ubiquitous use of smartphones by those in the parental age (nearly 9 in 10 cell phone-using adults in the 25- to 34-year age group use smartphones, according to a 2015 marketing study [MarketingCharts, 2015], the nudges that seem to work well are simple ones, using the technology of text messages that was available some decades earlier.

Helpful Hints for Media Mentors

Can new technology, especially smartphones, allow us to do more? We present below some suggestions for using nudges that exploit technology in a more complex way.

Summary of Helpful Hints for Providing a Nudge

- Keep messages short, clearly written, and aligned with standards.
- Provide a weekly tip on how to incorporate activities in the home.
- Use existing technology programs and social media platforms that can automatically send reminders and tips.
- Incorporate content into the school day for alignment between the classroom and home activities.
- Use the collaborative features of an online learning management system.

Our first suggestion draws on research from the successful early childhood interventions demonstrating that text messages promote reading in the home (Mayer et al., 2015; York & Loeb, 2014). Early childhood providers can also leverage social media, knowing that many parents are accessing social media on cell phones and are receiving "push notifications" (i.e., nudges) to provide reminders to parents related to basic paperwork requirements, center and community events, updates on what is happening in the classroom, and tips for how to promote children's learning at home. Given the research, we recommend keeping messages short, clearly written, and aligned with preschool or early learning standards. Specifically, educators could provide a weekly tip for parents on how to incorporate lessons from the week into activities in the home. For example, if the focus is on learning letters, educators could provide examples on how parents can turn walks or car drives into "letter hunts."

Another way educators can promote parent engagement is to "nudge" parents by providing information on already existing technology programs that automatically send reminders and tips (i.e., nudges) to parents, such as ReadyRosie. This particular program sends daily links to a video that provides instructions on how the parent can engage in an activity with the child (Daugherty, Dossani, Johnson, & Wright, 2014). Early childhood educators can also incorporate this content into the school day so that there is alignment between the classroom and home activities and continue nudging parents to use these types of programs via social media or text messages. If early childhood educators are utilizing ReadyRosie or another parent engagement tool, they can provide additional nudges to parents by sending reminder messages on social media or using text-messaging software to promote use of the tool.

A final suggestion involves the use of a number of features of online learning management systems (LMS) that most K–12 schools and an increasing number of ECE providers use. These offer forums for two-way communication in groups, student assessments, and multi-media material archiving. Suppose that a parent discussion forum on the LMS (moderated by the teacher) is created for the purpose of discussing which books are suitable to read with the child. Earlier, we noted several attributes that a parent would want such a book to contain: age-appropriate in its content, gender-sensitive, relates to a theme, contains lively multimedia content in a range of technology settings (from cut-outs in a book to multimedia digital images on a laptop), and the like. Through the discussion forum, the teacher can present the parents with her recommendations on each of these attributes, resulting in a far richer set of information than a simple "yes/no" recommendation. Such information allows the parent not only to become better educated about what is important but to make choices that are better suited to her child. The discussion forum can then help parents go "beyond the nudge": For instance, it can be used to create groups of those parents who have chosen the same book so that they can share their children's experiences and discuss supplementary material.

The above suggestions are intended to show that more can be done using technology. As technology allows more complex choices to be made, the challenge will be to support parents in ways that are low-cost and time-efficient for both teacher and parents. The nudge may well be the solution that delivers.

References

Albarran, A. S., & Reich, S. M. (2014). Using baby books to increase new mothers' self-efficacy and improve toddler language development. *Infant and Child Development, 23*(4), 374–387.

Anthony, J. L., Williams, J. M., Zhang, Z., Landry, S. H., & Dunkelberger, M. J. (2014). Experimental evaluation of the value added by Raising a Reader and supplemental parent training in shared reading. *Early Education and Development, 25*(4), 493–514.

Auger, A., Reich, S. M., & Penner, E. K. (2014). The effect of baby books on mothers' reading beliefs and reading practices. *Journal of Applied Developmental Psychology, 35*(4), 337–346.

Castleman, B., & Page, L. (2015). Beyond FAFSA completion. *Change: The Magazine of Higher Learning, 47*(1), 28–35.

Daugherty, L., Dossani, R., Johnson, E., & Wright, C. (2014). *Families, powered on: Improving family engagement in early childhood education through technology.* Santa Monica, CA: RAND Corporation, RR-673z5-PNC.

Diener, M. L., Hobson-Rohrer, W., & Byington, C. L. (2012). Kindergarten readiness and performance of Latino children participating in Reach Out and Read. *Journal of Community Medicine and Health Education, 2*(133), 2.

Dynarski, S. (2015, January 17). Helping the poor in education: The power of a simple nudge. Retrieved November 13, 2015, from www.nytimes.com/2015/01/18/upshot/helping-the-poor-in-higher-education-the-power-of-a-simple-nudge.html

El Nokali, N. E., Bachman, H. J., & Votruba-Drzal, E. (2010). Parent involvement and children's academic and social development in elementary school. *Child Development, 81*(3), 988–1005.

Fan, X., & Chen, M. (2001). Parental involvement and students' academic achievement: A meta-analysis. *Educational Psychology Review, 13*(1), 1–22.

Forry, N., Bromer, J., Chrisler, A., Rothenberg, L., Simkin, S., & Daneri, P. (2012). *Family-provider relationship quality: Review of conceptual and empirical literature of family-provider relationships,* OPRE Report #2012-46, Washington, DC: Office of Planning, Research and Evaluation, Administration for Children and Families, U.S. Department of Health and Human Services.

Gelber, A., & Isen, A. (2013). Children's schooling and parents' behavior: Evidence from the Head Start impact study. *Journal of Public Economics, 101*, 25–38.

Halgunseth, L., Peterson, A., Stark, D. R., & Moodie, S. (2009). *Family engagement, diverse families, and early childhood programs: An integrated review of the literature.* Washington, DC: The National Association for the Education of Young Children.

High, P. C., LaGasse, L., Becker, S., Ahlgren, I., & Gardner, A. (2000). Literacy promotion in primary care pediatrics: Can we make a difference? *Pediatrics, 105* (Supplement 3), 927–934.

Hoover-Dempsey, K. V., & Sandler, H. M. (1997). Why do parents become involved in their children's education? *Review of Educational Research, 67*(1), 3–42.

Klass, P. (2015, August 17). Bedtime stories for young brains. Retrieved November 13, 2015, from http://well.blogs.nytimes.com/2015/08/17/bedtime-stories-for-young-brains/?_r=2

Love, J. M., Kisker, E. E., Ross, C., Raikes, H., et al. (2005). The effectiveness of early head start for 3-year-old children and their parents: Lessons for policy and programs. *Developmental Psychology, 41*(6), 885–901.

Malhotra, N., Michelson, M. R., Rogers, T., & Valenzuela, A. A. (2011). Text messages as mobilization tools: The conditional effect of habitual voting and election salience. *American Politics Research, 39*(4), 664–681.

MarketingCharts. (2015, February 17). Smartphone penetration, rising in all age and income demos: Hits 75% of the U.S. mobile market. Retrieved November 13, 2015, from www.marketingcharts.com/online/smartphone-penetration-rising-in-all-age-and-income-demos-hits-75-of-us-mobile-market-51585/

Mattila, A. S., & Wirtz, J. (2008). The role of store environmental stimulation and social factors on impulse purchasing. *Journal of Services Marketing, 22,* 562–567.

Mayer, S. E., Kalil, A., Oreopoulos, P., & Gallegos, S. (2015). *Using behavioral insights to increase parental engagement: The parents and children together (PACT) intervention* (No. w21602). National Bureau of Economic Research.

McWayne, C., Fantuzzo, J., Cohen, H. L., & Sekino, Y. (2004). A multivariate examination of parent involvement and the social and academic competencies of urban kindergarten children. *Psychology in the Schools, 41*(3), 363–377.

Mendelsohn, A. L., Mogilner, L. N., Dreyer, B. P., Forman, J. A., et al. (2001). The impact of a clinic-based literacy intervention on language development in inner-city preschool children. *Pediatrics, 107*(1), 130–134.

Miedel, W. T., & Reynolds, A. J. (2000). Parent involvement in early intervention for disadvantaged children: Does it matter? *Journal of School Psychology, 37*(4), 379–402.

PEW Research Center. (2015). U.S. smartphone use in 2015. Retrieved November 13, 2015, from www.pewinternet.org/files/2015/03/PI_Smartphones_0401151.pdf

Puma, M., Bell, S., Cook, R., & Heid, C. (2010). *Head Start Impact Study: Final report.* Administration for Children & Families. Washington, DC: U. S. Department of Health and Human Services.

Reich, S. M., Bickman, L., Saville, B. R., & Alvarez, J. (2010). The effectiveness of baby books for providing pediatric anticipatory guidance to new mothers. *Pediatrics, 125*(5), 997–1002.

Reich, S. M., Penner, E. K., & Duncan, G. J. (2011). Using baby books to increase new mothers' safety practices. *Academic Pediatrics, 11*(1), 34–43.

Reich, S. M., Penner, E. K., Duncan, G. J., & Auger, A. (2012). Using baby books to change new mothers' attitudes about corporal punishment. *Child Abuse & Neglect, 36*(2), 108–117.

Reynolds, A. J. (2000). *Success in early intervention: The Chicago child parent centers.* Lincoln, NE: University of Nebraska Press.

Shapiro, J. R., Bauer, S., Hamer, R. M., Kordy, H., Ward, D., & Bulik, C.M. (2008). Use of text messaging for monitoring sugar-sweetened beverages, physical activity, and screen time in children: A pilot study. *Journal of Nutrition Education and Behavior, 40*(6), 385–391.

Sharif, I., Rieber, S., & Ozuah, P. O. (2002). Exposure to Reach Out and Read and vocabulary outcomes in inner city preschoolers. *Journal of the National Medical Association, 94*(3), 171.

Thaler, R. H., & Sunstein, C. R. (2009). *Nudge: Improving decisions about health, wealth, and happiness.* New York: Penguin Books.

Vogel, C., Brooks-Gunn, J., Martin, A., & Klute, M. M. (2013). Impacts of early head start participation on child and parent outcomes at ages 2, 3, and 5. *Monographs of the Society for Research in Child Development, 78*(1), 36–63.

Walker, K., Gooze, R., & Torres, A. (2014). Connecting the dots: Raising A Reader builds evidence base for its parent engagement and early literacy program. *Child Trends.* Retrieved November 13, 2015, from http://www.childtrends. org/?publications=connecting-the-dots-raising-a-reader-builds-evidence-base-for-its-parent-engagement-and-early-literacy-program

York, B. N., & Loeb, S. (2014). *One step at a time: The effects of an early literacy text messaging program for parents of preschoolers* (No. w20659). National Bureau of Economic Research.

Zuckerman, B. (2009). Promoting early literacy in pediatric practice: Twenty years of reach out and read. *Pediatrics, 124*(6), 1660–1665.

Resources

- California's Preschool Learning Foundations www.cde.ca.gov/sp/cd/re/psfoundations.asp
- *One Step at a Time: The Effects of an Early Literacy Text Messaging Program for Parents of Preschoolers* www.nber.org/papers/w20659.pdf
- Parents and Children Together (PACT) www.institutefamily.org/programs_PACT.asp
- Raising a Reader www.raisingareader.org/
- Reach Out and Read www.reachoutandread.org
- ReadyRosie http://readyrosie.com/
- Ready4K! http://news.stanford.edu/news/2014/november/texting-literacy-tips-111714.html
- *Smartphone Penetration, Rising in All Age and Income Demos, Hits 75% of the US Mobile Market,* MarketingCharts www.marketingcharts.com/online/smartphone-penetration-rising-in-all-age-and-income-demos-hits-75-of-us-mobile-market-51585/

Learn More...

- "T" is for Technology Publications and Relevant RAND Research, 2014 www.rand.org/education/projects/t-is-for-technology/publications.html
- Using Early Childhood Education to Bridge the Digital Divide
  - Getting on the Same Page: Identifying Goals for Technology Use in Early Childhood Education
  - Moving Beyond Screen Time: Redefining Developmentally Appropriate Technology Use in ECE
  - How Much and What Kind? Identifying an Adequate Technology Infrastructure for Early Childhood Education

- ◦ Getting Early Childhood Educators Up and Running: Creating Strong Technology Curators
- ◦ Families, Powered On: Improving Family Engagement in Early Childhood Education Through Technology
- ◦ Harvard Family Research Project www.hfrp.org
- Office of Head Start, Parent Family and Community Engagement http://eclkc.ohs.acf.hhs.gov/hslc/tta-system/family
- *Uses of Technology to Support Early Childhood Practice,* Office of Planning, Research, and Evaluation, Administration for Children and Families, 2015 www.acf.hhs.gov/programs/opre/resource/uses-of-technology-to-support-early-childhood-practice-full-report

---

Spotlight on Engagement

How Parents as Teachers and the USC School of Social Work Make Virtual Parent Education a Reality

One of the greatest hurdles to engaging parents in their children's health, early learning, and development is getting them connected to professionals who can provide mentoring and support. And often the problem for professionals is gaining access to parents. Geography, scheduling, and even apprehensions about allowing someone new into their home can present barriers that delay or even prevent parent engagement from happening. Just as smartphones, laptops, and tablets have transformed the ways in which young families shop, bank, and connect with their friends and families, those same devices will enable professional parent educators to reach more parents through home visiting and family support in the digital age.

Parents as Teachers, with the largest service footprint of the national evidence-based home visiting models, and the University of Southern California (USC) School of Social Work, launched a partnership in 2015 to develop virtual parent education. The project will provide digital access for parent educators to meet with families, in real time, using Web-based video sessions and telemedicine technology to build relationships between professionals and parents and "virtually" bring them the benefits of evidence based home visiting. The intent is to expand services to hard-to-reach families in underserved communities and provide more options for parents to receive the support they need to be their child's first and most impactful early teachers in an easy and available format.

"For decades, we have taken the position that there is no delivery system as powerful as one-on-one, personal visits by trained parent educators," said Scott Hippert, president and CEO of Parents as Teachers.

> Today, technology has the potential to foster relationships between parents and professionals, and to make valuable parent education services easily accessible. We can't underestimate the importance of digital relationship building. It may very well be that the parents themselves initiated their

relationship through online dating. So as technological advancements provide opportunities for us to extend our model to better serve today's culture, or expand access to underserved populations, it is incumbent upon us to do so. It is our intent to use this platform to expand the number of families we can serve utilizing telehealth technology, and to deliver high-quality services with the same high standards, whether the visit is in person or via an electronic device.

Parents as Teachers programs annually serve more than 200,000 families. The model is delivered by professionally trained parent educators who provide parents of children from prenatal through the kindergarten year with tools and mentoring to improve parenting practices and parent knowledge of child development, provide early detection of developmental delays and health issues, prevent child abuse and neglect, and improve children's school readiness, early literacy and learning skills.

During the live, web-based video sessions, a dedicated parent educator will mentor and support parents on their child's health and development, as well as their personal parenting challenges and accomplishments. They will be connected with additional resources based on individual family needs. Multiple studies confirm the Parents as Teachers model produces numerous long-term positive impacts for children and parents, including greater family stability and well-being, more parents being engaged in their children's development and education, and more families connected to their communities and to one another.

The Parents as Teachers/USC three-year virtual parent education initiative began in late 2015 with the training of USC School of Social Work Telehealth practitioners as parent educators in the Parents as Teachers curriculum and model. A pilot program working with 65 families in Southern California has begun and will continue through 2017. This demonstration project will focus on engagement and implementing the four program components of the Parents as Teachers Model through a video conferencing platform. The pilot initiative includes evaluation, which will inform future practice and service delivery.

Contributed by Jill Saunders, Scott Hippert and
Donna Hunt O'Brien of Parents as Teachers

Learn More...

- Parents as Teachers www.parentsasteachers.org
- Ready4K http://news.stanford.edu/news/2014/november/texting-literacy-tips-111714.html

Part II

Technology Tools and Techniques for Empowering Educators and Families

Editor's Introduction

In Part I, the focus was on broad issues and opportunities with technology and young children including: why media mentorship matters; the role of diversity in media and family engagement; how technology and digital media can be tools for teaching and learning, and the implications for technology-mediated family engagement; a new framework for developmentally appropriate technology integration; the importance of re-imagining children's engagement with technology, frameworks for parent, family, community engagement; the power of nudges; and examples of effective and innovative approaches to improving communication, strengthening the home–school connection, increasing parent involvement and enhancing family engagement to support young children, parents, and families in the digital age. Part II focuses on technology tools and techniques for empowering educators and families.

Junlei Li opens Part II and Chapter 6 by exploring the legacy of Fred Rogers and the strategies he used in his children's television program, "Mr. Rogers' Neighborhood," and in his communications with parents on the air, in person, and through his letters. He describes how Fred's messages of affirmation, encouragement, and empowerment were gently and consistently delivered to young children and to the caring adults in their lives. He explains how Fred believed there were no "magic answers" to parents' questions about parenting but that real answers could be found in the parents' own striving to understand and meet the needs of their child. Lessons learned from Fred's approach offer guidance for educators and parents today and advance the goal of deepening and enhancing family engagement in the digital age.

Weather forecasting is used as a metaphor by **Kate Highfield** in Chapter 7 to describe the obstacles and opportunities that educators and parents face in guiding young children through the digital age. She suggests that childhoods are changing and how young children use technology and media is a significant part of the change in the weather felt by parents, families, and children. Stories of successful technology use and mindful technology integration are connected to quality education, child outcomes, and family engagement goals, and Kate offers helpful hints to educators as media mentors and classroom meteorologists.

Chapter 8 by **Kristy Goodwin** describes how the digital age has created new concerns for parents and families with young children and explores the risks of digitized childhoods in the context of using technology and digital media wisely to support, not stifle, young children's development. Strategies for establishing healthy media habits in the home are presented for parents and for the media mentors who support them. Kristy describes technology-related health concerns and the need for caution and offers strategies for media mentors to share with parents and families.

The role of educators in supporting parents as media mentors in the digital age is the focus of Chapter 9 by **Devorah Heitner.** She comments on the need for media mentors, describes a culture of mentorship, and identifies six factors in supporting mentorship in an early childhood environment. Devorah offers helpful hints for media mentors to empower parents as media mentors and practical advice for working with parents and families raising young children in the digital age. She advocates for an inquiry-based relationship with technology that models creativity and creating media, not just consuming it.

Chapter 10, by **Michael Rich** and **Kristelle Lavallee**, provides the informed perspective of a pediatrician and children's media thought leader from the Center on Media and Child Health. The goal of the center is to educate and empower children and those who care for them to create and consume media in ways that optimize children's physical, mental, and social health. Research-based evidence from science is translated into practical strategies for raising and educating healthy children in the digital age. Three principles of integrating new media technologies into classrooms are offered along with hints for media mentors about how to use technology tools to provide opportunities for discovery, support learning, and model communication.

Chapter 6

"What Did Mister Rogers Do?"

Fred Rogers' Approach to Parent Engagement

Junlei Li

Introduction

Of the thousands of pieces of viewer mail collected in the archive at the Fred Rogers Center, the excerpt below reminds me the most about the needs of parents in our digital age and the important themes of this book.

> Dear Mr. Rogers,
>
> My two sons, [name] aged 2½ and [name], 9 months, and I are regular television neighbors of yours and very much enjoy our visits with you.
>
> ... A very serious matter has come to my attention and I would like to share it with you. [A for-profit toy manufacturer] and [a non-profit children's media producer] have collaborated on a series of video games for three- to seven-year-old children. I am extremely worried about children in this particular age bracket being exposed to and becoming "hooked on" video games. I believe that pre-school children need plenty of varied, concrete play experiences and that, far from helping children to "practice important early-learning skills such as letter matching and problem solving", these particular "toys" will harm those youngsters who use them because they will not be learning how to get along with others, how to tell good from bad, a sense of self and self worth as well as many other vitally important social skills.
>
> ... I feel certain that you do not think video games should be part of a pre-school child's experience. My friend and I intend to protest ... about these "toys". ... If you could lend us your encouragement and support I would be most grateful. ...
>
> Yours sincerely,
> [Mom of the two children]

This letter was received in 1983, the year SONY produced the first CD to distribute music, Apple manufactured its first personal computer called "Lisa," and Microsoft first released the word processing software "Word" (Computer History Museum, 2015). And, as the letter attests, video games were beginning to be advertised as "learning" tools and being marketed into young children's lives. Clearly, technologies have evolved and, in most cases, become even more personal and intertwined into the lives of families. Yet, parents' questions and concerns remain similar in nature to what was conveyed in this letter, even as all of us become both more accepting of and resigned to the idea that technological gadgets are a significant part of our children's play as well as the working and living of our own adulthood.

Early childhood educators continue to field these tough questions from their children's parents—and often, struggle with such questions themselves. How do educators best engage in such important conversations with parents? At the Fred Rogers Center, we explore this question in the same way we approach nearly every issue that impacts children and families: by asking ourselves, "What did Fred Rogers do?"

There are at least three important sources from which we at the Fred Rogers Center learn about how Fred engaged families. First, there are the thousands of viewer mails and Fred's responses. In a typical year when "Mister Rogers' Neighborhood" was on the air, more than 4,000 viewer mails arrived at the office of Family Communications—the nonprofit founded by Fred not only to produce educational television programs but to facilitate meaningful conversations in families. Fred, his wife Joanne, and his long-time colleague Hedda Sharapan read and replied to nearly all the letters over the years. Some of the letters and responses are compiled into a wonderful small book called *Dear Mister Rogers, Does It Ever Rain In Your Neighborhood?* (Rogers, 1996).

Second, there were Fred's books and booklets for parents about how families grow, how children develop, and how we can help children get ready for everyday moments such as welcoming a sibling or going to school or the hospital. There are three books that collected together the evolving understanding and interactions Fred had with parents: *Mister Rogers Talks with Parents* (Rogers & Head, 1983); *How Families Grow* (Rogers & Head, 1988); and perhaps the simplest and most concise version, rewritten and compiled by Fred after his retirement from television programming, *The Mister Rogers' Parenting Resource Book* (Rogers, 2005).

Third, there were the countless and still incoming stories of families' personal encounters with Fred. Every time my colleagues and I have the opportunity to speak about the Fred Rogers legacy in a public setting, invariably at least one person would come up afterward to offer his or her own memory of the time they met Fred at a street corner, a lobby, a traffic light, or a restaurant. They would tell us in vivid recollection what Fred said and, more important, how they felt at the time. Those feelings are very real and very present, regardless of the number of years that have transpired since the encounters.

It is tempting to attribute much of Fred's unique ability to connect with children, parents, and families to something "magical." However, Fred would be the first to remind us that there is no "magic" in human relationships and that anything worth doing requires us to do it with intention, discipline, and persistence. So, putting aside my own profound sense of awe and admiration for the Fred Rogers legacy, I started to look across the letters, books, and stories for consistent and recurring themes in Fred's approach to engaging parents.

No Easy Answers

Parents often wrote to Fred with their concerns and questions, eagerly awaiting the advice from the trusted expert or, at least, the expert's affirmation of their own hunches and instincts. Fred's consistent approach was to not give easy answers: "The more I work with children, the more humble I feel about giving specific advice" (Rogers, 1996, p. 162). He felt that, just as children who experience the same struggles may have many different reasons, there would be just as many different ways for parents to help children. Fred did not assume that he as the "trusted expert" had the answers to parents' questions. Often, when parents describe the great difficulties they were experiencing, Fred would reply with the phrase, "I can only begin to imagine what it's like for you (or your child) to ..." He made it clear that while everyone could offer empathy, no one could fully understand everything that another person or family was going through.

He understood the need and the urgency with which parents sought advice and the noisy advices parents already receive from the self-help marketplace:

> We've all been bombarded with books on how to raise children. Many of them tell us, "In such and such situation, this is what you say." But no two people in a relationship are the same as any other two people. I don't think that the words are nearly as important as the wanting. I'm very much afraid of formulas. So many of us want shortcuts. What is really important is the basic relationship, and that we must work on all the time.
>
> Fred Rogers (2006), p. 82

In addition to being wary of the inappropriate application of formulaic advice to vastly different children and families, there is something even deeper in Fred's resistance to offering "magic answers." Fred believed, and he wanted parents to believe, that the real answers were to be found in the parents' own striving to understand and meet the needs of their children: "Parents have to trust their instincts and try to think of the children's needs as well as their own needs. That's what makes parenthood such a challenge" (Rogers, 1996, p. 151). Fred respected and trusted that parents had the opportunity to know their own children best, and from that knowing, most parents were in the best position to decide, explore, and reexamine what might be helpful to the children and the family.

But what about parents who do not feel that they know their child best and parents who struggle so hard that they do not have the confidence to search for the answers?

You Aren't Alone in Your Struggles

Fred wanted parents to know that struggling is an integral part of parenting for *everyone*. Mrs. Joanne Rogers, in the very personal and touching introduction to a book of Fred's thoughts on parenting, *Many Ways to Say I Love You* (Rogers, 2006), recalled the following:

> Parenting is a struggle. I was always touched when people would tell me how much they've learned from Fred that's helped them in their parenting, but I have a hunch that they thought he had some magical gift with children. He and I had to work at being good parents … just like everyone else.
>
> Fred Rogers (2006), p. 1

Even though Fred was a very private person, he felt the need to let parents know—especially those who felt so imperfect—that he was not the always gentle, patient, quiet, and even-tempered parent they imagined him to be. In letters and books, he would describe the struggles of one parent (including his own) to another or to the parent readers, making struggle both a normal part of parenting and a worthy undertaking in our own growing as parents. To a young man (soon to become a parent) asking for "the best piece of advice" on being a father, Fred sent the following excerpt of his own reflection:

> Looking back over the years of parenting that my wife and I have had with our two boys, I feel good about who we are and what we've done. I don't mean we were perfect parents. Not at all. Our years with our children were marked by plenty of inappropriate responses. Both Joanne and I can recall many times when we wish we'd said or done something different. But we didn't, and we've learned not to feel too guilty about that. What gives us our good feelings about our parenting is that we always cared and always tried to do our best.
>
> Fred Rogers (2006), p. 2

And with every opportunity, Fred looked for and affirmed the "best" in parents.

Your Child is Fortunate to Have a Parent Like You

In every encounter, in nearly every speech, and in almost every letter, Fred looked for and affirmed what was "best" in the person who was reading and listening. It was not the hollow or superficial cultural caricature of the "I am okay and you are okay" type of affirmation but a sincere and insistent discipline to ground any effort of communication by finding the best in one's neighbor. This is the basis of Fred's engagement and communication with parents.

After one of my presentations about Fred Rogers and the importance of early childhood educators' work, a tall, broad-shouldered African American teacher found me in the aisle and wanted to tell me about the encounter he had with Fred in the lobby of WQED Public Television office building where Fred worked. It was his second encounter with Fred, actually—the first had happened years earlier when, as a teen driving his first car, the young man saw Fred Rogers pulling up next to him at a traffic light, motioned for him to lower the window, and gently told him that the blasting car radio might hurt the young man's ears. Nervous and excited, as most people were when they came face to face with the "Real Mister Rogers," the man recounted for Fred the earlier encounter. Fred did not remember but sat down to ask him all about his life, his family, and his children. They talked in the lobby for a good 45 minutes before Fred bid him goodbye. As the man walked off to the elevator, Fred called him back, looked him in the eyes, and said, "I just wanted to tell you how fortunate your children are to have a father like you." The man held himself together just long enough to say goodbye a second time and found tears streaming down his face. He had to find the nearest restroom to compose himself before heading to his own meeting. Even as he told me this story some 20 years later, his voice quivered and his hands trembled with a happy sort of excitement. Meeting that person gave me a real glimpse of what so many parents must have felt when they received a reply from Fred Rogers that contained the phrase, "[Child's name] is indeed fortunate to have a father/mother like you."

One of the challenges Fred felt he had in responding to viewer mail was that he could not see their face, hear their voice, and know as much as he wanted to know about their families. He would pay minute attention to the handwriting, the paper used, the way the envelope was addressed to imagine who the person was. Even so, Fred wanted to find the best in a parent, even in letters in which the parents expressed great need, distress, or concern. In no uncertain terms, Fred reflected the "good" he noticed in the letter back to the person who wrote. The affirmation was never a formulaic compliment without substance. Before or after the phrase "your child is fortunate to have you as a parent," Fred would always write specifically what he noticed: "You were so sensitive to your son's questions and that you were willing to help him think the issues through"; "Just your wanting to help him can be most important of all"; "The love she feels from you and her father is surely important for her now and as she grows" (Rogers, 1996).

Fred was not ignoring the obvious difficulties that were conveyed in the parents' letters. But he believed, for parents and perhaps for all human beings, our capacity to learn and grow is founded upon the recognition by ourselves and those we trust that the "bedrock of our very being is good stuff."

Tips: Helpful Hints for Media Mentors

I started with the word *tips* in quotation marks but then I crossed it out because it seemed antithetical to speak of tips after the discussion about Fred's insistence on not giving easy answers, sharing struggles, and affirming the strengths that are already inside people. In Fred's last parenting book (Rogers, 2005), he used the phrase "Helpful Hints" at the end of each section to offer ideas for parents. That feels more fitting.

Early childhood educators are among the group of professionals that Fred Rogers calls "children's helpers" and regarded as his "heroes." Even as we reflect on the legacy of Fred Rogers and ask questions such as "What did Fred Rogers say?" or "What did Fred Rogers do?" it is important to remember that we do not need to be "Mister Rogers" to our children or the parents we partner with. The best gift we have to offer, as Fred would say, "is our honest selves."

When parents wrote Fred asking for help, Fred often made it clear that, while he was willing to listen, he was only a "television friend" and that "the most meaningful help comes from someone who can know us in a real and ongoing way." For many parents, that "someone" is an early childhood educator. Unlike Fred, who often felt that he did not know enough about the child or the parent through letters alone to craft a good response, early childhood educators have in-depth knowledge about the children and have face-to-face relationships with the parents. Just as Fred was trusted by parents as the television neighbor for children, educators are trusted by parents in the most sacred way—they leave their *children* with us!

Naturally, parents can also trust educators with their own struggles with parenting in the technological age. Their inquiries may revolve around themes such as "Is there too much technology use in my child's life?"; "Is there not enough technology in my child's learning?"; "How do I choose what is good?"; or "How can my child and I use technology together and appropriately?" As urgent as the parents' desire for direct answers and as eager as educators are to meet such questions with our expertise and experience, it may be helpful to remember that our first opportunity to engage parents might be our *listening*. For Fred Rogers, the viewer letters represented first and foremost an opportunity for him to listen to, hear, and understand the families. Through our listening to the parents' concerns, sharing how we ourselves have listened to the children in our care, and encouraging the parents to listen to their children's concerns and questions, we may be preparing the important foundation for meaningful conversations within families about all sorts of important questions, including technology.

Just as important as listening is our willingness to *not* be the expert. Imagine what it might feel like to a parent if our answer began with, "You know, I have often wondered (or struggled) with what is the best way to use technology in the classroom." Just as Fred wanted to encourage children to feel comfortable to talk about "anything" with their parents, by our sharing our challenges, we might encourage parents to feel comfortable to talk about their difficulties and doubts as well as what they consider to be successes and growth.

Educators also have far more opportunities than Fred did to notice, reflect, and affirm the "best" in their children's parents. Educators are in this great position because they have real experiences with the children and the parents to recognize and affirm in ways that are *specific* and *concrete*. The story of the young father who was moved to tears by Fred's remark in the office lobby reminded me how rarely parents get to hear a specific, concrete, and affirming message about their parenting—and, in a similar way, how infrequently educators receive such recognition for their own work. Educators have an important information source to offer such affirmation to parents that neither Fred nor the parents have: We can observe and see their children for many hours during the day. Children's learning and growing even in the smallest ways might reflect the earnest striving of their parents. Just as some parents are devastated about their own parenting to hear from educators about their children's "problems," they can be enormously encouraged to hear from educators about their children's positive development—no matter how small and incremental.

And last, just as Fred trusted that parents ultimately will have the intuition to know and explore what the right answers are, educators are in one of the best positions to help parents to develop the confidence that they have what it takes within themselves to decide what technology to use, how much, and how often is appropriate for their own children. "Parents have feelings, too," as Fred Rogers reminded, and that it is important for parents to follow their own feelings about what is appropriate and inappropriate and for parents to teach children to respect such feelings even if children do not yet understand all the reasons for what a parent might permit or limit.

Just as children grow, parents and educators need time to grow as well. The relationships between children and parents and between parents and educators are the most important ingredients in support of such growth. The following passage by Fred Rogers is as fitting for parents as it is for educators:

Society is asking so much of parents and caregivers in today's world: "Make sure your child is safe and healthy"; "Develop routines"; "Set limits"; "Read to your child each night at bedtime"; "Help your child feel secure and loved." And all that is added to other things we're already doing in our lives. Many adults feel that they are falling short in one, if not all, of the "assignments" of their lives. They often feel they are failures. Well, people are not failures when they're doing the best they can. If parents are managing to cover most of the important bases most of the time, they have every reason to feel good about who they are and what they're doing. Our performance doesn't have to be measured against anyone else's—just against our own abilities to cope.

Fred Rogers (2006), p. 80

And now, back to the letter that started this reflection. How *did* Fred Rogers reply?

Dear Ms. [Name],

Your warm and thoughtful comments were deeply appreciated. It helps us in many ways to know how children and their families are building on what we offer.

I have long believed the best use of television happens when the program is over, and people integrate what has been presented. You are facilitating that in important ways for your children because you obviously care about them, and you are available to them… Your sons are very fortunate to have a mother like you who is so deeply invested in what is important to them.

… I do share your misgivings about children spending a great deal of their time in front of machines, working at destructive games or purely cognitive skills… You might have expected my reply to be along those lines. But there is more, and the response that I am adding now might surprise you… In much the same way (as television can be used to communicate positively about children's growth), we feel there is tremendous potential for the computer to provide much more than drills and violent games… We are hopeful that we can offer another avenue for play and creative expression, for work on feelings and fears, as well as a tool for discussion about what is important to families.

This all has been a new learning experience for us… But as we have observed children playing at computers, we have felt there is great value in producing material for this new technology that can be a healthy factor in children's development… I hear your strong objections to what is on the market, and I would like to ask you to consider visiting a store in your area where you can have the opportunity to experience some of the pre-school software for yourself. That would give you first-hand experience for your own judgment. Granted, some of your criticism is justified, but you also might be interested in the possibilities of using the computer to provide positive play activities for children.

Thank you for all that you shared with us… If you would like to write again and let us know your reactions to our comments, we would always welcome hearing from you.

Here are pictures for [children's names]. We will remember with great pleasure that your family is watching.

Sincerely,
Fred Rogers

Acknowledgment

I wish to thank Hedda Sharapan for her insights and guidance on the development of this chapter. For over three decades, Hedda worked alongside Fred. She continues to teach around the country about Fred's work.

Editor's Note: Junlei used the phrase "Helpful Hints", instead of "Tips" in his chapter. I agreed that it was more fitting, and we are all using "Helpful Hints for Media Mentors" throughout the book.

References

Computer History Museum. (2015). *Timeline of computer history.* Retrieved from www.computerhistory.org/timeline/1983/

Rogers, F. (1996). *Letter to Mister Rogers: "Dear Mister Rogers, does it ever rain in your neighborhood?"* New York: Penguin Books.

Rogers, F. (2005). *The Mister Rogers' parenting resource book.* Philadelphia, PA: Running Press.

Rogers, F. (2006). *Many ways to say I love you: Wisdom for parents and children from Mister Rogers.* New York: Hyperion.

Rogers, F., & Head, B. (1983). *Mister Rogers talks with parents.* New York: Barnes and Noble Books.

Rogers, F., & Head, B. (1988). *Mister Rogers' how families grow.* Pittsburgh, PA: Family Communications.

Resources

- The Fred Rogers Center for Early Learning and Children's Media at Saint Vincent College www.fredrogerscenter.org
- The Fred Rogers Company www.fredrogers.org/
- Daniel Tiger's Neighborhood www.fredrogers.org/media/daniel-tigers-neighborhood/
- Mister Rogers' Neighborhood www.fredrogers.org/media/mister-rogers-neighborhood/
- Professional Development Newsletter Subscription www.fredrogers.org/professional/signup/
- Professional Development Resource Library www.fredrogers.org/professional/video/

Learn More...

- *What I learned from Fred Rogers.* Hedda Sharapan, Fred Rogers Center Blog, March 21, 2013 www.fredrogerscenter.org/blog/what-i-learned-from-fred-rogers/
- *The willingness to fail.* Fred Rogers Center Blog, Junlei Li, 2013 www.fredrogerscenter.org/blog/the-willingness-to-fail/
- *The tail wagging the dog: Using technology in children's learning.* Remaking Learning: Blog of the Pittsburgh Kids+Creativity Network, Junlei Li, 2012. http://remakelearning.org/blog/2012/08/30/guest-junlei-li/

Chapter 7

Weather Forecasting in the Digital Age

Changing Childhoods

Kate Highfield

Introduction: Childhoods Are Changing

This chapter draws on the analogy of "weather forecasting" to explore how parents and educators as media mentors obtain information about effective technology use in early childhood, spotlight stories that exemplify thoughtful practice and engagement with technology in ways that extend, enrich, and enhance effective learning.

Take a moment to reflect on your childhood. My childhood was filled with outdoor time, with summers spent swimming and on picnics in the outdoors. We were free to ride around the neighborhood on our bikes, with the only rule being to make sure we were home before nightfall. I grew up at a time where there were only four channels on the television and when the idea of a computer in the home was considered an unnecessary expense. In this time, grocery shopping meant visiting a shop, where more than likely the shopping assistant who processed your order knew your name and asked after the family. Reading a book meant a visit to the library, where we would spend hours poring over which titles to borrow. My childhood was happy, but in comparison to the childhoods of today, it could be considered a simple life.

When we compare this to children growing up today, it is undeniable that for many the world has changed considerably. Frequently, independent time spent outdoors or riding bikes is no longer an option, due to safety concerns or increased urbanization and limited access to green space. Choice in television viewing has expanded exponentially, and video on demand (VOD) services and streaming tools have provided an almost unlimited variety of viewing options. Even grocery shopping and visiting the library are now available digitally, with books delivered wirelessly and, in most suburbs, grocery orders can be placed online and delivered with ease.

Navigating these changes and harnessing the best of these technological developments for young children is challenging, particularly when conflicting "evidence" is presented in media and research. This chapter examines some of the messages that parents and educators are presented with and highlights suggested areas to focus on as we make decisions about best use of technology with young children. Here, strategies are suggested for technology use that enables children to develop skills in problem solving, creativity, and higher-order thinking.

Technology and Media Use Changing Over Time

There is no doubt that the current generation of young children is engaging with more technology and media than previous generations. Increased use of media and technology is seen in most countries and spans age groups. Current statistics suggest significant daily use of technology and media. In the United States, Common Sense Media (2015) suggests that children aged 8 to 12 years spend an average of 4:36 hours of screen time each day, with teenagers spending on average 6:40 hours each day. In a similar Australian study, it is noteworthy that "screen time" is no longer watching one traditional television screen but now includes simultaneous use of screens, with approximately 74 percent of children aged from 2 to 15 years (sample size of 1,620) frequently using multiple screens at once (Zrim, 2015).

This trend of increasing use is related to a number of elements.

- The growing prevalence and use of mobile and tablet technologies: In 2015, it was estimated that 92 percent of American adults owned a cell phone, and nearly half (45 percent of American adults) had access to a tablet device (Anderson, 2015).
- Increasing classification of media and technology as "educational": Hirsh-Pasek et al. (2015) raise concerns that "80,000 apps are classified as education and learning based" (Apple, 2015).
- Increased choice in children's media, particularly media designed specifically for children: Common Sense Media (2013) suggests that 58 percent of parents in the United States reported that they had downloaded apps specifically for their children.
- Affordable access to resources, with free access to video via sites such as YouTube and a plethora for Video on Demand Services: Software affordability has also altered access to technology with many apps available for a low cost or for free. Increasingly, developers are adopting a "freemium" model of app sales, where an introductory component to the app is initially free with full access available at a price.

As technology has become more affordable, use by children and the integration of technology in children's toys has grown. Further, the mobile nature of tablets and hand-held devices enables increasing amounts of time using technology and media, as children can now use the technology outside their home and learning contexts.

When we narrow our focus to young children, a recent survey by Dubit (Kleeman, 2016) with approximately 2,000 parents responding, suggested that approximately 80 percent of children (ages 2 to 15 years) have regular access to a tablet device. The touch-sensitive nature of these tools enables young children easy access to technology, without the mediation of a keyboard or mouse. A survey of parents in the United Kingdom (Marsh et al., 2015) reported that children younger than age 5 used tablets for a mean of 1 hour 19 minutes on an average weekday. Weekend use was slightly higher—a mean of 1 hour 23 minutes on an average weekend day. This study is noteworthy as it provides evidence of current technology use by young children, including children aged from birth to 2 years. The study also examined parent selection of apps, and parents indicated that they were most motivated to download apps that would support their child's learning (60 percent of parents of children ages birth to 2 years and 64 percent for parents of children ages 3 to 5 years) and to encourage play and creativity (57 percent of parents of children ages birth to 2 years and 65 percent for parents of children ages 3 to 5 years).

Seeking Guidance

Given the increasing use of technology and the dramatic changes we are observing between generations, many parents and educators are seeking guidance. However, a quick scan of your newspaper, online news, or television news shows that many parents and educators are being presented with an alarmist perspective on children's technology and media use.

Parents and educators are at times bombarded by headlines such as: "The FaceTime babysitter" (March 18, 2015, *New York Times*); "Teens spend an average of 9 hours a day with media" (November 3, 2015, *Associated Press*); "Screen time and your child: what every parent needs to know" (September 12, 2015, *The Times*, London); and "Too much screen time for children causing depression" (January 22, 2015, *The Times*, London). Indeed, as I am writing this chapter, the Australian media is awash with articles about "Hello Barbie," an Internet-connected doll. Headlines were largely alarmist; for example, "Hello Barbie: Wi-Fi-enabled doll labelled a bedroom security risk" (November 28, ABC News Australia). The questions then arise: How do parents respond to these types of information and where can they obtain appropriate information about young children and media use? Who can they turn to as a media mentor?

Indeed, there are many areas of technology use that educators and parents should be aware of when they focus on healthy media and technology engagement. These include concerns with excessive screen time, posture, electromagnetic radiation exposure, and concerns with vision and hearing. Awareness of these concerns, and sensible responses such as those presented in Chapter 8 by Kristy Goodwin, are needed. However, parents also need to go beyond the headlines and need media mentors including educators, researchers, and the media to guide our children and families toward healthy media use.

Technology and the Weather

Should We Be Concerned With the "Storms in the Sky" and Where Are the Weather Forecasters?

I like watching the weather on my evening news. I like to plan my week, knowing which day is most likely to get rain or be sunny. I also like that my weather forecast is based on science: Though I don't have the knowledge or skills of a meteorologist, I like to know that they do have the ability and scientific knowledge to be able to interpret and predict weather systems. For this reason, I choose to watch the weather on the news rather than reading the weekly forecast in a newspaper. To me, this feels like a more accurate way to obtain information. Before you wonder why there is an apparently random paragraph about my preference for science-based weather, allow me to draw an analogy, linking the science of weather to young children's use of media.

In some ways, the conglomeration of factors that enable increasing technology and media use by young children can be seen as a "perfect storm": an accumulation of components forming together to see unprecedented use of technology and media. Here, the storm analogy is apt, with storms bringing both potential benefits, such as rain so plants and crops can grow, but also having potential to bring harm, such as too much rain causing floods or damage from high winds. To extend this analogy, as with most storms, we generally have forewarning; we are able to both watch clouds looming in the sky and access weather forecasts (even on a weather app on a mobile device)—using this information to inform our decisions. However, when it comes to benefits and concerns with children's technology and media use, where do we obtain information? When is technology seen as a tool for growth in young children's lives, and when is it a cause for concern? Who are the "forecasters" providing information, and where can we as educators and parents look for science-based guidance? And what role do media mentors play in predicting the weather and making sure young children are prepared?

Focus on Technology to Enable Quality Early Childhood Pedagogy or Your Philosophy of Childhood

As parents and educators, we often relate to a philosophy of learning or a belief structure about how children thrive and learn. In considering technology use, we should ensure that we choose technologies that align with this philosophy or belief structure, rather than allowing technologies to overtake our belief system. For example, if you choose a play-based philosophy of learning where children's outdoor play is valued, then it would be best to use technology to document this play or extend learning through research, rather than allowing technology to "take over" or disrupt children's play. Here's a story that describes how one teacher used technology to do this.

Spotlight on Outdoor Play and Technology

Michael [pseudonyms used for all names] was an educator, working with a group of 4-year-old children. Michael was a degree-trained teacher who had been working as the lead educator (including the role of creating programs and documenting learning for his class) for 4 years. In these years of experience, Michael developed a belief about using the environment as the third teacher, a concept arising from Reggio Emilia. Now he believes that children learn best as they engage with the natural environment, building gardens, working together to create structures from sticks and natural materials, and exploring learning and problem solving through play. In this context, when the iPads were given to his children, he became quite concerned that the children would be attracted to the iPads and want to play games on them instead of spending time outside. After considering this carefully, Michael initially decided to limit the iPad use, not allowing children to use them outside at all. Michael stated, "First I banned them outside, then I realized that perhaps I was missing an opportunity." He then changed tactics, and after a class meeting decided to work with the children on how they could use them while outside, to extend their play. Michael commented,

> Allowing the iPads outside was actually amazing. The children used ChatterPix [an app that allows children to animate images] and extended their play by taking photos and then imagining and acting out what the items in their photos would say... we also (teachers and children) used the iPads to take photos of the children's play in the sandpit and their water paintings; this was especially great as the children could look back at their photos and talk about their creations, even after their sand structures and water paints had gone.

In Michael's story, we see him as a reflective teacher, carefully considering how he will use the technology to support learning. Drawing on our analogy of weather, Michael observed his environment (the classroom context) and used this to help him plan. His prior understanding and beliefs acted as a guide to manage the technology in his context. Here, his belief that the children should be active participants in their learning is evidenced by the use of a class meeting to discuss this. In turn, enabling this conversation he built the children's ability to reflect, a key tool as we help children to regulate their own media use. We can also see that he has integrated technology in a way that aligns with his personal philosophies and beliefs, in this case using the technology to extend outdoor play.

Also key here is the idea that Michael was actively engaged as a reflective practitioner. He recognized that his initial concept to not use the iPads outside was not working, reflected on this, and reconsidered his approach. In our roles as educators, media mentors, and parents, we should reflect and evaluate, changing our practice as needed—as Michael has done here.

**The quotation from author and poet, Maya Angelou, "Do the best
you can until you know better. Then when you know better, do better"**
can be helpful as we adopt the role of reflective practitioners and media
mentors.

Focus on Quality Education and Engagement

When we work with children, we start by knowing the children, their
interests, skills, and abilities; we then build on this, extending learning
through practices such as scaffolding their learning or "Sustained Shared
Thinking." The Sustained Shared Thinking concept arises from a project in
the United Kingdom and can be defined as "when two or more individuals
work together in an intellectual way to solve a problem, clarify a concept
[or] evaluate an activity... Both parties must contribute to the thinking and
it must develop and extend the understanding" (Sylva, Melhuish, Sammons,
Siraj-Blatchford, & Taggart, 2004, p. 6).

Linking to our analogy of weather, as educators, parents, and media
mentors we can draw on our understanding of learning sciences as we
integrate technology, just as meteorologists use their scientific understanding.
Sustained Shared Thinking and the use of technology to prompt reflection is
modeled in Alishay's story.

Spotlight on Documenting with Technology

Alishay is 3 years old and painting on an easel. Her teacher, Mary, is observing
and notes that Alishay is exploring colors and mixing red and yellow to make
orange on her paper.

Alishay carefully paints a red dot, then quickly adds yellow, mixing on the paper
with excitement—but unfortunately in mixing the paints she becomes frustrated
as the paper tears. Mary engages her, and they discuss the problem, trying again,
with the same situation occurring: "Uh oh, it ripped again" says Alishay. Eventually,
they find a plastic lid, and Alishay makes her orange color there before painting.
While this occurred, Mary carefully took photos on the preschool's tablet.

The following day, Mary and Alishay write a story, using Book Creator (an app
that allows you to create stories). Mary encourages Alishay to tell her story, using
the photos to recall what happened. They create a story, with images and typed
text before choosing to email it to Alishay's grandparents who live in another state.

Mary commented, "I make stories all the time, I've always done it—but I used
to have to take the camera to the computer, download the photos, print them
out and stick them on the book... We used to write the book by hand and keep
it here... Now I can make a book and have the child choose the photos and help
with the text. I think this is great 'cause it's not my learning anymore; it's the child's."

In this example, we see the educator extending learning with technology, using it as a tool for reflection and helping to share learning beyond the walls of her classroom. Her understanding of the role of relationships and attempt to engage the child is sustained shared thinking, and scaffolding her learning is evidenced. It is important here that the teacher was able to balance her role as a documenter of learning while also focusing on quality engagement with the child. The child, her engagement with the child, and her learning were paramount with the technology in a supporting role. The technology was a more efficient tool for the educator to document learning but was carefully used so that it didn't inhibit relationships or active engagement in extending learning.

Key Messages from the Joint Position Statement

Early childhood educators always should use their knowledge of child development and effective practices to carefully and intentionally select and use technology and media if and when it serves healthy development, learning, creativity, interactions with others, and relationships.

NAEYC & Fred Rogers Center (2012), p. 5

Focus on Technology to Promote Both Academic and Intellectual Goals

When we consider educational goals, it is often easiest to focus on specific curriculum areas and set skills that children need to acquire as they move into more academic learning. This could include many skills such as learning letters and sounds, blending letters to form words, understanding numbers, or combining numbers and learning basic number facts. These discrete skills could be called content knowledge, or Katz (2010) suggests that they could be referred to as academic goals. While these skills are important, we should also consider the role of intellectual goals: activities that focus on enabling children to develop skills in "reasoning, hypothesizing, predicting, the quest for understanding and conjecturing, as well as the development and analysis of ideas" (Katz, 2010, p. 2). The following *Spotlight on* story overleaf is presented as an example of the use of technology to assist in the development of an academic goals and as an example of how a parent used this as a "springboard" into developing intellectual goals.

Many children's apps can be very engaging; their use of rewards, cause and effect, and action and reaction can appeal to many young children. Here, children can consume content and at times limit opportunities to create (see Dwyer & Highfield, 2015, for further examination of the continuum of consume and create). While consuming premade content can be harnessed as a tool to develop curriculum or academic goals, it is important to have a balance of technology that also allows children to create or use technology as a prompt of behavior off-screen. In this example, Sia's parents carefully

---

Spotlight on Technology in Support of Academic Goals

Sia is in her first year of school. Her parents recently attended a teacher–parent interview and found that Sia was occasionally finding counting challenging. Her teacher suggested that Sia would benefit from more practice.

Sia's parents (her father worked as a math professor) worked hard to practice counting. They tried to count as they went through their everyday activities, such as counting steps or counting apples as they placed them in a bag at the grocery store. They counted buttons and fingers and flowers in the garden. Sia quickly lost interest in counting aloud with her parents.

After reading about an app online, Sia's parents decided to try an alternate strategy—using an app called Tiggly Chef. This is a counting app whereby children count items into a bowl as dictated by the "recipe." As children count, they have to touch each item (or use a counting accessory). Sia's parents noted with interest that she could happily play this app for extended periods without becoming bored or frustrated; they surmised that she was amused by the character's "funny voices" and "silly recipes."

Sia's parents were concerned, however, that her extended engagement with this app was only focusing on one key skill and so used the "silly recipes" in the app as a prompt to cook together in real life, away from the screen. Here Sia and her parents created their own recipes for crazy milkshakes—inadvertently developing intellectual goals of reasoning, hypothesizing, and predicting by asking questions such as: "What do you think that will taste like?" and "What will happen if we…?" as they cooked together.

---

researched counting apps online, and they found their "weather guide" and used this in their engagement with technology. Sia responded to the app to practice her counting skills, but it was her activity creating milkshakes that enabled her to engage with higher-order thinking including reasoning, communicating, and creating.

> Sometimes we become anxious about children consuming media or playing games that are premade and engage children in consuming educational content or are considered "drill and practice." Though this is something to monitor, it can also be an opportunity for learning or an opportunity for off-screen activities.

The Forecast Is in: Digital Childhoods Are Here to Stay

Within this chapter, we've explored a number of stories wherein technology—when used well—can enhance and extend learning and engagement. In each of these stories, the educators and parents have drawn on their understanding of learning science, their teaching philosophies, and research to find ways of harnessing technology use with young children. These exemplars show people who have read the weather forecast and made informed decisions based on this. In these examples, we see movement toward changing digital childhoods—where the technology and media use are not something to be feared but something that can be meaningfully used.

Helpful Hints for Media Mentors

- Seek out and share research with parents and colleagues about technology and use. Whether this be reports from Common Sense Media, links to the Technology in Early Childhood (TEC) Center videos, or information from other sites, use this research to help inform the discussion about technology and media use; this enables you to be a leader and help parents with their "weather forecast."
- Invite parents and children to share their favorite apps and games and consider using these as a prompt for investigations and play. For example, one teacher found a child was fascinated by an app called "Cut the Rope" (an app that frequently uses a rope pendulum and problem solving to complete levels such as swinging rewards to a character). Though the app was designed for older children and adults, the teacher was surprised that the child had developed knowledge of pendulums and early physics by playing the game. She worked with the child and a small group to create their own "real life" version of the game, using string and resources from her center
- Don't be afraid to play. Technology and media are changing, many of the shows and characters are different, and the games and apps are constantly evolving. For us to know about these and share with children in their digital childhoods, we have to engage with children as they watch and play. Co-engagement, playing with children as they engage with technology, is a great opportunity to learn but also to engage and communicate with children as they become the teachers and lead our play.
- Carefully consider technology, reflect on its use, and encourage children to reflect. As with any activity or resource, some will work beautifully, while others won't be as effective. As parents and educators, we need to reflect, evaluate, and change where needed; we also need to encourage children to reflect on and begin to self-regulate their use of technology and media.

Parent and Teacher Takeaways

- Technology is here to stay, and though this is a significant change from many parents and educators' lived experiences, it can be an opportunity to extend, enhance, and engage children.
- While research is key as we use technology (it is our 'weather forecast'), we can also integrate our knowledge of children, pedagogy, and learning science as we integrate technology.
- Ensure that you're using technology and media to enrich current practice, rather than allowing the technology to lead practice.

References

Anderson, M. (2015). *Technology Device Ownership: 2015*. Pew Research Center, October, 2015, Retrieved from www.pewinternet.org/2015/10/29/technology-device-ownership-2015

Apple. (2015). *iPads in Education*. Retrieved from http://www.apple.com/education/apps-books-and-more/

Common Sense Media. (2013). *Zero to eight: Children's media use in America—A Common Sense research study*. Retrieved from www.commonsensemedia.org/research/zero-to-eight-childrens-media-use-in-america-2013

Common Sense Media. (2015). The Common Sense census: Media use by tweens and teens. Common Sense Media. Retrieved from www.commonsensemedia.org/sites/default/files/uploads/research/census_researchreport.pdf

Dwyer, N., & Highfield, K. (2015) Technology, our tool not our master. *Every Day Learning, 3*(4), 1–28.

Hirsh-Pasek, K., Zosh, J., Michnick Golinkoff, R., Gray, J., Robb, M., & Kaufman, J. (2015). Putting education in "educational" apps: Lessons from the science of learning. *Psychological Science in the Public Interest, 16*(1), 3–34.

Katz, L.G. (2010). STEM in the early years. Early Childhood Research and Practice. Collected Papers from the SEED (STEM in Early Education and Development) Conference. Retrieved from http://ecrp.uiuc.edu/beyond/seed/index.html

Kleeman, D. (2016). iSpy 2016: Five things we're keeping an eye on. Presentation for Kids@Play conference. Retrieved from http://www.slideshare.net/dubit/ispy-2016-five-things-were-keeping-an-eye-on

Marsh, J., Plowman, L., Yamada-Rice, D., Bishop, J. C., et al. (2015). *Exploring play and creativity in pre-schoolers' use of apps: final project report*. Retrieved from www.techandplay.org

National Association for the Education of Young Children, & Fred Rogers Center for Early Learning and Children's Media at Saint Vincent College. (2012). *Technology and interactive media as tools in early childhood programs serving children from birth through age 8*. Washington, DC: NAEYC; Latrobe, PA: Fred Rogers Center for Early Learning and Children's Media at Saint Vincent College.

Sylva, K., Melhuish, E., Sammons, P., Siraj-Blatchford, I., & Taggart, B. (2004). *The Effective Provision of Pre-School Education (EPPE) Project: Findings from Pre-school to end of Key Stage 1*. Retrieved from eppe.ioe.ac.uk/eppe/eppepdfs/RBTec1223sept0412.pdf

Zrim, L. (2015). *Nielsen Australian eGeneration Report*. Retrieved from www.neilsen.com/ai/en/insights

Resources

- Book Creator, Red Jumper www.redjumper.net/bookcreator/
- ChatterPix, Duck Duck Moose www.duckduckmoose.com/educational-iphone-itouch-apps-for-kids/chatterpix/
- Cut the Rope, zeptolab www.cuttherope.net
- Tiggly Chef, Tiggly www.tiggly.com/tiggly-chef
- YouTube www.youtube.com

- Digital camera: Most smartphones and tablets have a range of camera tools including "slow motion" and "time lapse." Slow motion can be a great way of recording fast activities such as a marble moving down a marble track or an animal scurrying. This tool allows you to slow the movement down (and so observe more closely).

Recommended Sites for Research and Reviews

- Common Sense Media shares tips, resources, research, and reviews for parents and educators. www.commonsensemedia.org/
- The Technology in Early Childhood (TEC) Center at Erikson Institute has links to current research and a growing library of "show me" videos that connect research and practice. http://teccenter.erikson.edu/
- Review sites such as Children's Technology Review (http://childrenstech.com/), Know Before You Load App Reviews from the Australian Council on Children and Media (http://childrenandmedia.org.au/app-reviews/), and Common Sense Media's Reviews (www.commonsensemedia.org/reviews) can help parents and teachers read reviews about apps before purchasing them.

Resources from Early Childhood Australia

- The digital business kit www.earlychildhoodaustralia.org.au/our-work/digital-business-kit/
- Learning modules www.earlychildhoodaustralia.org.au/our-work/digital-business-kit/digital-business-kit-module-1/
- Video collection www.earlychildhoodaustralia.org.au/our-work/digital-business-kit/digital-business-kit-module-2/
- Live Wires www.earlychildhoodaustralia.org.au/our-work/digital-business-kit/live-wires/

Learn More...

- Dwyer, N., & Highfield, K. (2015) Technology, our tool not our master. *Every Day Learning, 3*(4), 1–28.
- Armstrong, A., Donohue, C., & Highfield, K. (2015). Technology integration: Defining what is appropriate for young children. *Exchange 225,* 28–33.
- Highfield, K. (2014). Stepping into STEM with young children: Simple robotics and programming as catalysts for early learning. In Donohue, C. (Ed.), *Technology and digital media in the early years: Tools for teaching and learning* (pp. 150–161). New York: Routledge and Washington, DC: National Association for the Education of Young Children.

- Goodwin, K., & Highfield, K. (2013). A framework for examining technologies and early mathematics learning. In English, L.D. & Mulligan, J.T. (Eds.), *Reconceptualising early mathematics learning* (pp. 205–226). New York: Springer.

Chapter 8

Helping Children and Families Develop Healthy Media Habits

Kristy Goodwin

Digitalized Childhoods

Young children today are experiencing "digitalized childhoods." Technology has become a ubiquitous feature in children's socio-cultural landscape. It's changing many aspects of childhood, including ways that young children play, interact with others, form relationships, move, physically develop, and learn language. The impact of children's digitalized childhood is contingent upon how technology is used with and around young children.

An extensive corpus of research was cited in the NAEYC and Fred Rogers Center Joint Position Statement (2012) to confirm that when technology is used intentionally and in developmentally appropriate ways, it can support children's learning and development. However, there are concerns among many parents, educators, health professionals, and researchers that young children's digital immersion may have adverse developmental consequences. These concerns are possibly warranted if technology isn't used in ways that are commensurate with young children's developmental and physical needs. Therefore, parents and educators need to explore what constitutes intentional and appropriate technology use and guide children as to how to best use media in ways that help, not hinder, their development.

This chapter explores how families and educators, as media mentors, can help young children form healthy media habits, early in life, by formulating media management plans. These plans ensure that children's digital habits promote, not impede, their learning and development and allow children to develop healthy and sustainable media habits.

Key Messages from the Joint Position Statement

To make informed decisions regarding the intentional use of technology and interactive media in ways that support children's learning and development, early childhood teachers and staff need information and resources about the nature of these tools and the implications of their use with children.

NAEYC & Fred Rogers Center (2012), p. 5

Using Technology to Support, not Stifle, Young Children's Development

Research on the long-term and developmental impacts of young children's use of technology is still in its infancy. There's a paucity of longitudinal or empirical research that provides insights about how media-rich childhoods are impacting children's development. Instead, mapping research-based principles of children's developmental needs to the technologies currently available helps parents and educators determine safe and effective ways to use technology with young children.

Teaching and modeling healthy media habits ensures:

- that young children's technology practices support, not stifle, their development, and
- healthy, lifelong media habit patterns will be established early in life and are more likely to be perpetuated.

Mapping research-based principles of children's developmental needs to the technologies currently available helps parents and educators determine safe and effective ways to use technology with young children.

Healthy Media Habits

There's been an historical reluctance to use technology with young children, as there were entrenched philosophical concerns that technology wasn't appropriate for young children. As a result, many teachers and families avoided or banned technology with young children. However, this approach doesn't help to prepare young children to succeed in the digital world they'll inherit. Pleasingly, in recent times the conversation and research agenda have shifted. The debate no longer centers on whether we should use technology with young children but rather how we can best utilize technology with young children. This shift in focus enables parents and educators to consider the best ways to utilize the available technologies with young learners, and this requires a media management plan.

The debate no longer centers on whether we should use technology with young children but rather how we can best utilize technology with young children.

Just as we teach children about healthy eating habits, modern parents and educators must also teach young children about healthy media habits. There's little doubt that digitally overloaded childhoods can pose developmental risks to our children. Much as excessive or unhealthy food consumption is detrimental to children's physical health, the overuse or inappropriate use of technology can also derail a child's development. In order for parents and educators to teach children the best ways to leverage new technologies, they need access to research-based information about how children's development intersects with digital technologies.

Media Management Plans

Parents and educators need to formulate and implement media management plans to give careful consideration to how to use technology in ways that will support children's health and development. A media management plan minimizes the chances of using technology in an ad hoc or inappropriate manner with young children. For example, iPads are much less likely to be used as a "digital pacifier" if parents and/or educators have clear guidelines and principles that guide their use.

Parents and educators need to mindfully plan and consider seven broad areas when formulating a media management plan:

1 What media will young children use?
2 When will young children use media?
3 With whom will young children use media?
4 Where will the media be used?
5 Why will the media be used?
6 How will the media be used?
7 How much time will be devoted to media?

What Media Will Young Children Use?

Lisa Guernsey (2012) identifies three Cs to consider when selecting media for young children: content, context, and child. Providing access to quality content is essential when it comes to young children's forming healthy media habits and using technology in ways that will support their learning and development.

It's important to consider what young children watch, play with, or create with technology. In fact, what children are doing with technology is possibly more important than simply quantifying how much time they're spending with screens. Previously, researchers, early childhood practitioners, and families tended to focus predominantly on how much screen time young children consume. It's critical that parents, educators, and researchers continue the renewed focus on examining what young children's media experiences look like qualitatively as opposed to relying exclusively on quantitative measures that simply gauge how much time children spend with media.

For example, a 3-year-old may spend 30 minutes watching rapid-fire cartoons with vocabulary and concepts that are unfamiliar to the child. Alternatively, he or she could spend the same amount of time reading an interactive fairytale as a book app, where the reader is invited to interact and respond to the story through various activities such as puzzles, matching activities, recording the story, and replaying their narration. These are qualitatively very different experiences that would demand different levels of cognition and language.

To ensure that young children's media habits are aligned with their developmental needs, we need to provide them with technology experiences that:

- support language skills
- facilitate social interaction
- support play, and
- allow them to create content in addition to consuming content.

Consuming and Creating Content

Research confirms that young learners benefit from active involvement in the learning process (Chaille & Britain, 2003; Department of Education, Employment and Workplace Relations, 2009), so many early childhood practitioners have feared that technology displaces or erodes these hands-on, exploratory, active learning experiences. However, thanks to technological advancements such as touch screen devices, there's more interactive and engaging media tools now available for young children to use.

Young children now have access to a plethora of apps, software, and websites that allow them to create music, animations, slideshows, digital storybooks, multimedia flashcards, puppet shows, and movies. Content creation engages higher-order thinking skills as children need to plan, implement, and evaluate their plans; problem-solve; use language; and often collaborate with others. This active involvement is different from the lower levels of thinking required by more passive media activities, where children are often merely observing.

Spotlight on Creating Media

Using the app Kids Flashcard Maker by INKids Education, preschoolers created and shared multimedia flashcards about insects they'd been researching. In small groups, the students read books, used magnifying glasses to observe insects in their natural environment, watched online videos, and retrieved information from a variety of online sources about an insect of their choice. They then made a Play-Doh model of their chosen insect, took a photograph of their creation, and embedded the photo into the app, where they also typed the name and recorded their voice to state the name of the insect. They also embedded a short David Attenborough–inspired video that they'd recorded, providing a verbal information report about the insect they'd been researching. These multimedia flashcards were saved on an iPad that was then placed in the Literacy Corner of the classroom for their peers and parents to watch.

Content That Promotes Language Skills

Research confirms that young children need language-rich environments for optimal development to occur in the early years (Hart & Risley, 2003; Medina, 2010).

When carefully selected, technology experiences can promote children's language development. For example, young children can create digital puppet shows using Puppet Pals or Sock Puppets apps, where they get to rehearse and improve their language skills.

Television can be an alternative technological tool to facilitate language development. For example, children can learn new vocabulary when watching age-appropriate content, especially if parents or educators are "co-viewing" (watching the media with young children). Well-designed, educational TV programs often elicit children's participation, as on-screen characters pose questions to the viewer throughout the episode. For example, Dora the Explorer often asks children questions or encourages them to repeat phrases or words throughout the show to ensure active participation. In this sense, the on-screen characters act as animated pedagogical agents and can help children learn new vocabulary.

Young children also develop parasocial relationships with online characters, which are the one-sided relationships children have with on-screen characters. Research confirms that when children form parasocial relationships with characters, it increases the likelihood that children will learn from the characters (Gola, Richards, Lauricella, & Calvert, 2013; Richert, Robb, & Smith, 2011). Young children are much more inclined to learn language and concepts from characters with whom they form parasocial relationships. Parents and educators need to source media content that allows children to build these parasocial relationships.

Content That Facilitates Social Interaction

Parents and educators also need to look for media opportunities that support social interactions. Children benefit from serve-and-return and interactions with peers, siblings, and adults (Farzin, Hou, & Norcia, 2012; Kuhl, 2004). Digital technologies provide additional and alternative ways for young children to form and sustain relationships and engage in these ping-pong interactions.

For example, video-chat technologies enable children to have relationships with family members living abroad and connect with parents who travel. Research also confirms that socially contingent interactions help young children learn language when using media (Roseberry, Hirsh-Pasek, & Golinkoff, 2013). Technology is certainly no substitute for real, in-person interactions (real "face time"), but it can complement these opportunities, especially if family members live abroad or parents have to travel for work.

Spotlight on Technology to Connect Family, Culture, and Community

In an inner-city, multi-cultural school in Sydney, Australia, a kindergarten class was learning about each of the children's countries of origin. The teacher used Google Earth on the interactive whiteboard (IWB) to enable the students to show their peers from which country their family had originated. The children "pinned" their countries of origin on a physical map using Google Earth. Next, the teacher organized a virtual field trip, where the students pretended to board an airplane (rows of seats in front of the IWB) and fly to each country, using Google Earth.

When the class arrived in Japan, the teacher had organized with one of the children's grandparents to connect via a Skype call. The students posed questions to their peer's grandfather, who answered them in real time. In addition, the grandfather took the children on a live tour of his house and then took them on a walk through his local neighborhood. The level of excitement was tangible among the students, and the questions they asked their Skype partner and the insights they gleaned from the interview were impressive, according to their teacher.

Content That Supports Children's Play

There's ample research evidence that confirms that young children learn best through play (Barnett, 1990; Ginsburg, 2007; Marcon, 2002). Through play, young children develop a host of skills critical for their development: improved cognitive abilities and communication competencies, enhanced creativity, physical development, and emotional skills. Play will always be essential, and play in the digital age should be supported and enhanced by technology, not displaced or replaced by it.

Play will always be essential, and play in the digital age should be supported and enhanced by technology, not displaced or replaced by it.

In fact, technology can offer new play experiences. Many young children are now playing in the digital landscape and with "techno-toys." Digital play experiences offer new opportunities to extend or enrich young children's play. Interactive TV, apps, and gaming consoles can facilitate alternative ways for young children to play. Young children can enter and explore new worlds, create music, books, videos, and animations, in ways that traditional play opportunities would not have afforded.

Sourcing Age-Appropriate Content

Given that technology is rapidly evolving, it's imperative that educators and parents stay up-to-date. Here are some resources that help parents and educators source quality content for young learners:

- Common Sense Media provides wonderful resources, tips, and reviews of children's media to enable parents and educators to keep abreast of new content available and suitable for young learners. In particular, their Kids Media app, available on both iOS and Android platforms, is essential for all parents to download on their smartphone.
- Children's Technology Review is an online subscription service offers independent reviews of a range of interactive digital media designed for children, based on sound developmental principles.

Spotlight on Augmented Reality, Saving, and Sharing

Toca Boca Hair Salon Me was used by 3-year-olds in a child care center. The augmented reality app enables children to "play" hairdressers without risking the permanence of a "bad" haircut. The children inserted a photograph of themselves and then used a range of tools to create elaborate haircuts and designs. The finished images were saved and sent to parents via a text message so that they could discuss their child's creation at home (which further extended the children's language skills). The educators also imported the saved images into ChatterPix Kids app, and the children then recorded their voices to provide a description of their haircuts.

When Will Children Use Media?

In order for children to benefit from using technology, it should ideally be used when children's attention and focus are at their prime. The use of screens around nap and sleep times should be avoided, or at least minimized, as research is confirming that screen use before sleep can have adverse impacts on the duration and quality of sleep.

Identify the Best Times to Use Screens

Parents and educators need to be intentional about *when* technology is used. While there is no universal time that's ideal for children to use technology, explicitly planning the use of technology ensures that it's not used in a haphazard manner or used as a digital pacifier.

Adults need to observe and monitor how children respond to technology throughout different times of the day. Identify specific times when it's best to use media with young children. Parents and educators also need to be flexible and responsive to other times throughout the day, when it may be suitable to use technology with young children.

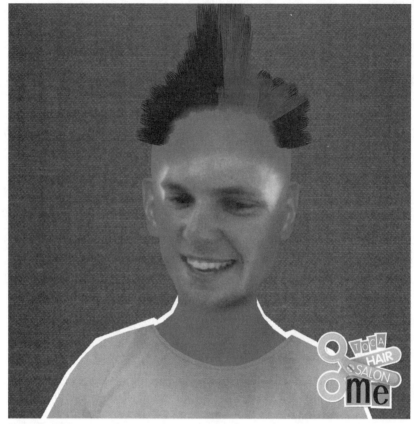

Figure 8.1 Toca Boca Hair Salon Me
(Courtesy of Toca Boca)

Sleep and Digital Devices

Young children require sleep to ensure healthy brain development and to allow their developing bodies time to recuperate. Inadequate or poor-quality sleep can negatively impact children's mood; cause behavioural issues; diminish their alertness and capacity to learn; impair memory formation, emotional health, concentration, immunity, reaction times, and impulse control; and increase their chances of obesity (Molfese et al., 2013; Sadeh, Gruber, & Raviv, 2003).

There are mounting concerns that young children's screen habits are jeopardizing the quality and amount of their sleep. The use of screen-based technologies, especially touch screen devices such as tablets and smartphones, before sleep or naptime and the presence of technology in sleep areas is problematic. The research has shown that screen time before sleep (or naptime for younger children who still nap) can delay the onset of sleep (Hale & Guan, 2014; Li et al., 2007).

Screen activities can stimulate and excite the brain, especially if the content is rapid-fire, fast-paced action. A stimulated brain makes the onset of sleep more difficult, as children need to be relatively calm to induce sleep.

Screen use in the 90 minutes before sleep can also interfere with the body's circadian rhythms (set by a light–dark cycle over a 24-hour period) and can prevent the onset of sleep. Mobile devices are particularly problematic as they emit blue light that inhibits the body's production of melatonin, which helps children fall asleep quickly and easily. Insufficient melatonin production results in sleep delays and, over time, these delays can accumulate into a sleep deficit impeding children's capacity to learn and develop.

Helpful Hints for Media Mentors to Share with Parents and Families

- Give digital devices a bedtime, too. Ideally, this would be at least 90 minutes before nap or sleep time.
- If it's not possible to avoid technology in the 90 minutes before sleep time, dim the brightness of the screen, increase the distance between the child and the screen, and/or avoid the use of fast-paced screen activities before sleep.

With Whom Will Children Use Media?

There's a strong corpus of research that confirms that co-viewing technology is beneficial for young learners (Leibham, Alexander, Johnson, Neitzel, & Reis-Henrie, 2005). Co-viewing mitigates the possible negative media effects on children, as it reduces the likelihood of exposure to inappropriate content and allows adults to help children make meaning from what they've seen on-screen and extend learning beyond the screen.

Parents and educators need to explicitly plan for opportunities that allow children to use media with an educator, parent, caregiver, peer, or sibling where possible. When adults use media with young children, they can then source resources to enable children to make sense of the on-screen experience, and they can extend children's learning beyond the screen. For example, a young child may watch a YouTube clip about giraffes with a parent. To extend the experience further, the parent could take the child to the zoo to see a giraffe or could read books about giraffes. They could also use their physical environment to show the child the actual height of a giraffe in real life. These off-screen experiences extend learning and enable parents and educators to capture the "teachable moment." However, such experiences are possible only when co-viewing takes place.

Where Will the Media Be Used?

Parents and educators need to think carefully about the design of children's physical spaces, especially when using technology.

Given the ubiquity of mobile devices, it's now easy for technology to permeate many parts of children's homes and classrooms. However, young children also need "tech-free zones." In particular, they need places to play, eat, interact, and learn, where they won't be disrupted by technology. The mere presence of screens in these areas can disrupt children.

Families and teachers also need to consider the physical layout of spaces where technology will be used to ensure that it facilitates co-viewing (easy for more than one child to use the digital device at a time) and also meets healthy ergonomic principles. In particular, parents and educators need to carefully consider a child's posture when using devices and the demands on their eyes. (See further details about posture and vision in the section, "How will the media be used?")

It's not only important to consider the placement of the digital devices that young children will use; families and teachers also need to carefully think about their personal use of devices around young children. Background media and adults' use of media can impact on a child's play and capacity to focus. Research confirms that background TV can impact on young children's play experiences and hamper their language development (Lapierre, Piotrowski, & Linebarger, 2013).

Adults also need to establish and enforce boundaries around how they'll use technology when in the presence of young children. Young children emulate adults, so parents and educators must ensure that they're not perpetually tethered to, or distracted by, digital devices, as young children are highly likely to replicate these behaviors.

Helpful Hints for Media Mentors to Share With Parents and Families

- Establish "tech-free zones" in classrooms and homes.
- Have designated "tech zones" where devices can be used. Make sure these zones are appropriately lit (see the section on "Vision"), have ergonomic work stations set up such as beanbags or cushions (see the section on "Musculoskeletal Problems"), and devices are easily accessed by multiple children and/or adults to facilitate co-viewing.
- Be mindful of adults' use of technology. Young children emulate adults' technology habits, so we need to ensure that we're modeling healthy habits.

Why Will the Media Be Used?

Parents and educators need to carefully consider why technology is being used with young children. There are mounting concerns from psychologists and educators that some children are gravitating toward screens in order to self-regulate their emotions.

Technology should allow young children to learn, play, collaborate, and create in ways different from those in traditional media.

Digital media should offer benefits to young learners. There needs to be some "value-add" in order to justify the use of technology with young children. Otherwise, parents and educators can fall into the trap of using technology for the sake of it. Technology should allow young children to learn, play, collaborate, and create in ways different from those in traditional media.

Ideally, when considering why parents and teachers use media with young children, they should be seeking innovative technology experiences that couldn't be replicated off-screen or using traditional media.

Spotlight on Technology to Connect Families and Generations

Using the Kindoma Storytime app, Sydney grandmother Jan reads digital books in real time with her grandson, Lucas, who lives in Canada. Both Jan and Lucas can see each other within the app via pop-up video chat windows that appear on-screen. They read the story together and engage in a dialogic reading experience. A similar example is the Quality Time app.

How Will the Media Be Used?

We're potentially flirting with physical developmental dangers if technology is used excessively or inappropriately with young children. In this section, four areas related to children's physical health will be explored:

- electromagnetic radiation (EMR) exposure
- vision
- hearing, and
- musculoskeletal problems.

It's important to note at the outset that research in this area is in its infancy. There's an absence of longitudinal or empirical evidence that shows how young children's media habits are impacting their development.

Electromagnetic Radiation and the Do No Harm Principle

Wi-Fi and wireless technologies have become increasingly popular. Many electronic devices are connected to computer networks wirelessly using radio waves or EMR that are invisible electrical and magnetic forces. Public concern about potential health effects associated with EMR exposure, especially from Wi-Fi, have been raised.

In 2011, the World Health Organization (WHO) and the International Agency for Research on Cancer classified radiofrequency electromagnetic fields as Type 2B Possible Carcinogen (possible cancer risk to humans; International Agency for Research on Cancer, 2011).

It's important to note that despite the WHO classification, there's still scientific uncertainty about the impact of EMR on human health. There's a lack of experimental studies with humans that confirm "safe" levels of EMR exposure, coupled with some studies that suggest there may be long-term adverse health effects from EMR exposure. However, the WHO advises that a precautionary approach be adopted, especially with young children because of possible risk of harm.

Helpful Hints for Media Mentors to Share with Parents and Families

- Increase the distance between children and the device (at least 16 inches away from the body). A simple mantra to teach young children is, "No apps in laps."
- Switch tablet devices to airplane mode when Wi-Fi connectivity isn't required. Most children's apps don't require an Internet connection, so switch the device to airplane mode.
- Switch off Wi-Fi routers when they're not in use.
- Keep modems away from high-traffic areas of the classroom or home.

Vision

Anecdotally, ophthalmologists are reporting increasing numbers of young children who present with myopia, which is near-sightedness, and computer vision syndrome (CVS). Children's early exposure and their increasing time spent with screens may put them at increased risk of both myopia and CVS. Research in this area is still in its infancy, but medical professionals suggest that simple preventative measures are implemented to reduce any possible adverse impacts associated with young children using screens.

Helpful Hints for Media Mentors to Share with Parents and Families

- Implement the 20-20-20-20 rule. Every 20 minutes encourage young children to take (at least) a 20-second break away from the computer, blink 20 times, and look at something at least 20 feet away and do something physical for 20 seconds (star jumps, run on the spot, stretch). This reduces eye fatigue associated with screen use.
- Encourage children to blink more often when using screens, as we blink up to 66 percent less when we use screens. Increased blinking helps to lubricate eyes and prevents CVS symptoms.

- Minimize external glare by closing blinds, shutters, or curtains when screens are being used. Avoid the use of screens under direct fluorescent lights or direct sunlight, as these place greater demands on the eyes and cause eyestrain.
- Balance "green-time" with screen-time. It's imperative that young children still have ample time playing in nature. This green-time allows their eyes to develop the full range of vision.
- Teach young children basic visual ergonomics. When using "fixed" screens (such as laptops and computers), the center of the screen should be 4.5 to 8 inches below their horizontal line of sight and should be 16 to 28 inches away from the body. Smaller screens such as gaming consoles and touch screen devices should be no closer than 16 to 20 inches from their eyes.

Hearing

The WHO estimates that 1.1 billion people worldwide could be affected by noise-induced hearing loss because of unsafe use of personal music devices, including mp3 players and smartphones and exposure to noisy entertainment venues (WHO, 2015). Young children are particularly vulnerable to noise-induced hearing loss because they're using headphones at younger and younger ages and sometimes for excessive amounts of time and exceeding safe decibel levels.

Research confirms that consistent use of headphones beyond 75 decibels (dB) can cause permanent hearing loss with that damage being cumulative (Melnick, 1979; Passchier-Vermeer & Passchier, 2000). Young children are particularly vulnerable to acoustic injuries because their ears are developing. However, at the time of publication, most commercial mp3 players have volume limits that exceed 130 dB (contingent upon the model of mp3 player and brand of headphones used).

Helpful Hints for Media Mentors to Share With Parents and Families

- Set up device restrictions. While it is difficult to specify a precise decibel level on most commercially available headphones, teach young children about healthy volume levels. As a general rule, children should be able to hear someone talking in a normal speaking voice when they're an arm's distance away (when using speakers or ear buds). Check with individual manufacturers as to how to set up restrictions.
- Limit children's headphone use to fewer than 60 minutes/day.
- Use noise-cancelling, earmuff-type headphones with young children. Children are less likely to blast the volume if some of the background noise is diluted. Set the maximum level to 80 percent.

Musculoskeletal Problems

Health professionals from a range of disciplines are reporting increasing numbers of children presenting with musculoskeletal problems and repetitive stress injuries (RSI), which they attribute to children's rising use of screens. Young children are spending increasing amounts of time with devices, and they may be sitting, or lying incorrectly, placing their developing bodies under unnecessary strain. Research from Australia showed that more than 30 minutes of touch screen time per day could sow the seeds for potential neck and back issues in adulthood (Coenena, Howiea, Campbella, & Strakera, 2015).

Some young children are also suffering from RSI especially if they're spending excessive amounts of time performing repetitive tasks or using incorrect movement patterns with gadgets.

The overuse of screens can displace other essential developmental tasks, such as fine-motor skills. Parents and educators need to ensure that children's media habits don't encroach on their off-screen experiences where they can refine and develop essential fine-motor skills such as cutting, tearing, twisting, drawing, and threading.

Helpful Hints for Media Mentors to Share With Parents and Families

- Teach children about healthy digital postures. Bring digital devices to slightly below a child's eye level by propping screens or adjusting chairs and desks accordingly.
- When using tablet devices, encourage children to use them lying on their stomachs (as this keeps their necks in a neutral position and they also lie for limited amounts of time on their elbows) or sitting upright in a tear-shaped beanbag (just remember to switch off Wi-Fi if the device is in their lap).
- Balance off-screen, hands-on activities with screen activities.

How Much Time Will Be Devoted to Media?

While adults need to establish "screen-time" limits, it certainly shouldn't be the only thing that parents and educators consider when it comes to young children using technology.

It's important to note that there's no evidence that confirms safe amounts of screen time. Just as it's impossible to specify an exact number of calories for children to consume each day, so too is it impossible to prescribe "healthy" or safe amounts of screen time. Using time as a metric for healthy media use is too simple and not supported by empirical studies that substantiate such limits. By focusing narrowly on how much screen time children consume/use, parents and educators can possibly overlook other really critical considerations (already explored in this chapter, such as what children are watching or creating and when they're using screens). These aspects are even more important to address than simply focusing on quantifying screen time.

Parents and educators can certainly use current guidelines proposed by the American Academy of Pediatrics (Brown, Shifrin, & Hill, 2015; Strasburger et al., 2013) and other bodies as a basis from which to make decisions about how much screen time young children should have each day. However, these should be a starting point for families and educators and not a benchmark that they necessarily need to achieve.

Most important, when considering how much screen time young children experience, parents and educators must consider the opportunity cost of screens. What are young children not doing when they're using a screen? What experiences does technology displace? Or is the time spent with screens enhancing their development?

Helpful Hints for Media Mentors to Share With Parents and Families

- Monitor children's screen-time by using media tokens (see Figure 8.2); this could be as simple as milk bottle lids with time amounts written on them and placing them in a container or paddle pop sticks in a cup) or a printable weekly media planner (see Figure 8.3).
- Establish and enforce screen time limits that are appropriate for individual children. This will need constant revisions over time, as children develop and their needs change.

Takeaways for Teachers and Parents as Media Mentors

- Think carefully and intentionally plan how technology will be used with young children to help them form healthy media habits from the outset.

Figure 8.2 Media Tokens
(Courtesy of Kristy Goodwin)

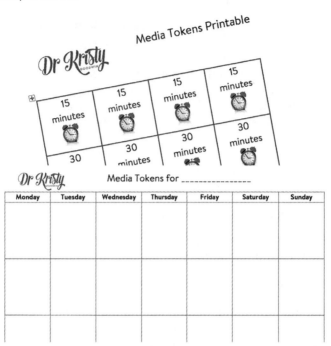

Figure 8.3 Printables from Every Child to Learn
(Courtesy of Kristy Goodwin)

- Establish media management plans to proactively design learning experiences that consider what, when, with whom, where, why, how, and how much media will be used with young children. This ensures that media are used in meaningful ways and is congruent with children's developmental needs.
- Expand thinking and research beyond how much screen time children encounter. Instead, consider broader questions related to young children's screen habits, such as what they watch, when they're using media, and how they're using devices.
- Always start with child development principles and then consider how technology can be used to support children's development.

References

Barnett, L. A. (1990). Developmental benefits of play for children. *Journal of Leisure Research*, 22(2), 138–153.

Brown, A., Shifrin, D. L., & Hill, D. L. (2015). Beyond "turn it off": How to advise families on media use. *AAP News, 36*(10), 54. doi:10.1542/aapnews.20153610-54

Chaille, C., & Britain, L. (2003). *The young child as scientist* (3rd ed.). Boston, MA: Allyn & Bacon.

Coenena, P., Howiea, E., Campbella, A., & Strakera, L. (2015, August). Mobile touch screen device use among young Australian children—first results from a national survey. In *Proceedings 19th Triennial Congress of the IEA*, vol. 9, p. 14.

Department of Education, Employment and Workplace Relations. (2009). *Belonging, being and becoming: The early years learning framework for Australia*. Canberra, Australia: DEEWR.

Farzin, F., Hou, C., & Norcia, A. M. (2012). Piecing it together: Infants' neural responses to face and object structure. *Journal of Vision, 13,* 6.

Ginsburg, K. R. (2007). The importance of play in promoting healthy child development and maintaining strong parent–child bonds. *Pediatrics, 119*(1), 182–191.

Gola, A. A., Richards, M. N., Lauricella, A. R., & Calvert, S. L. (2013). Building meaningful relationships between toddlers and media characters to teach early mathematical skills. *Media Psychology, 16,* 390–411. doi:10.1080/15213269.2013.783774

Guernsey, L. (2012). *Screen time: How electronic media—from baby videos to educational software—affects your young child*. Philadelphia, PA: Basic Books.

Hale, L., & Guan, S. (2014). Screen-time and sleep among school-aged children and adolescents: A systematic literature review. *Sleep Medicine Reviews, 21,* 50–88.

Hart, B., & Risley, T. R. (2003). The early catastrophe: The 30 million word gap by age 3. *American Educator* (Spring), 4–9.

International Agency for Research on Cancer. (2011). *IARC classifies radiofrequency electromagnetic fields as possibly carcinogenic to humans*. Press release, 2008.

Kuhl, P. K. (2004). Early language acquisition: Cracking the speech code. *Nature Reviews Neuroscience, 5,* 831–843.

Lapierre, M. A., Piotrowski, J. T., & Linebarger, D. L. (2013). Background television in the homes of US children. *Pediatrics, 130*(5), 839–846.

Leibham, M. E., Alexander, J. M., Johnson, K. E., Neitzel, C. L., & Reis-Henrie, F. P. (2005). Parenting behaviors associated with the maintenance of preschoolers' interests: A prospective longitudinal study. *Journal of Applied Developmental Psychology, 26*(4), 397–414.

Li, S., Jin, X., Wu, S., Jiang, F., Yan, C., & Shen, X. (2007). The impact of media-use on sleep patterns and sleep disorders among school-aged children in China. *Sleep, 30,* 361.

Marcon, R. A. (2002). Moving up the grades: Relationship between preschool model and later school success. *Early Childhood Research & Practice*. 4(1).

Medina, J. (2010). *Brain rules for baby*. Seattle, WA: Pear Press.

Melnick, W. (1979). Hearing loss from noise exposure. *Handbook of noise control*. New York: McGraw-Hill.

Molfese, D. L., Ivanenko, A., Key, A. F., Roman, A., et al. (2013). A one-hour sleep restriction impacts brain processing in young children across tasks: Evidence from event-related potentials. *Developmental Neuropsychology, 38,* 317–336. doi:http://dx.doi.org/10.1080/87565641.2013.799169

National Association for the Education of Young Children, & Fred Rogers Center for Early Learning and Children's Media at Saint Vincent College. (2012). *Technology and interactive media as tools in early childhood programs serving children from birth through age 8*. Washington, DC: NAEYC; Latrobe, PA: Fred Rogers Center for Early Learning and Children's Media at Saint Vincent College.

Passchier-Vermeer, W., & Passchier, W. F. (2000). Noise exposure and public health. *Environmental Health Perspectives, 108*(1), 123.

Richert, R. A., Robb, M. B., & Smith, E. I. (2011). Media as social partners: The social nature of young children's learning from screen media. *Child Development, 82*(1), 82–95.

Roseberry, S., Hirsh-Pasek, K., & Golinkoff, R. M. (2013). Skype me! Socially contingent interactions help toddlers learn language. *Child Development, 85*(3), 956–970. doi:10.1111/cdev.12166

Sadeh, A., Gruber, R., & Raviv, A. (2003). The effects of sleep restriction and extension on school-age children: What a difference an hour makes. *Child Development, 74*, 444–455.

Strasburger, V. C., Hogan, M. J., Mulligan, D. A., Ameenuddin, N., et al. (2013). Children, adolescents, and the media. *Pediatrics, 132*(5), 958–961.

World Health Organization. (2015). *Make listening safe*. Geneva: World Health Organization. Retrieved from www.who.int/pbd/deafness/activities/MLS_Brochure_English_lowres_for_web.pdf

Resources

- ChatterPix Kids, Duck Duck Moose www.duckduckmoose.com/educational-iphone-itouch-apps-for-kids/chatterpix/
- Children's Technology Review http://childrenstech.com/
- Common Sense Media www.commonsensemedia.org/
- Dora the Explorer, Nick Jr. www.nickjr.co.uk/shows/dora/
- Google Earth www.google.com/earth/
- Google Search www.google.com/
- Kids Flashcard Maker, INKids Education, http://inkidseducation.com/kids-flashcards-maker/
- Kids Media App, Common Sense Media www.commonsensemedia.org/mobile
- Kindoma Storytime http://kindoma.com
- Puppet Pals, Polished Play www.polishedplay.com/apps/puppet-pals.html
- Quality Time, ZeroDesktime www.qualitytimeapp.com/about/
- Sesame Street www.sesamestreet.org
- Sid the Science Kid http://pbskids.org/sid/
- Skype www.skype.com
- Sock Puppets, SmithMicro Software http://my.smithmicro.com/sock-puppets-description.html
- Toca Boca Hair Salon Me http://tocaboca.com/app/toca-hairsalon-me/
- YouTube www.youtube.com

Learn More...

- American Academy of Pediatrics www.aap.org/
  - Beyond "Turn it Off": How to advise families on media use http://aapnews.aappublications.org/content/36/10/54.full
  - Children and Media—Tips for Parents www.aap.org/en-us/about-the-aap/aap-press-room/pages/Children-And-Media-Tips-For-Parents.aspx

- ◦ Growing Up Digital: Media Research Symposium www.aap.org/en-us/Documents/digital_media_symposium_proceedings.pdf
- Every Chance to Learn, Dr. Kristy Goodwin www.everychancetolearn.com.au
- World Health Organization www.who.int/

Spotlight on Engagement

Enabling Family Engagement at A Distance: There is an App for That

Grazi is a 4-year-old girl who recently immigrated to Canada from Argentina. Every evening while her father is working and her mother is putting her baby brother to sleep, she video calls Grandma in Argentina from her iPad using the Kindoma Storytime *App*.

Distance makes family engagement particularly difficult. Today, roughly half of grandparents live more than 200 miles away from their grandchildren. More than 60 percent of households have two working parents, and one in three children live away from a biological parent. Some families struggle with distance due to challenges such as hospitalization, incarceration, military service, or work-related travel.

The team at Kindoma has been working on enabling family engagement at a distance for almost a decade. Research shows that telephone and Skype interactions with a young child are usually brief, as children don't have the conversational skills nor are they interested in chitchat.

Figure 8.4 Kindoma Storytime
(Courtesy of Carly Shuler, Kindoma)

Kindoma re-imagines video chat for families in a way that supports cooperative play and learning. The Storytime app allows young children and their loved ones to read together over video calls. The app includes a number of innovative practices that enforce family engagement, as described below in the context of Grazi and her family:

Include a Shared Activity

"What book do you want to read tonight, Grazi?" her grandmother asks. "Three Little Pigs!" exclaims Grazi, her chubby finger adeptly selecting the classic fairy tale from the library of books. The book opens simultaneously on both iPads.

Our research has shown that the inclusion of a shared activity increases the length of video calls with a young child by an average of more than 15 minutes. As one parent told us, "It's so much better than just a Skype call as he actually SITS still and listens!"

Enable Dialogic Reading and Inquiry

"What's that animal, Grazi?" Grandma asks, pointing to a pig. A shadow hand appears indicating where the grandmother is pointing. "A pig!" answers Grazi. "Yes," says Grandma. "Do you remember when we saw a pig at the farm?"

Educational research demonstrates that the more children talk about a book during the reading experience, the better their vocabulary development. In the case of Kindoma Storytime, the shared shadow hand encourages this back-and-forth discussion, making the book the basis for engagement and conversation.

Avoid Unnecessary Technology-Based Interactivity

"What does the cow say?" asks Grandma. Grazi, used to interactive hot spots in most apps and eBooks, presses the cow again and again, waiting for it to Moo. Nothing happens. Through the shadow hand, Grandma sees that Grazi is touching the cow. She encourages Grazi again, "Does a cow say Oink?" "Grandma!" Grazi giggles, followed by a loud "MOOOO."

With Kindoma, the goal is for humans to provide the interactivity and scaffolding. Unnecessary technology-based interactivity such as animations and sounds is avoided. As one parent told us, "I love the simple interface that does not distract my child and keeps him focused on the book."

The book gives Grazi and her Grandma something to do together and something to talk about, much as they used to when they were together in Argentina. Grandma is thankful to be meaningfully connecting with Grazi on a video call, rather than fighting to hold her attention. Grazi is excited to be using the iPad, and to be reading a story that she loves. Her mother is thankful that she has a few minutes to put down Grazi's brother and grateful for family support from across the globe.

Contributed by Carly Shuler and the Kindoma team

Learn More...

Kindoma www.kindoma.com

Chapter 9

Digital-Age Family Engagement

Supporting Parents as Media Mentors

Devorah Heitner

Abundance Versus Engagement: A Tale of Two Technology Strategies

At many preschools and primary grade schools, defining an approach to technology is an important part of the school's outward-facing brand. Schools may emphasize their approach on their website or with images. Some schools overtly or subtly emphasize the *lack* of technology as a guarantor of quality while others emphasize the integration of technology or a "state-of-the-art" high-tech environment as a signifier of quality. Often, schools promote their approach to integrating (or abstaining from) technology without deep considerations for current or potential parents' questions about the role digital devices might play in inquiry, documentation, exploration, collaboration, and play at the school.

Depending on the ideology and pedagogical approach of the school, the language that schools and child care programs use to describe integration of technology can be very different. In early childhood education, ideas about developmental appropriateness and relevance vary widely, and this variety is evident in how schools describe their approach to technology on their websites or in their brochures.

Terms such as *state of the art* may signify an abundance of technology but not necessarily developmentally appropriate or thoughtful engagement. As a parent and educator, I am less interested in the tools to which my child might have access but more interested in the thoughtful planning, engagement, and sensitivity of the educators who are working with the children and communicating with their families.

More of the Same: Updates From the "TV Prohibition" Days

As Ellen Seiter's canonical article "Power Rangers in Preschool: Negotiating Media in Early Childhood Settings" (1999) demonstrates, attitudes toward technology can range from antithetical to media literacy. I've seen it go beyond simple literacy, to ardent evangelism. Seiter shows how an approach to media or "rules about television" in schools or child care environments "help produce status differences and stratify/segment the childcare market." Seiter offers an ethnographic account of two child care settings: (1) a Montessori school frequented by more affluent and upper-middle-class families and (2) a child care center employed by more working-class and lower-middle-class families. At the Montessori school, children were forbidden from watching television, and their families were instructed to limit their viewing outside of school. Play based on characters in television was not allowed, nor was clothing with television characters. Although when Seiter looked deeper, she found that girls were sometimes allowed some character-based play, but the boys' TV character-based play was deemed more disruptive and was forbidden.

While her television-focused examples may seem dated (although TV is still an important slice of the media pie for young children!), the attitude and rules about media are equally, if not more, significant in a world that now includes interactive media experiences and applications as a differentiator between programs in the early childhood marketplace. The ways media use is associated with the prestige or "branding" of a school or child care setting is very applicable to our present moment, and it is a cautionary reminder for parents.

In Seiter's article, the Montessori school gains its prestige partly by eschewing television and not allowing play based on TV characters—or even clothing with TV characters on them. Higher tuition and more affluent population of students is also part of the prestige package, of course. In contrast, the child care director that Seiter studied used television as a time to settle kids down after lunch and at the end of the day. She was familiar with the characters in the kids' favorite shows and allowed them to play games based on their shows. She was observed entering into conversations about both the shows themselves and the kids' imaginative world built on top of the shows' storylines. Seiter contrasts the media literacy approach of the center with the marginalizing approach of the Montessori school as well as the way the Montessori school sought to brand itself as a refuge from a media-saturated world.

This example shows how deeply educators' personal beliefs and ideologies about media, mass culture, and technology can influence their assumptions about what constitutes quality. As educators, we need to double-check the ways we use technology to market and brand different educational environments.

The Result? Mixed Messages

Parents are in a very confusing situation when they try to decide what kinds of technology engagements are positive for kids. As I've described, schools use their ideologies around technology to create their brand. Because everyone from pediatricians to grandparents has a differing perspective on parents' choices for media and digital access for young children, these mixed messages are often laced with guilt. Yet, as Alexandra Samuel's research suggests, to be able to truly mentor our kids in the digital age, we have to put aside our "technology shame" and not leave ourselves open to hypocrisy (Samuel, 2015). It's probably safe to assume that at least some of the Montessori parents still allowed television in their homes. Making them feel guilty seems less productive than offering recommendations for quality shows and methods for joint media engagement.

Parents often are looking to early childhood educators and school leaders for guidance in raising their children. Indeed, especially for first-time parents, it makes sense to think of an experienced early childhood program director as a trusted sage. Therefore, the intensity of many educators either as techno-optimists or techno-cautionists can be influential.

Thankfully, in many early childhood settings, educators recognize that mentoring parents is crucial. Some settings are still able to marshal the resources of a home visit. As a parent, my recollections of the preschool teacher's home visit was that it formed an essential connection between home and school. Her snapshot of our home life, our child's setting, and his way of relating to us at home offered crucial information. Home visits are resource-intensive and may not be possible for all early childhood educators, but the impulse behind them and the focus on the importance of understanding and supporting parents as part of the mission for quality early educators is compelling.

Over the past several months, I've interviewed numerous educators about the factors that are most crucial for kids' learning and thriving with tech integration. I've found that the attitude and openness toward learning new things and to supporting families where they are with technology go a long way toward empowering parents to mentor their children.

Supporting Parents as Media Mentors: Preschool in the Digital Age

In order to set parents up for a successful path to parenting in a technology-rich world, early childhood educators want to encourage media mentorship and engagement with kid's technology. We want parents to "play what their kids play" and to plan for screen engagements that emphasize creativity and creation over consumption. While some control is also important (unsupervised Internet access or unlimited device time isn't good for any preschooler), a mentoring approach and an open, curious attitude will go a long way in cultivating a positive family life in the digital age.

Since I have identified mentorship as a crucially distinguishing approach, I've worked to identify the factors for cultivating and disseminating a culture of mentorship around human/technology interactions in educational settings.

Playgrounds Versus Playpens

As Marina Bers describes, the most desirable and stimulating digital experiences for young kids are applications and engagements that function more like "playgrounds" than "playpens" (2012). Bers makes this distinction between applications and environments that simply contain children (such as a playpen) versus more complex and challenging environments that are still kid-friendly enough and intuitive enough that children can roam freely within these spaces. She characterizes playground-like digital experiences as allowing for "playful learning, autonomous decision making (even if as adults we know that they will lead to initial failure), and risk taking" (Bers, 2012, p. 28). Much of the "edutainment" available to preschoolers and young children is more playpen like, it doesn't foster developmental autonomy, it simply focuses on capturing attention and perhaps on teaching literacy or numeracy, often in developmentally inappropriate ways. On the other hand,

> playground technologies support children in using their creativity and imagination, discovering, and inventing while making their own projects in a playful way.
>
> We are focusing here on the playpen as a metaphor the conveys lack of freedom to experiment, lack of autonomy for exploration, lack of creative opportunities and lack of risks...[...] The playground promotes while the playpen hinders, a sense of mastery, creativity, self-confidence and open exploration....
>
> From a developmental perspective, most of today's technologies for young children are playpens and not playgrounds.
>
> Bers (2012), p. 23

Parents can observe in a school environment whether students are creating with technology, such as a marvelous photobooth I saw near the dressup area in a preschool classroom, or in the "take apart station" I observed in another preschool, or just using tablets or other technology to play an alphabet game. Bers points out, and I agree, that many playpen-type experiences are harmless, but they are not offering children a chance to grow their self-esteem by taking risks and increasing autonomy and mastery (Bers, 2012).

Use the Tools You Already Have: You Don't Need a Ton of Money

With Bers's playpen metaphor in mind and with an eye to being cautious about preschool "branding in relation to technology," I want to assert an important truth about excellent use of technology in early childhood settings. You don't need a tremendous amount of money or technology to do it well. I've worked with child care centers that had a very limited budget for technology and used photographs and documents of children's work in many innovative ways to support learning, teacher assessment, and parent engagement. Many teachers have cameras on their personal cell phones or devices. Simply documenting student work to increase parent engagement, especially ephemeral creations such as block buildings or stages of projects such as the take apart station, or action shots, are incredibly helpful uses of technology. These images can help students expand on their creations by making books using images of their work to illustrate a story or as part of a visual schedule that helps children anticipate transitions. Video is incredibly useful for a teacher's own development. In the moment, it can be hard to catch things in the highly spontaneous environment of an early childhood setting, so video can be a wonderful tool for documenting activities, events, and interactions. For educators, video offers an opportunity to see both their successes and missed opportunities, disconnections, and the like.

Six Factors to Support a Culture of Mentorship

I have identified mentorship as a crucially distinguishing approach—internally a culture of mentorship between teachers and with students and parents.

In my work with schools on parent engagement and digital citizenship, I encourage schools to empower teachers to be media mentors, approach parents as mentors, and also to empower parents to mentor their own children. I've identified six factors that schools and early childhood settings can use to self-evaluate their approach to cultivating a climate of mentorship.

Factors to Support a Culture of Mentorship

1. Tech environment.
2. Technology habits.
3. Spirit of inquiry.
4. Ideologies about child development.
5. Ideologies about technology.
6. Behavioral integrity.

Factor 1: Tech Environment

I start with this one because it's the single biggest governing factor when it comes to technology use. Access to technology, whether at home or in class, makes a huge difference in the way that kids, their parents, and their teachers interact. This can range from rules to habits, and experienced educators have done this for years in the analog world when "curating their classroom." They know what makes a good environment to promote learning and active engagement.

When parents are looking for an early childhood environment, they want to see a welcoming space for their kids. Creativity is key—even the draftiest, darkest church basement can be a welcoming preschool with some great thought put into textiles, lighting, and classroom design. In terms of technology, where devices live, and children's autonomy and responsibility around any digital devices, says a lot about the culture of a school. Look for images of student work in the classroom for students to use, in the hall for parents to see, and on the website.

Access Is Everything

In order to have access to technology in a specific environment, it must be physically available, and rules (governmental, institutional, parental) must allow the person to use it.

For example, in order for a student to use Wi-Fi on a school bus, the bus must be equipped with Wi-Fi, the student must have a device on the bus, and the student must be able to log in. Home visits and conversations with parents are important so that educators understand media exposure and access and when possible, can support families in making excellent choices.

Different Spaces, Different Rules

Schools need to understand children's environments including as much as possible about the homes students live in, which is why many excellent early childhood programs still do a home visit. Seeing for yourself the kinds of toys, books, electronics as well as food, furniture, and ratio of people to space tells a lot for educators. This understanding of the home and family context can help educators consider how best to communicate with parents. Is their widespread access to Wi-Fi in your community? Is email a good way to communicate with parents, or is text? Posting information to a bulletin board at your school is a good way to share information with parents who don't have access to the Internet or a device.

Factor 2: Technology Habits

We all need to take stock of how frequently and desperately we check our email, scroll through Facebook feeds, or interact in other digital spaces. It is hard even to recognize our motivations, as many of us check compulsively without thinking about how often, how long, or who we're with.

Evaluate Yourself

A little honest self-reflection can really help, at any time. This goes for parents and teachers. For instance, what habits are parents modeling for young people when they text during mealtimes?

Transferring Habits From Analog to Digital

At this age, we help children make a schedule, and we are building habits. In the "real world," we teach them how to sneeze into their elbows, say please and thank you, and line up properly for excursions to other parts of the building. These and many other habits that we instill will serve children as they grow and make it easier for them to be part of society. Likewise, taking care of technology, putting it away, and knowing when it is appropriate to use are wonderful things to habituate preschoolers to.

Empathy for Parents, Too

Many schools have rules about parents using cell phones at drop-off or pickup. These are good rules and helpful boundaries, as it considers children's safety above all. But after safety is taken care of, we should always approach parents with compassion and understanding. The stresses of parenting, working, and surviving and all the other things that may be happening in life can be quite overwhelming for parents.

I would try to offer support to parents who struggle with this policy, but I would try not to guilt or shame them into changing their behavior. While sometimes we may worry about the damage to attachment, we should also wonder what is going on in the larger context.

Modeling a positive spirit of inquiry is an important way for early childhood educators to support parents.

Factor 3: Spirit of Inquiry

Mentoring is teaching. Therefore, another important thing to know in mentoring is how people respond to learning new things. Are they open to—and excited by—new challenges? Are they comfortable with not knowing something or being an expert?

We all have an immediate response to a situation where someone else knows more than we do. It can be anything from inspiring to threatening. Think back to your interactions with other educators at conferences and other public settings. How did you feel when another teacher seemed more savvy than you about technology? Do you feel comfortable learning on the fly and saying, "I don't know, let's find out." Some of us (myself included) prefer significant preparation, practice, and at least the illusion of mastery before we try something with students! Know yourself and what will work for you.

Modeling a positive spirit of inquiry is an important way for early childhood educators to support parents. Parenting can be stressful and overwhelming, and it can be easy in these times to feel fearful of getting it "wrong" or making a costly misstep. It is important for both parents and educators to be honest with themselves when doing a self-assessment. How much do we know, and what do we have to learn?

For help, look to your children. The child's model of inquiry is often very curious and open. It can serve as a very good model for adults when teaching early childhood or mentoring the parents of young children.

Factor 4: Ideologies About Child Development

Another factor I've identified that plays a huge role in how we mentor both kids and their parents in learning with technology is their parenting ideologies or their beliefs about childhood. In a moment, I'll also address their beliefs about technology. Both of these beliefs converge in the preschool environment.

Parents

On one hand, in a given community, you may have parents whose ideologies seem to be drawn from the book *Battle hymn of the tiger mother* (Chua, 2011) while, on the other hand, you may have parents who want to raise the "free-range kids" that Lenore Skenazy describes in her eponymous book and blog (2010). Not all parenting approaches are simply decisions … the influence of culture and especially class is huge. Sociologist Annette Lareau compares the concerted cultivation that the majority of affluent and middle-class parents employ, where kids do a lot of structured activities and parents intervene at school and attempt to nurture their children's specific talents, versus natural growth approach that many working class parents (2003). This method had some advantages, Lareu found, with kids having more independence and stronger sibling and extended family relationships, but they were less good at self-advocacy, which is a skill that can be helpful to getting ahead or even resolving problems at school and elsewhere.

Teachers

Educators also hold dear to these beliefs, and one often hears of people who long for a "Mark Twain" early childhood or even their own seventies childhood. It's natural to idealize our own experiences, but they may be reminded that some of their "free-range" unattended childhood was lonely and even frightening. Each era has its scourges and its pleasures. Teachers may respond differently to parents on the basis of how much they feel in alignment with their approach to child-raising.

Factor 5: Ideologies About Technology

Our belief system about how to raise our children used to be enough. But when the environment changed (see Factor 1), we needed to also look at our own response to the new technologies that are available today. Some of it enhances our world, to be sure—and some of it is not so good. Love it or hate it, it's not going away. And in order to be a good mentor, you have to have an understanding of it.

Are You Starting With Inherent Biases?

A self-examination of your technology disposition is required. How do you feel about technology? What informs your own approach to technology? What's your view of technology's purpose? Do you see it as a creative medium or merely a means to consume? Are you generally an early or late adopter? And, most important, are you open to change or not open?

Are You an Optimist or Cautionist?

This conflict is apparent to me when couples approach me at my parent education events. When one is deeply invested in technology for everything, the tech-optimist will find that it supports or constitutes most of her or his interests. Similarly, the tech-cautionist who is repulsed by technology and its effects will find support for all the reasons why social media are destroying society. The answer usually lies somewhere in the middle, and the big thing to remember is that our children's experience with technology is not the same as our own.

How Do Schools Respond to Parents?

There are plenty of books, websites, and blogs that exhort parents to be excited about "state-of-the-art" technology. Many of them offer tips for thoughtful integration, which can be very helpful. In a competitive market, keep in mind that schools do what they have to do, and they respond to what they *presume* parents want. Are we as parents sending the right message to our school administrators?

Factor 6: Behavioral Integrity

All the work that you put into creating a "culture of mentorship" can fall apart without the sixth factor: behavioral integrity. To be a good mentor, you have to be a good role model. Parenting has come a long way from, "Do as I say, not as I do." Your actions and choices must align with your stated ideals.

Key Messages From the Joint Position Statement

As they do for young children, educators have a responsibility to parents and families to model appropriate, effective, and positive uses of technology, media, methods of communication, and social media that are safe, secure, healthy, acceptable, responsible, and ethical.

NAEYC & Fred Rogers Center (2012), pp. 7–8

Accountability

As a school leader, am I responsive to email at all hours, or do I model the healthy boundaries I tell my staff that I expect them to have? Do I respond out of defensiveness quickly to communications with colleagues, or do I take some time to think—or see them in person if the conversation seems likely to be triggering, challenging feelings, or emotional reactions?

Consistency

If I expect kids to have limits and boundaries, do I have any boundaries on my own time? Having behavioral integrity does not mean that you need to have the same rules for yourself that you have for your children. But there is logic to the reasons behind the rules. Your own habits and behaviors should, at base, adhere to the same reasons or logic. These are your core values that inform everything you do—for yourself *and* as a mentor.

Helpful Hints for Media Mentors to Empower Parents as Media Mentors

- **Share blogs and resources about kid's apps.** As the authors of *Tap, Click, Read* point out, the "educational app" market is a Wild West of applications, many of dubious quality and minimal correspondence to what we know about child development and learning (Guernsey & Levine, 2015). So for any early childhood educator to be able to recommend a few great TV shows and apps that are recommended by _____ (fill in someone you would trust) is a great start.
- **Try to get beyond a parent's initial assumptions** about "state-of-the-art tech will prepare my kid for the Ivy League. Or...tech is bad and I am a bad parent because my child has played with my phone or seen a TV show.

  o If they ask about your approach to technology, find out what they really want to know. They may be concerned that tech integration is a way to raise class size. They may be concerned that their child will do nothing else if offered access. Find out more.
  o If a parent is a programmer or designer or does something else with technology, is there something they can share with kids? Can you use technology to make classroom visits accessible to parents who cannot get away from work to drop in?
  o As you do build resources for technology in your program, don't spend all of your resources on technology. Be sure to spend more on professional development than devices. Better to share a few devices, but make sure all the teachers have been

well-supported than to have many devices and minimal professional development.

○ In a non-guilt-inducing way, emphasize to parents that their own technology use is a model for their kids and that the always-on culture of today's workplace can be hard on family life and requires active management. This can be done in a sympathetic, non-accusatory way.

Conclusion

Early childhood environments offer an excellent opportunity to habituate students and their families to an inquiry-based relationship with technology. We can model creativity and finding ways to create more than we consume. We can help parents use excellent criteria to choose applications for their children to use. We can also help create school communities where unplugged activities are important and resist fetishizing technological devices for their "state-of–the-art" qualities and focus on what they are doing to support playful learning and documentation in our early childhood classrooms.

References

Bers, M. (2012). *Designing digital experiences for positive youth development: From playpen to playground*. Oxford: Oxford University Press.

Chua, A. (2011). *Battle hymn of the tiger mother*. New York: Penguin Press.

Guernsey, L., & Levine, M. H. (2015). *Tap, click, read: Growing readers in a world of screens*. San Francisco, CA: Jossey-Bass.

Lareau, A. (2003). *Unequal childhoods: Class, race, and family life*. Berkeley, CA: University of California.

National Association for the Education of Young Children, & Fred Rogers Center for Early Learning and Children's Media at Saint Vincent College. (2012). *Technology and interactive media as tools in early childhood programs serving children from birth through age 8*. Washington, DC: NAEYC; Latrobe, PA: Fred Rogers Center for Early Learning and Children's Media at Saint Vincent College.

Samuel, A. (2015, November 4). *Parents: Reject technology shame*. Retrieved from www.theatlantic.com/technology/archive/2015/11/why-parents-shouldn't-feel-technology-shame/414163

Seiter, E. (1998). *Television and new media audiences*. Oxford: Clarendon Press.

Seiter, E. (1999). Power Rangers at preschool: Negotiating media in child care settings. In Kinder, M. (ed.), *Kids' media culture*. Durham, NC: Duke University Press.

Skenazy, L. (2010). *Free-range kids: How to raise safe, self-reliant children (without going nuts with worry)*. San Francisco, CA: Jossey-Bass.

Resources

- *Screen Time: How Electronic Media—From Baby Videos to Educational Software—Affects Your Young Child.* Lisa Guernsey www.lisaguernsey.com/screen-time.htm
- *Tap, Click, Read: Growing Readers in a World of Screens.* Lisa Guernsey and Michael H. Levine www.tapclickread.org

Learn More...

- Raising Digital Natives. Dr. Devorah Heitner www.raisingdigitalnatives.com
- *Children's learning from educational television: Sesame Street and beyond.* Shalom Fisch. (2004). New York: Routledge.
- *Connecting Wisely In The Digital Age: Social/emotional Insights & Skills For Plugged-in Kids.* Devorah Heitner & Karen Jacobson, Youthlight, Incorporated www.chapters.indigo.ca/en-ca/books/connecting-wisely-in-the-digital/9781598501728-item.html
- *Empathy and Research: Engaging Parents with Tech Initiatives.* Devorah Heitner, edutopia www.edutopia.org/blog/engaging-parents-with-tech-initiatives-devorah-heitner
- *Exposure and use of mobile media devices by young children.* Kabali, Irigoyen, Nunez-Davis, Budacki, & Mohanty. Pediatrics Oct 2015, DOI:10.1542/peds.2015-2151.
- *Feeling Overwhelmed By All the Apps? Here's a Guided Tour of Your Kids' Digital World.* Devorah Heitner, Raising Digital Natives www.raisingdigitalnatives.com/overwhelmed-by-apps-cant-keep-up-how-to-make-sense-of-it-all/
- *Top 10 Parent Concerns.* Devorah Heitner, Raising Digital Natives http://raisingdigitalnatives.com/top-10-concerns-about-children-and-technology/
- *What to Ask Before Buying Tech Tools for Kids.* Devorah Heitner, PBS Parents www.pbs.org/parents/experts/archive/2012/12/what-to-ask-before-buying-tech.html

Chapter 10

The Mediatrician's Advice for Today's Media Mentors

Michael Rich and Kristelle Lavallee

Introduction

As educators and as members of society, we are facing a dramatic sea change in the way we learn, communicate, teach, and live in the world. The digital revolution has yielded technologies that were hardly imagined even a decade ago. Because such technologies are now inexpensive and accessible to people of any socioeconomic status, they are nearly ubiquitous in workplaces, homes, and even our pockets. As a result, classrooms preparing children for the world of tomorrow feel pressured to introduce screen media earlier and earlier in children's education. Unfortunately, the enthusiasm that society and administrators may feel about integrating screen media into early childhood education is not always supported by theory or by the experiences of the educators who must implement it.

The Center on Media and Child Health (CMCH) at Boston Children's Hospital aims to educate and empower children and those who care for them to create and consume media in ways that optimize their physical, mental, and social health. To achieve this mission, CMCH translates scientific evidence into strategies for raising and educating children. It conducts and collects research, translates its findings into practical action steps for parents and educators, and builds on that knowledge to innovate with media technologies in ways that support and enhance the cognitive, social, and emotional growth of children.

As part of this effort, CMCH offers Ask the Mediatrician, an online advice column that addresses questions faced by children, parents, clinicians, and educators as they navigate the digital landscape. CMCH answers these questions on the basis of research, addresses both the potential benefits and the potential risks of using particular technologies, and presents possible solutions that are feasible for readers, whether parents, professionals, or both. In the following example, we provide such guidance to an early childhood educator. We recognize that we must build on existing theory and research, but also learn from one another and our mistakes as we explore an ever-changing technological and social environment.

Spotlight on Advice for Media Mentors

Dear Mediatrician:

I'm a Pre-K teacher in a public school that was recently awarded funding for new classroom technologies. I have been given new tablets to use with my students (nearly one per child). I am not sure how to use these devices most effectively in my classroom because they have never been a part of my curriculum before. I don't want to use them in ways that will displace critical learning, but I also understand that technology is and will be an essential part of my students' lives. I realize that I can limit tablet use to a free-play center, but my goal is to help my students use them to learn as part of an integrated curriculum throughout the school year. Is there any advice you can offer on how to do this?

~ Teacher Tablet Trouble, NH

Dear T3,

You have already taken the most important step toward using technology effectively in your classroom: You are treating it as a tool for teaching.

To address your concerns, first make sure that you aren't attributing any special powers, good or bad, to electronic technologies. Instead, we need to look at digital devices in the same way we look at textbooks or pencils: They are tools that help shape and structure the learning process and the educational interaction that occurs between teachers and students. The teacher and the curriculum remain the central and most important components of the educational process. Digital technologies cannot replace either—but can be used to enhance them. Technology is only as important as its ability to support and enhance the human-to-human learning process.

As educators, we must choose learning tools that best support each of our varied learning goals rather than seeking a single tool that can support all of them. That holds true for digital technologies as well, which are sometimes touted as supereducators. As an example, many apps and computer programs claim to teach preschoolers math skills, but manipulatives may be more effective for children in this age group. Unlike tablets, manipulatives provide concrete experiences, which means that children can feel them and weigh them and play with them in ways that aren't possible with an image on a two-dimensional screen.

However, such technologies can be quite effective as learning tools when used to reinforce and expand what you can do with traditional learning tools. For example, when learning about ants, you can explore the underground architecture of ant colonies online and then go to the playground and find ants building a nest and ferrying food to it. This multiple-perspective approach can strengthen your lesson and expand students' understanding in new ways. Ultimately, discussing and processing this multisource, multidimensional information through questions, answers, and hypothesis testing will allow students to discover and "own" knowledge, which is the core of the learning process.

You mentioned that you don't have enough tablets for each student to have one, and I'm glad to hear it. If there were enough tablets that students did not have to share, they would miss out on an important opportunity for social emotional growth. A key developmental task (Kliegman, 2016) of preschoolers is to progress from solo, individual activities and parallel play to partnering with others in collaborative tasks and shared play. Problem-solving activities that encourage students to work together on a single device can help build their interpersonal communication, cooperation, and collaboration (Arnott, 2013;

McManis & Gunnewig, 2012)—and research has shown that children learn more when they synergize and learn together (Bransford, Brown, & Cocking, 1999).

Regarding where in the classroom to locate the tablets, I would urge you *not* to place them or any technology in a free-play center. First, leaving them in that space would encourage your students to think of them as toys rather than as the powerful tools they are. Second, supervision and collaborative media use will help your students learn to use these devices in positive, productive ways (Christakis, 2014). Finally, by taking devices out for certain activities and putting them away after those activities are finished, you model that these are tools like other tools they use—to be implemented effectively to perform a particular task and turned off and stored to perform another task with a different tool. Digital devices are not used for everything, and they should not be used in the classroom for diversion.

Although it's true that play is learning and learning is play, especially during the preschool years, remember that at home young children will get, and may already be getting, plenty of time playing on screen media (that is, using it without particular educational goals). School provides the opportunity to use these tools in more directed ways, with consciously selected content. To make that possible, digital devices should be seamlessly integrated into the parts of school day and classroom environment where they effectively support the process, rather than as distractions or ways to fill the time. Remember that just as you can use a spoon for both meals and dessert, you can use a digital device for both achieving particular learning goals and for entertainment. In either case, it is the content and intent of the activity that matters.

This shift may be challenging at times for your students, who come into your class with their own experiences, expectations, and understandings of technology. Recent research shows that three-fourths of children younger than age 4 own, and most have used, interactive tablets or smartphones; most use the devices daily by age 2, and one third multitask with tablets and other media at age 4 (Kabali et al., 2015). This amount of usage means that young children can demonstrate facility with the devices. However, reading screens is more than just making the technology work. Toddlers can turn pages very early, but learning from digital devices, like reading a book, is a skill that can and should be taught to help develop literate, thoughtful, and reflective children of the digital age. Subsequently, be prepared to help re-tool or redirect preschoolers' media use in ways that best support learning, both in the classroom and at home (Hsu, Liang, Chai, & Tsai, 2013).

Finally, I want to applaud and encourage the inquisitiveness that led you to ask this question. Your desire to build an evidence-based curriculum that uses educational technology reveals an effective educator who is unafraid of the future and wants to step boldly into it with her eyes open. One of the challenges of doing so effectively is that schools and administrators have varied ideas about the importance of educators keeping up with technology, so training may or may not be available to you (Lawless & Pellegrino, 2007). You may need to be the driving force in seeking out and maintaining your professional development in educational technology. You may also find yourself at the beginning of an ongoing process of educating your colleagues, as well as yourself and your students, when it comes to new classroom technologies. You are starting the journey with your best foot forward, keeping your students and your learning goals for them in mind as you embark on integrating the digital domain into their education.

Enjoy your media and teach with them wisely.

~ The Mediatrician

In order to be successful media mentors, early childhood educators must first know how to select media technologies and integrate them into their classrooms. As noted in this Ask the Mediatrician question from the New Hampshire teacher, educators are often placed in a precarious situation when it comes to educational media. Should they immediately jump on the bandwagon and become modern, tech-savvy teachers or should they hold to tried-and-true tech-free techniques? As with most dichotomies, there is a third option. That is, educators should do what educators do best: rely on their knowledge of curriculum goals and of their students in order to select tools that will best support learning and development.

Educators should do what educators do best: rely on their knowledge of curriculum goals and of their students in order to select tools that will best support learning and development.

To most effectively rely on their essential pedagogical knowledge to decide how to use media tools to support student learning, educators can adhere to the following three principles:

1   choose the learning goal first, then select the media tool;
2   choose media that are intentionally designed to foster children's learning; and
3   choose media that encourage interaction.

Applying these principles is crucial for classroom education using media. They can help educators avoid adopting new technologies simply on the basis of "educational" labels (which are used primarily for marketing purposes, typically are not backed by scientific research, and few classification systems exist; Cherner, Dix, & Lee, 2014; Shuler, 2009) or as "just for fun" or free-play options (Maddux & Cummings, 2004).

Principle 1: Choose the Learning Goal First, Then Select the Media Tool

No matter what their underlying educational goal, new items in the classroom will draw students' attention. Whether it's a terrarium introduced to watch the life cycle of a frog or a TV to deliver a Spanish-language lesson, novelty will often garner enthusiasm and interest from students. However, just because students are entranced by the newest classroom gadget or display doesn't mean that they are learning the intended information or skills. Many media devices, apps, and platforms for children are designed to grab and hold their attention as long as possible; however, what the child learns from spending time with them may not align with the educators' goals. Like all classroom and learning tools, media should be selected and used for a predetermined purpose before being made accessible to students.

Both pre-scripted (such as TV shows) and open-ended (such as music apps) media can be used for such purposes.

- **Pre-scripted media:** These are media that are predetermined and remain unchanged despite users' interaction with them. Using such media can advance student learning when their goals align with the educator's. Curriculum focused on fostering children's prosocial skills can benefit from integrating an episode of a research-based educational television series such as *Sesame Street* (Zielinska & Chambers, 1995). Choosing media such as *Sesame Street*, which is designed to help young children learn how to cooperate while recognizing and appreciating others' differences, can bolster students learning about these topics in ways that are developmentally optimal (Truglio, Lovelace, Segui, & Scheiner, 2001).
- **Interactive media:** Media in which the user's choices and actions drive the experience can cultivate students' creativity, self-expression, peer-collaboration, and even problem-solving skills (Geist, 2012; Kucirkova, Messer, Sheehy, & Fernández Panadero, 2014). Examples include students working in peer groups to solve a digital puzzle or discovering, on their own, how to use an eraser tool in a drawing app to edit their artwork.

Choose screen media only when they are the right tools for the job. Although learning an instrument may be fun using a tablet's digital keyboard, playing a tangible keyboard or piano may better allow students to understand harmony, reverberations, and even duets (such as by sitting side by side on a piano bench) than can even the most advanced app. Educators must apply their knowledge, experience, and skills to ensure that the tools they select for their students optimize the achievement of their learning goals.

Principle 2: Choose Media That Are Intentionally Designed to Foster Children's Learning

Early childhood educators choose classroom materials, texts, and supplies based on their ability to effectively support students' learning and development. This same rigorous screening and selection process applies when integrating technology. Whether a tablet, app, or computer game, each new medium should be introduced to students after the teacher has purposefully and mindfully chosen the tool to fit the students' needs.

New devices and apps are continually being marketed for classroom learning, but it's not always clear which ones are actually effective. When seeking out technologies, look for those that engage the following techniques, which have proven to be successful at achieving desired learning outcomes in early childhood education:

- **Use repetition:** Young children enjoy engaging in new or interesting experiences again and again: Consider how often they request the same story or song. They do so both for pleasure and because it helps them master knowledge or a new skill. Take advantage of this tendency by choosing media that are deliberately designed for repetitive use. Each episode of *Blue's Clues* is designed to be viewed daily for five days in a row (and is broadcast that way). When used as designed, young viewers' grasp of the learning goals increases with each viewing (Anderson et al., 2000). The customizability, mobility, and responsive interface of tablets can allow young students to control the content, which can include interacting with the same content again and again for as long as they would like, helping them reach their learning goals at their own pace.
- **Communicate learning goals clearly:** By explicitly stating their learning goals and presenting those goals in formats that are easy for the child to understand (Falloon, 2013), pre-scripted media such as TV programs help children focus their attention on salient points rather than on non-central features of the episode. *Sesame Street* begins (and ends) each episode by stating that the program is "brought to you by" a specific letter. That letter is used in a variety of contexts throughout the episode in an effort to teach the child how to identify, say, and understand it as part of his or her alphabet and language (Fisch & Truglio, 2014). Because the goal is stated up front, the child is more likely to pay attention to the use of that letter.
- **Integrate instructions and provide feedback:** Young children do best with technologies that are easy and intuitive for them to use. Media that provide clear instructions and explicit teaching elements, such as corrective feedback and the ability to interact, support young children's learning (Falloon, 2013). Direct feedback for both correct and incorrect responses in an educational app helps kindergarteners learn intended lessons by providing encouragement when they succeed and letting them know when their answers need to be revised. These applications must be selected on the basis of students' ability level in order to keep children engaged and to help them achieve the desired learning goals (Muis, Ranellucci, Trevors, & Duffy, 2015).
- **Avoid distracting content:** Media technologies engage children with a variety of different features. Although these features can be used to reinforce learning, they can also distract from educational goals by engaging children's attention with superfluous features. It's for this reason that enhanced e-books, those that contain a variety of multi-media features in addition to the story, can be less effective at achieving learning goals than their print or basic e-book counterparts. Clickable images, sound effects, and games can divert from, rather than support, the intended educational goals (Chiong, Ree, Takeuchi, & Erickson, 2012).

Principle 3: Choose Media That Encourage Interaction

Interactivity is often heralded as an essential feature of quality educational media. Defined by the National Association for the Education of Young Children (NAEYC) and the Fred Rogers Center for Early Learning and Children's Media as "content designed to facilitate active and creative use by young children and to encourage social engagement with other children and adults" (National Association for the Education of Young Children & Fred Rogers Center for Early Learning and Children's Media, 2012), the term *interactive* can refer both to interaction with the medium itself and to interaction with peers, teachers, and caregivers that the medium facilitates.

Early childhood is a time when children are learning about their world primarily through observation and interaction. Because interactive media provide platforms where children can relate to and work with others (even if that "other" is a digital character), such media can help children learn and practice skills such as taking turns, sharing, compromising, and even empathizing.

The term interactive *can refer both to interaction with the medium itself and to interaction with peers, teachers, and caregivers that the medium facilitates.*

Different forms of interactivity have different benefits for children's learning:

- **Interactivity by design:** Media of all kinds can be designed to elicit user interaction. Applications on tablets and smartphones may require interaction by asking the user to swipe, tap, or even speak to the device. Educational apps such as PBS KIDS's *Super Why!* aimed at building literacy skills, react to user's engagement and provide feedback and incentives for correct answers (Chiong & Shuler, 2010).

  Even TV, once considered a passive medium, now has an entire industry dedicated to educational interactive programming for children. *Dora the Explorer*, a popular educational program for preschoolers, makes the viewing experience interactive by pausing to ask viewers questions or to ask them to participate with characters in a song, dance, or other activity. Such viewer participation can increase children's learning, even though the program remains unchanged by the viewers' response (Anderson et al., 2000; Calvert, Strong, Jacobs, & Conger, 2007).

- **Interactivity with peers:** Many media have the capacity to support social development because they encourage users to engage and cooperate with peers (Hsin, Li, & Tsai, 2014). Multiplayer video games can encourage young children to cooperate and work together in achieving game objectives (Infante et al., 2010).

  Even watching an interactive TV show (such as *Dora*) with peer groups can support learning. Children will often try to respond together, expand on one another's answers, and discuss the episode with each other. Such peer-to-peer interaction not only enhances children's learning of the show's intended educational goals but creates new learning opportunities through sharing the experience and listening to others' ideas (Takeuchi & Stevens, 2011).

- **Interactivity with adults:** Children's learning with educational technologies can be amplified and enriched by an educator scaffolding their experience (Fisch, 2004).This type of learning, referred to as "joint media engagement," takes place when individuals learn together with media (Takeuchi & Stevens, 2011). When an educator actively mediates play of an educational video game, rather than leaving the child to explore it on his or her own, student learning is dramatically increased (Takeuchi & Stevens, 2011).

  Adult mediation of pre-scripted educational TV can also increase children's learning and afford them a deeper understanding of the material (Fisch & Truglio, 2014). When adults watch *Sesame Street* with children, asking them questions tied to the show's educational content (such as, "What else begins with the letter L?"), and providing feedback to the child ("That's right, the word 'lollipop' does begin with the letter L"), they directly enhance the child's understanding of the show's desired learning goals (Reiser, Tessmer, & Phelps, 1984).

While drawing upon their defined principles and relying on their own teaching expertise, educators must take on the challenge of meeting students where they are and be prepared to guide their media use to optimize learning and development.

Bringing It All Together

Knowing the three principles of integrating new media technologies in their classrooms—*determine* the learning goal first, then select the media tool; *choose* media that are designed to foster children's learning; and *use* media that motivate interaction—is a critical strategy for early childhood educators. However, just as the Mediatrician advised the NH teacher, educators must also understand that their young students enter the classroom with their own experiences, expectations, and understanding of technology. While drawing upon their defined principles and relying on their own teaching expertise, educators must take on the challenge of meeting students where they are and be prepared to guide their media use to optimize learning and development.

As part of this challenge, educators must recognize that today's children are growing up exposed to, using, and consuming more media than any other generation (Rideout, 2013). Media use is now a ubiquitous part of children's lives, and it deeply affects how they learn, develop, and grow. Although the

American Academy of Pediatrics discourages screen media use for children younger than age 2 and recommends limiting entertainment screen media to less than 1 to 2 hours per day (Strasburger et al., 2013), what constitutes "entertainment" is often not clear given the burgeoning "edutainment" market. Children's combined media use and ambient exposure at home, at school, and now almost anywhere often exceeds these limits. A study of 350 children ages birth to 4 years old found that at age 4, 75 percent of children had their own device and half had their own TV. Perhaps even more telling is that most of the children ages 3 to 4 used their devices unsupervised (Kabali et al., 2015). Because children enter the classroom with varying backgrounds of media exposure, educators can assume that students will have some fluency with media devices and applications but that their understanding will vary significantly based on individual experience.

Children's media use at home is heavily influenced by parents' attitudes, beliefs, and behaviors. Influenced by "conventional wisdom" and anecdotal evidence rather than scientific evidence, many parents believe that children need to understand and use technology as early as possible so that they can function, or even have a "leg up," in our screen-saturated society. These parents see media use as a necessary experience of childhood, an influence that will benefit their child as opposed to hindering or harming their development (Wartella, Schomburg, Lauricella, Robb, & Flynn, 2010). However, parental concerns over violence, desensitization, and lack of social development still loom, making news headlines and driving sales of products that monitor or limit children's access to media content. Confused by these conflicting views, parents are walking the tightrope of wanting to help their child become tech-savvy while also protecting them from exposure to harmful content.

Many parents hand children devices or place them in front of screens as a way to calm them or keep them busy (Kabali et al., 2015). Such digital distraction often occurs when parents are unable to attend to their child or while out in a public setting. On these occasions, media can displace essential learning, because children focus their attention on the screen instead of observing the world around them, using their imaginations, or interacting with parents or peers. As a result of this common parenting practice, young children may enter the classroom expecting to use media as a diversion, rather than as a learning tool.

The early childhood educator is in a unique position to become a true media mentor, integrating conscious training in effective media use as part of twenty-first-century education. Influencing mindful and focused media use can have comprehensive positive effects on students' learning and development in their homes as well as the classroom.

The early childhood educator is in a unique position to become a true media mentor, integrating conscious training in effective media use as part of twenty-first-century education.

Helpful Hints for Media Mentors

To positively influence students' understanding of and engagement with media, given their powerful potential and challenges, we recommend that educators:

- **Recognize that children bring prior media experience to school.** Educators can help children access that expertise in the classroom by asking them about media and, when appropriate, having them demonstrate what they know.
- **Create clear classroom rules and expectations** that clarify differences between classroom and home uses of media. Children's understanding of media and how to use them may need to be examined and relearned, especially for the classroom, so that they can use these tools in purposeful ways.
- **Provide students with skills** necessary for using media mindfully, in ways that are developmentally optimal for learning.
- **Provide parents with clear, concrete resources and guidance** for using media at home in the same ways and with the same goals that students use them in the classroom.

Conclusions

Technologies available to early childhood educators provide remarkable opportunities for expanding children's worlds without traveling, for supporting rote learning without endless drilling, for student-with-student and student-with-educator collaboration, and for modeling and scaffolding interpersonal communication. We should neither incorporate electronic screen media as a substitute for educators nor summarily reject them as pale imitations of pedagogy. Instead, we must see media devices and applications for what they are—tools—just as slate and chalk, pencil and paper, and violin and bow are tools.

We must seek to understand and use screen media to do what they do best. We should use them to support learning tasks when, and only when, they do so more effectively than other tools. We should put screen media aside when other tools are more effective or even equivalent. As educators, we can use these powerful tools to broaden and deepen children's understanding and mastery of the world—and we can also teach children to use them in ways that are creative, innovative, and true to these devices' strengths, exploring their potentials and avoiding their pitfalls. As they grow up, the children we teach will need to know how to use these and vastly more advanced tools in effective and productive ways. More important, however, they will need flexibility of mind and quality of character to address the technologies and demands of the future as smart, passionate, and productive citizens of a better world. As educators, we can help them develop those characteristics through our own use of media in the classroom.

Acknowledgments

We gratefully acknowledge the input of Jill R. Kavanaugh, MLIS, who constructed and performed the literature search and provided suggestions throughout the process of developing this chapter.

We also gratefully acknowledge the contributions of Lauren L. Rubenzahl, EdM, who helped conceptualize the chapter and craft its recommendations as well as providing editorial support.

References

Anderson, D. R., Bryant, J., Wilder, A., Santomero, A., Williams, M., & Crawley, A. M. (2000). Researching Blue's Clues: Viewing behavior and impact. *Media Psychology, 2*(2), 179–194. doi:10.1207/S1532785XMEP0202_4

Arnott, L. (2013). Are we allowed to blink? Young children's leadership and ownership while mediating interactions around technologies. *International Journal of Early Years Education, 21*(1), 97–115.

Bransford, J. D., Brown, A. L., & Cocking, R. R. (1999). *How people learn: Brain, mind, experience, and school* (pp. 79–113). Washington, DC: National Academy Press.

Calvert, S. L., Strong, B. L., Jacobs, E. L., & Conger, E. E. (2007). Interaction and participation for young hispanic and caucasian girls' and boys' learning of media content. *Media Psychology, 9*(2), 431–445. doi:10.1080/15213260701291379

Cherner, T., Dix, J., & Lee, C. (2014). Cleaning up that mess: A framework for classifying educational apps. *Contemporary Issues in Technology and Teacher Education, 14*(2), 158–193.

Chiong, C., Ree, J., Takeuchi, L., & Erickson, I. (2012). Print books vs. e-books: Comparing parent–child co-reading on print, basic, and enhanced e-book platforms. *The Joan Ganz Cooney Center.* Retrieved from http://www.joanganzcooneycenter.org/wp-content/uploads/2012/07/jgcc_ebooks_quickreport.pdf

Chiong, C., & Shuler, C. (2010). *Learning: Is there an app for that?* Paper presented at the investigations of young children's usage and learning with mobile devices and apps. New York: The Joan Ganz Cooney Center at Sesame Workshop.

Christakis, D. A. (2014). Interactive media use at younger than the age of 2 years: Time to rethink the American Academy of Pediatrics guideline? *JAMA Pediatrics, 168*(5), 399–400.

Falloon, G. (2013). Young students using iPads: App design and content influences on their learning pathways. *Computers & Education, 68*, 505–521. doi:dx.doi.org/10.1016/j.compedu.2013.06.006

Fisch, S. M. (2004). Children's learning from educational television: Sesame Street and beyond. New York: Routledge.

Fisch, S. M., & Truglio, R. T. (2014). *G is for growing: Thirty years of research on children and Sesame Street.* New York: Routledge.

Geist, E. A. (2012). A qualitative examination of two-year-olds interaction with tablet based interactive technology. *Journal of Instructional Psychology, 39*(1), 26.

Hsin, C.-T., Li, M.-C., & Tsai, C.-C. (2014). The influence of young children's use of technology on their learning: A review. *Journal of Educational Technology & Society, 17*(4), 85–99.

Hsu, C.-Y., Liang, J.-C., Chai, C.-S., & Tsai, C.-C. (2013). Exploring preschool teachers' technological pedagogical content knowledge of educational games. *Journal of Educational Computing Research, 49*(4), 461–479. doi:10.2190/EC.49.4.c

Infante, C., Weitz, J., Reyes, T., Nussbaum, M., Gómez, F., & Radovic, D. (2010). Co-located collaborative learning video game with single display groupware. *Interactive Learning Environments, 18*(2), 177–195. doi:10.1080/10494820802489339

Kabali, H. K., Irigoyen, M. M., Nunez-Davis, R., Budacki, J. G., Mohanty, S. H., Leister, K. P., & Bonner, R. L. (2015). Exposure and use of mobile media devices by young children. *Pediatrics, 136*(6):1044-50. doi: 10.1542/peds.2015-2151

Kliegman, R. M. (2016). *Nelson textbook of pediatrics.* Philadelphia, PA: Elsevier.

Kucirkova, N., Messer, D., Sheehy, K., & Fernández Panadero, C. (2014). Children's engagement with educational ipad apps: Insights from a Spanish classroom. *Computers & Education, 71,* 175–184. doi:dx.doi.org/10.1016/j.compedu.2013.10.003

Lawless, K. A., & Pellegrino, J. W. (2007). Professional development in integrating technology into teaching and learning: Knowns, unknowns, and ways to pursue better questions and answers. *Review of Educational Research, 77*(4), 575–614. doi:10.3102/0034654307309921

Maddux, C., & Cummings, R. (2004). Fad, fashion, and the weak role of theory and research in information technology in education. *Journal of Technology and Teacher Education, 12*(4), 511–533.

McManis, L. D., & Gunnewig, S. B. (2012). Finding the education in educational technology with early learners. *Young Children, 67*(3), 14–24.

Muis, K. R., Ranellucci, J., Trevors, G., & Duffy, M. C. (2015). The effects of technology-mediated immediate feedback on kindergarten students' attitudes, emotions, engagement and learning outcomes during literacy skills development. *Learning and Instruction, 38,* 1–13. doi:dx.doi.org/10.1016/j.learninstruc.2015.02.001

National Association for the Education of Young Children, & Fred Rogers Center for Early Learning and Chidren's Media. (2012). Technology and interactive media as tools in early childhood programs serving children from birth through age 8. Retrieved from http://www.naeyc.org/files/naeyc/PS_technology_WEB.pdf

Reiser, R., Tessmer, M., & Phelps, P. (1984). Adult–child interaction in children's learning from "Sesame Street". *ECTJ, 32*(4), 217–223. doi:10.1007/BF02768893

Rideout, V. (2013). *Zero to eight: Children's media use in America 2013.* San Francisco, CA: Common Sense Media.

Shuler, C. (2009). *Ilearn: A content analysis of the itunes app store's education section.* Paper presented at the New York: The Joan Ganz Cooney Center at Sesame Workshop.

Strasburger, V. C., Hogan, M. J., Mulligan, D. A., Ameenuddin, N., et al. (2013). Children, adolescents, and the media. *Pediatrics, 132*(5), 958–961.

Takeuchi, L., & Stevens, R. (2011). *The new coviewing: Designing for learning through joint media engagement.* New York: The Joan Ganz Cooney Center at Sesame Workshop.

Truglio, R. T., Lovelace, V. O., Segui, I., & Scheiner, S. (2001). The varied role of formative research: Case studies from 30 years. In S. M. Fisch & R. T. Truglio (Eds.), *"G" is for growing: Thirty years of research on children and sesame street.* Mahwah, NJ: Earlbaum.

Wartella, E., Schomburg, R., Lauricella, A., Robb, M., & Flynn, R. (2010). Technology in the lives of teachers and classrooms: Survey of classroom teachers and family child care providers. Retrieved from http://cmhd.northwestern.edu/wp-content/uploads/2015/10/TechInTheLivesofTeachers-1.pdf

Zielinska, I. E., & Chambers, B. (1995). Using group viewing of television to teach preschool children social skills. *Journal of Educational Television, 21*(2), 85–99. doi:10.1080/0260741950210203

Resources

- Center on Media and Child Health http://cmch.tv
- Ask the Mediatrician www.AsktheMediatrician.org
- Boston Children's Hospital www.childrenshospital.org
- CMCH Database of Research http://cmch.tv/researchers/database-of-research/
- Rich, M. (2014). Moving from child advocacy to evidence-based care for digital natives. *JAMA Pediatrics, 168*(5), 404–406. doi:10.1001/jamapediatrics.2014.55

Learn More...

- American Academy of Pediatrics www.aap.org/
  - Growing Up Digital: Media Research Symposium www.aap.org/en-us/documents/digital_media_symposium_proceedings.pdf
  - Beyond "Turn it Off": How to Advise Families on Media Use www.aappublications.org/content/36/10/54.full
  - Children and Media—Tips for Parents www.aap.org/en-us/about-the-aap/aap-press-room/pages/Children-And-Media-Tips-For-Parents.aspx

Part III

Innovative Approaches to Technology-Enhanced Family Engagement

Editor's Introduction

While Part II focuses on technology tools and techniques for empowering educators and families, Part III focuses on innovative approaches to technology-enhanced family engagement in early childhood program administration; media literacy education; supporting dual language learners; providing an inclusive environment where every child belongs; the role of librarians as media mentors; public media strategies for engaging families; and the need to identify and mobilize new allies in support of media mentorship. Practical examples, case studies, success stories, and evidence of innovation and effectives put the spotlight on family engagement and technology in the twenty-first century.

Part III begins with Chapter 11 that includes a description from **Fran Simon** of technology tools and digital systems that facilitate communication, increase involvement, and enhance engagement with families. She offers a continuum of touch points that define important differences between communication, engagement, and involvement and offers guidance for whether, when, and how to use technology tools for engaging with families. A review of available tools for specific family communication strategies is presented, and three technology game changers for digital family engagement are identified. The need for educators to be intentional in selecting the tools and strategies they use with parents and families is emphasized.

Faith Rogow and **Cyndy Scheibe** make the case that media literacy education develops habits of inquiry, critical thinking skills, and skills of expression that young children need to grow, develop, and learn in the digital age. In Chapter 12, they offer effective approaches to media literacy teaching and learning for educators, parents, and families and describe key elements of a media literacy curriculum including core competencies and desired outcomes for young children. Specific examples of media messages and stories that address concerns about media in children's lives are offered, along with strategies for educators to model media literacy and promote habits of inquiry and skills of expression as media mentors for children, parents, and families.

Family engagement strategies that work for all families, all languages, and all cultures are the focus of Chapter 13 by **Amaya Garcia** and **Karen Nemeth**. The authors point out the while all families benefit from effective family engagement strategies, when educators are planning with diverse families, there are additional considerations to manage. These considerations include: sending comprehensible information to families; understanding communication from families; supporting families in their role as the child's first and most important educator; and including families as active members of the school community. Opportunities for digital-age educators to be media mentors and model the use of technology to work with children who are dual language learners and to work effectively with families across language and cultural barriers are identified and described.

Pamela Brillante describes new technology tools that support inclusive environments, welcome every child, and support the feeling of belongingness in Chapter 14. Her starting point is inclusion, and she introduces a universal design for learning (UDL) approach and enabling technology that offer new opportunities to rethink inclusive practices for educators and children. She explains how low-tech and high-tech solutions and assistive technologies are essential tools for integrating the UDL principles of multiple means of representations, multiple means of action and expression, and multiple means of engagement. The chapter ends with practical strategies for working with families and taking steps toward a UDL frame of mind and offers helpful hints for media mentors.

In Chapter 15, children's librarians **Cen Campbell** and **Amy Koester** explain how the concepts of media mentors and media mentorship have become part of the fabric of children's libraries and the practices of children's librarians. The implications for traditional library services to children, parents, and families in the digital age are discussed. Survey data on young children, new media, and libraries is shared, and key concepts from a white paper on media mentorship in libraries are identified. Media mentorship success stories from librarians and libraries connect emerging practice with new media and digital age technologies. Lessons learned from librarians as they embrace the role of media mentor and integrate media mentorship into their practice can inform classroom practice and enhance family engagement.

I play a different role as editor, having gathered and curated the case studies and stories in Chapter 16 that focus on the Department of Education's Ready to Learn program for innovative practices and the development of new technologies and media to improve school readiness and enhance learning at home for lower-resourced children, parents, and families. Lessons learned and promising practices from two research-based case studies of how public media can leverage transmedia approaches and digital technologies as effective tools for family engagement and to promote positive outcomes for young children are presented. Stories from two public television stations that participated in the Ready to Learn initiative are included to describe the experiences of participants engaging with the transmedia approach and tools and the role that public media can play in strengthening communities and families.

Chapter 17 by **Lisa Guernsey** and **Michael H. Levine** pulls together key concepts and big ideas that have been presented throughout the book. The book began in Chapter 1 with an essay on media mentorship by Lisa Guernsey and ends with this chapter co-authored with Michael H. Levine in which they present a case for necessary supports for media mentorship. A "big tent" approach with new allies to help educators and families navigate the digital age is described and discussed. Key players are identified along with their roles in building a responsive and effective infrastructure for policy and research. Strategies are offered for elevating the discussion of media mentorship, connecting research to practice, and taking steps to prepare a cadre of media mentors who can design, develop, and deliver technology-enhanced family engagement that supports young children, parents, families, and communities in the digital age.

Chapter 11

Selecting Digital Systems That Facilitate Family Engagement and Communication

Fran Simon

Introduction

Here's our starting point: Let's assume as you reach this point in the book that we all know the myriad reasons why family engagement and communication are important and agree that they matter. You are reading and I am writing this chapter because we are looking for better, more efficient, and practical ways to facilitate home/school exchange of information and authentic relationships with the families of the children we educate. This nexus is where technology can either help or be a hindrance. This chapter will help you sort out the tools and the strategies to make the most of the benefits of being an educator in a rapidly evolving digital era.

It's safe to say that both parents and early educators genuinely want to engage with one another. When it comes to their children's early learning programs, one of the most important factors for parents is knowing that their children are safe, healthy, and happy when they are in the care of other people. They want to know the details. And, in the twenty-first century, they want to be in touch in real time by using the communication methods with which they are most comfortable.

We know, too, that educators sincerely want to connect with parents. One of the top challenges most often expressed by early childhood educators is how to engage parents, caregivers, and families. So, you might think, "What's the problem? It's simple: Just communicate!"

Just communicating is easier said than done. Once upon a time, families and teachers were regularly able to connect in face-to-face conversations, and notes to home were logistical supports, not replacements for personal relationships. In addition to picking up their children regularly, most families could come in to participate. Teachers had smaller classes and fewer administrative duties. There were fewer options for communication, too—face-to-face conversations, telephone calls, and "satchel" notes. Now, many parents are challenged to balance work and home life and have fewer opportunities to come to school. Teachers are challenged to find the best ways to connect with families because there are so many options and so little time. The complicated and rapidly evolving digital age demands that we provide and receive information from families every day. It has never been as important to learn from families and inform them as it is now. The good news is that there are so many ways to connect. In fact, there are so many it can be overwhelming.

Key Message from the Joint Position Statement

Technology tools can help educators make and strengthen home–school connections. With technology becoming more prevalent as a means of sharing information and communicating with one another, early childhood educators have an opportunity to build stronger relationships with parents and enhance family engagement. Early childhood educators always have had a responsibility to support parents and families by sharing knowledge about child development and learning.

NAEYC & Fred Rogers Center (2012), p. 7

Spotlight on Angelica: *A Digital Native and a People Person*

A mom of two, Angelica recently told me that the reason she has not put her youngest son into preschool is that she is afraid of what might go on when he is in someone else's care. She has heard so many gruesome stories about abuse and neglect in early childhood programs that she is simply afraid to even look for a program. She expressed concern that she would lose touch with her child's learning and development and give over the important moments to other people. Angelica is a digital native and also a people person. While she relies heavily on digital communication, because of her fears and concerns, she also needs personal interaction. Angelica needs to know she can depend on communication with her child's teacher and the program administrators. How should her child's future teachers best connect with her? What can they do to share milestones, learnings, and build relationships with her?

Let's find out more about what digital media can do to help.

Communication, Engagement, and Involvement: A Continuum of Touch Points with Families

When early educators talk about relationships with families, they use the words *communication*, *engagement*, and *involvement* interchangeably but, in fact, we all have different visions of what these words mean. Case in point: In a recent conversation with a high-profile early education leader, we bantered about our visions of how to engage families. As the conversation unfolded, it became apparent he envisioned families being involved in the classroom, but I was focused on ways to facilitate communication and relationships. We were using similar words, but we had completely different visions. He was focused on the notion of families coming in to school to participate and help. I was thinking about engaging in reciprocal relationships and keeping families informed. As I reflected on the conversation, I developed the notion that there is a continuum of home/school relationships. The continuum in Figure 11.1 defines the difference between communication, engagement, and involvement.

Other authors describe a similar two-point continuum between involvement and engagement (Goodall & Montgomery, 2014). For the purposes of this discussion, I propose a three-point continuum in which existing digital tools can solve the complex problems of building relationships along a spectrum of touch points with parents.

As you can see in Figure 11.1, I envision a three-point continuum that begins with *communication*, the most basic type of contact educators must have with families, if for nothing else, logistics. The continuum progresses to the next step, which involved interpersonal interactions between teachers and families and/or families and other families: *engagement*. The third step is the most personal type of interactions: *involvement*.

Communication is needed just to make it possible for children to matriculate, arrive at school, function throughout the school day, and have everything they need. It is more transactional but can develop a foundation for emerging relationships. In this continuum, communication is primarily one way, from school to home, but often responses are needed from families for the most basic type of contact. But, our goal is to engage more deeply. Optimal parent engagement is reciprocal and two-way (National Association for the Education of Young Children, n.d.)

As you can see in Figure 11.1, the options for exchange of information and/or ideas between school and home become progressively deeper and more involved from left to right. All of the steps along the continuum are important—none are better or worse than the other. Because there are so many points for school-to-home connection along the continuum, you may use all of the techniques at one time or another depending on the circumstances and depending on the needs of the families in your program. Taking a look at all of the options at a glance may help you plan to select the tools that will result in deeper engagement. Just like children, families prefer different modalities for interpersonal relationships. Understanding those preferences will be critical elements of your selection of digital tools

In Figure 11.1, there are many digital techniques you can use to augment your parent engagement strategies. Let's be very clear here: Digital strategies should never replace personal interaction with families, but often circumstances demand the immediacy, access, and efficiency that technology

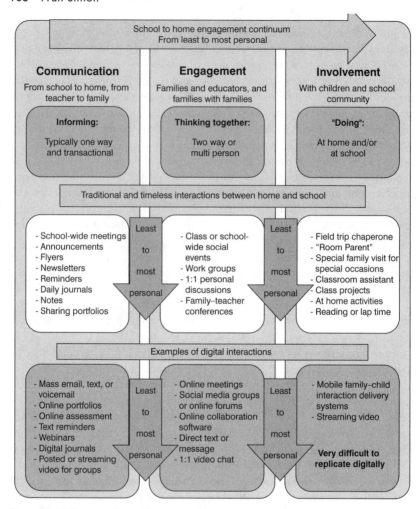

Figure 11.1 School to Home Engagement Continuum

can provide. For example, if families cannot come in for conferences, it is possible to hold the meetings via online meeting or streaming video chat. Or perhaps you would like to ensure families see the progress their children are making. Digital portfolios and online assessment systems allow you to share visual evidence and data with families regularly, even if they cannot come into the classroom. Perhaps you would like to provide families with activities they can do at home with their children to support your classroom studies; text, email, or voice messaging would be allow you to reach families, even if backpack notes don't end up in their hands.

The question is, how resourceful and digitally creative can you be with strategies that meet families' needs? As the professional in the relationship, it is up to you to find ways to make engagement possible, and technology along with traditional strategies can allow you to reach all families in one way or another.

Our communication toolboxes are full of options now. Tools range from handwritten notes to mobile applications and robust online portfolio tools. We are fortunate to have options that can connect us to families when, where, and how they want us to connect.

The Harvard Family Research Project frames parent engagement and involvement as "Anywhere, Anytime Learning" (Lopez & Caspe, 2014), a concept based on shared responsibility between teachers and parents. As you read this chapter, challenge yourself to use digital media to think beyond the limitations of the school walls and school-day hours to bring teachers and families together to share responsibility for children's learning. (Also see Chapter 4, "Logging in to Family Engagement in the Digital Age.")

Let's be very clear here: Digital strategies should never replace personal interaction with families, but often circumstances demand the immediacy, access, and efficiency that technology can provide.

When to Use Technology

As previously noted, it is important to consider technology as an additional support to face-to-face experiences. That being said, the myriad innovative, time-saving, and creative technology options grow every day, as do the reasons to supplement personal interactions with digital supports.

Technology has always been around. From the stones and sticks early humans used as tools to Google Glass, technology has always been about finding new, easier, and more effective ways to solve challenges. In this case, relating to and with parents is a challenge that demands innovation. Developers and companies have produced tools that help meet the challenge of relationship building and communication in general. Thousands have put their minds and investments specifically to home/school engagement.

People turn to technology at home or in the workplace when:

- current methods are not generating the **desired result**;
- there is **volume** that demands efficiency;
- there is a need to do something with more **sophistication and professionalism**;
- there is demand for an **easier process**; and
- there is simply **no other way** to accomplish what you need to accomplish.

Applying those principles to family engagement applications helps us define the circumstances in which we might select technology tools. For example, if the problem we are trying to solve is that families are not responding to notes sent home to announce important events, you will need to look for a better way: Would email or texts solve that problem?

It seems that technology could:

- help generate the **desired result** (parents responding);
- meet the need for **volume** communication (families in the program or families in a specific class or groups of classes);
- deliver very **professional** and **sophisticated** communication; and
- make it **easier** for educators to overcome the problem of lost, mangled, or misdirected notes and make it **easier** for families to respond accordingly.

One of the most important affordances of the use of digital media in family-to-school engagement is the ability to support families of children with special needs and those who speak languages other than our own. These are two examples of how digital innovations can make family engagement more efficient, productive, and possible. Selecting tools that help meet these needs will be imperative. (See Chapter 13, "Family Engagement Strategies for All Languages and Cultures," and Chapter 14, "Universal Design for Learning and Assistive Technology: Ensuring Every Child Belongs.")

Selecting Software, Apps, and Websites

Using Internet search engines to research applications and sites is a logical first step to find tools that solve your family communication problems, but it is important to consult reputable sites. By defining your needs for family engagement and communication first, it will be easier to narrow your search and dig deeper by finding reviews on reputable sites. You can make short work of your search by consulting

- Common Sense Media's site, Graphite;
- Cybrary Man's Educational Websites (the Educators page); and
- Teachers with Apps.

In addition to these great resources, using social media such as Twitter, LinkedIn, Facebook, Pinterest, and others to get ideas from experts is a great idea. One of the most prolific and resourceful experts on social media is Jerry Blumengarten, who carefully cultivates thousands of resources for educators. He is not only the brains behind Cybrary Man's Educations Websites, he is a Twitter legend for educators seeking information about technology resources. The website is not sleek, but the resources and insights are deep and rich. To get started, follow @cybraryman1 on Twitter.

Planning for Selection of Digital Engagement Tools

While doing research to select tools is imperative, you must first assess your family engagement strategies and identify areas you need to improve. Then, plan your objectives. Jessica Meacham, an experienced elementary school teacher, describes her process for planning to improve her family engagement strategies on her blog, *Mrs. Meacham's Classroom Snapshots*:

***

Spotlight on Jessica Meacham

My goal for next year is to increase and strengthen parent communication. I wanted to find an app that would meet the following goals:

1. allow me to share photos, links, and messages;
2. allow parents to respond to message;
3. allow me to message/share with a few select or all parents;
4. allow me to schedule events and notify parents of the events;
5. synchronize scheduled events to my Google Class Calendar;
6. allow me to schedule parent/teacher conferences;
7. share volunteer and wish list opportunities;
8. work on a variety of platforms (Web-based, smartphone-based);
9. cost nothing for Ps and Ts; and
10. have a variety of comprehensive supports for Ts.

I recently stumbled across two possible solutions… My initial thoughts were that they were very similar, but I wasn't sure, so I asked my FB, Twitter, and blog-follower #teacherfriends for feedback. My plea for help resulted in *more* app suggestions and a *lot* of questions!

More confused than ever, I sought out to research each app and create a spreadsheet that detailed each app's features. I signed up for accounts, started playing with each app's interface, devoured the support/help resources I found on their websites, and contacted the app developers (Meacham, 2015).

***

As you can see Jessica first established her goals, searched, consulted colleagues, refined her research, and tested the solutions. Great approach!

As with everything we do with children in early education, it is important to be intentional about engagement and communication with families. Coordinating tools, techniques, procedures, and policies that are school-wide or, better yet, system-wide is critical. Ensuring equity and consistency from one classroom, one program, and one school to the next will eliminate confusion for all involved. It will be important to develop a team of key stakeholders as you plan your program's guidelines.

Because digital communication often means planning for security and confidentiality, in addition to ensuring the tools you use are secure, your program should develop policies for the use of digital tools. The policies should take into account which devices, apps, and programs can be used and outline rules for their appropriate use. To get started developing your policies, purchasing, and implementing, you will need to break down the types of engagement you want to target and how you'd like to face the challenges. You can gather ideas for your policies by consulting books like *Smarter Clicking: School Technology Policies That Work!* (Wells, 2010) or Common Sense Education's *1 to 1 Essentials – Acceptable Use Policies* at https://www.commonsensemedia.org/educators/1to1/ phase1. While these resources were written from the perspective of a district administrator, they both include excellent examples and guidance that will help you develop your policies. You can also consult *Rethinking Acceptable Use Policies to Enable Digital Learning* (Consortium for School Networking, 2013) for sample policies and other concise guidance.

Considering a framework for determining your objectives is also an important first step. The National Association for the Education of Young Children published *Principles of Effective Practice for Family Engagement* (National Association for the Education of Young Children, n.d.) which is the result of the Engaging Diverse Families Project. Elements of the six principles are included in Figure 11.1 and should be considered as you think about your parent engagement strategies. Overall, the principals focus on reciprocity, shared decision making, meaningful activities, inclusion, advocacy, and comprehensive program-level family engagement programming.

One other effective way to begin your planning process is to consult the families to find out how they want to communicate and what they care most about. Remember, there may be families who do not have access to technology or may prefer other methods of communication. This means you might have to use several methods of surveying families: in-person, telephone, email connected to online surveys or tools your program already uses, and, yes, even paper surveys sent home in backpacks or lunch boxes! By asking families for their thoughts, you can authentically meet their needs, build trust, and begin developing reciprocal and inclusive channels of communication.

Technical Considerations

When selecting any digital system, website, or app that requires entering personal information, security is important. Reading the terms of service and security-related documents about the systems you select is imperative. That means doing research far beyond what is provided on the sites that offer apps for download or the marketing information offered by the vendor. You need to ensure that families' data are not shared or used by any third party except to deliver the services promised. Do your due diligence.

Considering the options for technical support is also an important factor to ensure you and the families can find information about how to use the tools you select. The options can range from telephone support (typically only for fee-based systems), to online documentation only, to no support at all! Be sure to check in order to avoid alienating the families with whom you are trying to connect.

You may wonder how to gauge whether the application or website works from a technical and practical perspective. First, consider professional reviews from trusted sources such as those mentioned earlier in this chapter. Following Jane Clare (2015), the owner and publisher of Teachers With Apps (TWA) on social media sites, and attending live twitter chats sponsored by TWA or #edtechchat are other methods you can use to rapidly learn about new tools and ask other teachers about their experiences. You can also look for testimonials and ratings on the source's websites. The descriptions in the iTunes and Google Play stores are very limited, so you will want to dig much deeper than what you see on those sites. Be sure to follow the link to the source's website for more information about security and functionality and consult online networks.

You will want to consider whether the equipment to which you have access will work for the strategies you have in mind and the tools to which parents have access. If your school or program is in an area that serves low-income families, digital tools may still play a part in your overall family engagement plan. Research indicates that despite disparity in in-home Internet access for low-income families, 90 percent of adults in the United States have a cellphone, and 65 percent own a smartphone. For many families in low-income areas, cellphones and smartphones are their only means of access to the Internet. This means text and email can play a part of your communication strategies, but you may rethink strategies that require a computer (Pew Research Center, 2014a). You should also select a mix of high-tech and high-touch strategies. In other words, pick multiple options so you can reach as many parents the way they prefer to be reached.

Once you set your goals and select your tools, proceed cautiously, because once you select appropriate tools, enter data, and convince parents to adopt the solution and use it, you will have invested a lot of time and energy. If the solution doesn't catch on with families, they cannot access it, or if it does not deliver the results you expected, you will have wasted your time and caused your family engagement efforts to stumble.

Promising Communication Applications That Bridge Home and School

There are thousands of options for educators to use to engage families. There are open source and proprietary applications that range from simple one-trick apps to complex organization-wide enterprise systems. They might be free, one-time purchase, or subscription services with monthly or yearly fees. The systems address all three of the needs along the Home/School Exchange Continuum in Figure 11.1. Because the youngest learners in our programs are naturally more dependent on their families, early educators have typically had more access and proximity for more person communication, and thus our adoption of technologically-mediated communication tools has been slow. Now we need to catch up.

Let's explore some of the options for technology tools to help you connect with families. In Table 11.1, I have included a comprehensive list of categories of tools. The examples of apps, websites, and systems is not exhaustive, because it would become rapidly out of date. The purpose of this table is to help you think about the tools and strategies that fit your program best and help you kick off your search for the right tools.

As you learned from Jessica Meacham's experience, one criterion that was important to her was that the apps had to be free. Free apps are great, but many of the options listed in Table 11.1 are fee-based. In Jessica's case, she made a decision to find a tool just for her class, and that worked in this case. However, there are times when administrators make selections for the entire program, and will invest in systems that range from affordable to expensive. In Jessica's case, the objective was easily met with free tools, but often some of the same objectives can be met by software, websites, and apps that are included in systems that are fee-based and may not be the primary use-case of the system. For example, the data management and child assessment systems included in Table 11.1 include parent communication tools, so if Jessica's school had used those systems, she could use those instead. Using school-wide systems can offer a lot of advantages, so it is important to audit the systems your program already uses to avoid duplicating efforts and missing out on the advantages. Whenever possible, if there is an option, it's best to coordinate program or school-wide technology adoption to ensure consistency from classroom to classroom.

Three Standouts and Game Changers for Family Engagement in Early Education

Portfolio Systems

While this era of mobile communication certainly offers incredible opportunities, several tools are simply revolutionary game-changers. One of the most powerful and impactful types of tools for early educators are those that allow teachers to create portfolios for each child and share them with families. Digital portfolios epitomize deep family engagement: By enabling educators to exchange information with families through observations and digital images of children in action or examples of their work (Bates, 2014). Families are empowered to share information as well as teachers, which adds depth to relationship building and information sharing. After all, aren't personal relationships reciprocal?

Table 11.1 Family Communication and Engagement Technology Supports

Categories of Family Communication and Engagement Technology Supports		
Type of Family Communication Tool:	Tools like:*	To consider:
Blogging	Wordpress, SquareSpace, Blogger	
Child Assessment Systems Online	GOLD, High Scope, Work Sampling Online, Preschool First	Web-based. In addition to scoring objectives, also include note taking (observations), portfolio development, photo sharing. Some have apps that make some functions mobile.
Child Data Management Systems or Student Information Systems	ChildPlus, EZ-care, ProCare, COPA	Program-wide systems that may include portfolios or other parent engagement functionality and child assessment.
Document Sharing	Dropbox, Evernote, Google Drive	
Education-Specific Collaboration Sites	Edmodo, BuzzMob	
Email/Office Clients	Outlook, Mail, Gmail, Yahoo	
IEP Online Systems	State specific tools available in many states and school districts. Brand names are not relevant	These systems are HIPPA (Health Insurance Portability and Accountability Act) compliant, which is always an important consideration when communicating about children with identified diagnoses.
Instant Messaging Apps	Class Messenger, Remind 101, Celly	
Learning Management Systems	Blackboard, Moodle, Google Classroom, Desire2Learn	
Mass Email Systems	MailChimp, Constant Contact	
Mobile Family–Child Interaction Systems or Home-Based Involvement Applications	ReadyRosie, BringingUp, Vroom!, Ready4K, Message From Me	An emerging set of systems that send educational content to families. Offered directly to parents, or to school systems. Message From Me sends messages and images created by children.

continued ...

Table 11.1 continued...

Categories of Family Communication and Engagement Technology Supports		
Type of Family Communication Tool:	Tools like:*	To consider:
Note Sharing	Notability, Evernote, Supernote, Paper Desk Pro, MyChild	
Online Meeting Solutions	Join.me, Any Meeting, GoToMeeting	
Photo Sharing	Snapfish, Shutterfly, Picassa, Homeroom	
Portfolio, Lesson, Daily Report Sharing/ Communication Systems	Bloomz, MyChild, Tadpoles, LifeCubby, Evernote	Typically include photo sharing, email newsletters, lesson sharing.
Public Social Media Platforms	Twitter, Facebook, Pinterest, Instagram, Periscope	
School Notification Systems	SchoolMessenger, OneCallNow, Alert Solutions	Mass text, voice, email messaging.
School or Program Customized Engagement Apps	Jigsaw School Apps, Crescerance	Customized portal specifically for schools or programs. Jigsaw includes translation.
Survey Systems	SuveryMonkey, Google Forms, Zoomerang, Polldaddy, ClassPager	
Text Messaging Apps	Class Messenger, Remind 101, LearningTree, SimplyCircle, ClassPager	
Translation Tools	Google Translate, iTranslate, SayHi Translate, Skype Translator	
Video Chat/Steaming Video	Skype, FaceTime, Hangouts	
Volunteer Scheduling	Signup Genius, Bloomz, Volunteer Spot, Doodle	
Webinars	GoToWebinar, AnyMeeting, Join.me	

*This list of software, apps, and websites is not exhaustive. The solutions included are simply examples.

Portfolio systems and other systems that include portfolio functionality allow teachers to replace an age-old, time-consuming, and space-intensive task with efficiency, speed, and no need for physical space in their classrooms. Now it's possible to replace the need to share teacher's pizza boxes full of work samples and observation notes with parents when they come into the classroom. Now, all that's needed is digital space in the cloud and Internet access. Well-designed portfolio systems should allow both families and educators to share the same information and should have mobile and computer interfaces.

The most fascinating, and yet confusing, aspect of digital family engagement and communication systems is how many of the tools overlap in functionality. The "standalone" mobile apps typically offer limited functionality, but the Web-based systems and websites (many that include mobile functionality) offer the functionality of many apps. It's important to note that some of the early education-specific child data management systems may include child assessment and email. The observation-based child assessment systems often include portfolio, email newsletters, and one-to-one email. The learning management systems, which are not specifically designed for early education, include some of the same functionalities of the data management systems with parent visibility, with less emphasis on information exchange. Designed for grades kindergarten and up through college, these systems, while used by some programs in K–12 settings, are more focused on homework assignments and grading. They have been successfully adapted by some early educators who have access to these expensive systems.

Home-Based Involvement Text Systems

Another highlight of digital developments in family engagement and involvement is the class of tools designed to facilitate interactions between families and children beyond school. Noted in Table 11.1 as Mobile Family-Child Interaction Systems, this category includes stellar examples of how simple text messages and mobile devices can offer families easy, practical tips and activities they can use with their children to stimulate conversation, cognitive and vocabulary development, media literacy, content creation, and play. Because we know cell phone and smartphone use is becoming almost ubiquitous among families, the applications in this rapidly developing category should become important tools in early educators' digital media toolbox.

A recent policy brief issued by the Rand Corporation (Daugherty, Dossani, Johnson, & Wright, 2014) highlights (among other promising digital trends) tools they define as "home-based involvement" applications. (See Chapter 5, "Families, Powered on: The Power of Nudges" for more information on the series of policy briefs from the Rand Corporation.) The two shining stars in this category called out in the report are ReadyRosie and Message From Me. ReadyRosie offers easily implemented and fun activities that parents can facilitate with their children in English and Spanish. Message From Me allows children to use technology tools at school to report on and visually record their experiences at school and send the messages to their parents in order to stimulate conversation at home. Early educators need to know about this emerging category of digital systems in order to guide families to use them. In fact, some of the systems are designed for educators to distribute to families. Each has a unique model for engaging families and educators.

Social Media

We also need to acknowledge and explore the power of social media for keeping families engaged and informed. Because educators who are interested in family engagement in this digital era need to "be" where parents congregate, it makes sense to narrow the wide world of social media to a handful of the most popular platforms. If you decide to use social networking sites to connect with families, select the sites where they are already connected so they don't have to have yet another place to log in. You might survey the parents in your program to find out which sites they regularly use.

In general, research shows that 65 percent of adults in the United States use social media (Pew Research Center, 2015). While the largest percentage of users are 18 to 29 years old, 77 percent of adults ages 30 to 49 (prime ages for parents) also network online. Research also shows that 50 percent of the adults in the 30- to 49-year age range access social media sites on their mobile phones, making digital networking immediate and pervasive. Social media allow educators to use video, photos, narrative, and links to share what is happening with the program, class, or a specific student, and it even connects families to one another. The ability to develop a sense of community even when families can't always come together is priceless and can enhance the work you do with the students.

Of adults participating in online social networking, Facebook, Twitter, YouTube, Instagram, Pinterest, and LinkedIn are the most commonly used, and families in the parenting age ranges primarily use them to stay connected with families and friends (Pew Research Center, 2014b). Your survey of families should be designed to reveal which networking sites are most popular with the families in your program.

Helpful Hints for Media Mentors

Being intentional is a hallmark of best practice in early education. Educators who aim to improve family engagement must be as intentional about selecting the tools and strategies they use to communicate as they are when they select curricula and classroom strategies.

- Improve your own media literacy and be an educated consumer of digital tools you use to interact with families. Use reputable sources and peer networks to inform your selection process.
- Plan carefully to balance your family engagement efforts with high-tech and high-touch approaches so you meet the needs of all of the families in the program.
- Coordinate your selections throughout the program or school.
- Make security and privacy top priorities when you select and use digital media to communicate with families.
- Stay informed about new developments in digital family engagement by subscribing to Common Sense Media and following the blogs and social media presences of thought leaders in educational technology.

With open hearts and minds, planning, and resourcefulness, you can use digital tools and traditional practices to develop deeper partnerships with that will positively impact students at home and at school. Get started by taking one step at a time.

References

Bates, C. C. (2014, September). Digital portfolios: Using technology to engage families. *Young Children, 69*(4), 56–57.

Clare, J. (2015). Retrieved from TeachersWithApps: www.teacherswithapps.com/

Consortium for School Networking. (2013). *Rethinking acceptable use policies to enable digital learning.* Washington, DC: Consortium for School Networking.

Daugherty, L., Dossani, R., Johnson, E., & Wright, C. (2014). *Families, powered on: improving family engagement in early childhood education through technology.* Santa Monica, CA: RAND Corporation, RR-673z5-PNC.

Goodall, J., & Montgomery, C. (2014). Parental involvement to parental engagement: A continuum. *Educational Review, 66*(4), 399–410.

Lopez, M. E., & Caspe, M. (2014). *Family engagement in anywhere, anytime learning.* Cambridge, MA: Harvard Family Research Project.

Meacham, J. (2015, July 14). *Mrs. Meacham's Classroom Snapshots,* Parent Communication App Review. Retrieved from http://jessicameacham.com/parent-communication-app-review/

National Association for the Education of Young Children. (n.d.). *Principles of effective practice in family engagement.* Retrieved from NAEYC Engaging Diverse Families Project: www.naeyc.org/familyengagement

National Association for the Education of Young Children, & Fred Rogers Center for Early Learning and Children's Media at Saint Vincent College. (2012). *Technology and interactive media as tools in early childhood programs serving children from birth through age 8.* Washington, DC: NAEYC; Latrobe, PA: Fred Rogers Center for Early Learning and Children's Media at Saint Vincent College.

Pew Research Center. (2014a). *Mobile technology fact sheet.* Retrieved from Pew Research Center: www.pewinternet.org/fact-sheets/mobile-technology-fact-sheet/

Pew Research Center. (2014b). *Social networking fact sheet*. Washington, DC: Pew Research Center.

Pew Research Center. (2015). *Social media usage: 2005–2015*. Washington, DC: Pew Research Center. Retrieved from www.pewinternet.org/2015/10/08/social-networking-usage-2005-2015/

Wells, C. W. (2010). *Smarter clicking: School technology policies that work!* Thousand Oaks, CA: Corwin.

Resources

- Consortium for School Networking (COSN) www.cosn.org
- Edutopia www.edutopia.org
- Facebook www.facebook.com
- Google Apps for Education www.google.com/edu/
- Google Play https://play.google.com/
- Instagram https://instagram.com/
- iTunes https://apple.com/itunes
- LinkedIn https://www.linkedin.com
- Message From Me www.MessageFromMe.org
- Mrs. Meacham's Classroom Snapshots http://jessicameacham.com/
- Pinterest https://www.pinterest.com
- ReadyRosie www.ReadyRosie.com
- SchoolTechPolicies.com http://schooltechpolicies.com
- Teachers with Apps www.teacherswithapps.org/
- Twitter https://twitter.com
- YouTube www.youtube.com

Learn more...

- Cybrary Man's Educational Websites http://cybraryman.com/
- ECETechNet www.ecetech.net
- Early Childhood Investigations Webinars www.earlychildhoodwebinars.com
- Graphite, Common Sense Media www.graphite.org/
- *How to Create Social Media Guidelines for Your School*. Edutopia. www.edutopia.org/pdfs/edutopia-anderson-social-media-guidelines.pdf
- NAEYC Engaging Diverse Families Project www.naeyc.org/familyengagement/about
- *NAEYC Principles of Effective Practice for Family Engagement* www.naeyc.org/familyengagement/principles
- PEW Internet and American Life Project www.pewinternet.org
- Teachers with Apps www.teacherswithapps.org/

Spotlight on Engagement

A "Daily Ding" from ReadyRosie

Janeth was seeking to sharpen her English skills and support her 2-year-old Isabella's development when she enrolled in the READ Family Literacy program offered in her northwestern Pennsylvania community. As part of her participation, Janeth began receiving daily emails from a resource called ReadyRosie. Every "daily ding" included links to short videos in English and Spanish showing actual families modeling learning games and activities. "As soon as Isabella heard the [ReadyRosie] music, she would stop what she was doing and get in my lap. We enjoyed the videos. She enjoyed trying to imitate what she saw."

Mattie McKines is the Family Literacy Coordinator for the Crawford County READ Program. She explains how the ReadyRosie videos support their two-generation approach: "Students have the opportunity to share aloud what they watched, the activity, the focus of the video (counting, word recognition, vocabulary, etc.) and how would they implement this activity at home." She adds, "ReadyRosie is used in the classroom not only to assist parents in getting their child ready for school but also in bonding with their child, knowing what their likes and interest are, where they are mentally, emotionally, and physically and how they learn. ReadyRosie truly helps bring families together full circle. It helps reinforce the importance of literacy, education, family, and equipping children with all the right tools that will lead to self-dependency."

Every time Janeth opens a ReadyRosie email and interacts with the videos, her usage is registered in the data provided by ReadyRosie to her program manager. In this way, coordinators such as Mattie can measure the reach and usage of the videos in addition to the anecdotal feedback collected in biannual surveys.

While technology plays a pivotal role in delivering and demonstrating best practices in early learning to families such as Janeth's, the broader mission behind ReadyRosie is that the technology will be the launch pad to equip and inspire parents and caregivers to engage in meaningful interactions with their children *outside* of technology.

According to Janeth, it's working. "ReadyRosie inspired me to take advantage of an opportunity for learning that I had previously overlooked. I now teach Isabella in the supermarket, on the playground, during trips, and wherever there is the opportunity. For example, when we are driving, I will ask her questions such as 'What do you see? What color are the cars?'"

She shares examples of ways she has been inspired to create her own games based on the videos. "One example is when I changed the video ["Pop Go the Bubbles"] into a counting game where I began to teach her numbers. As soon as she could walk, I would walk her to the laundry room with me. "Baby Basketball" was fantastic, and I saw a way to teach Isabella to put clothes in the laundry basket."

It is stories such as these that warm the hearts of the developers behind ReadyRosie, a team composed of educators who are also parents. Co-founder

Emily Roden states, "We love hearing about parents that go beyond our ideas to creating their own! We believe in the importance of finding a common ground among all families by recognizing that we all struggle to make language and learning a priority. This is not just an issue for families who qualify for services due to being classified within a specific demographic. We ALL need it! When you see video modeling from many different kinds of families in real-life settings, it gives dignity and community to parents with the need for support and the common goal of wanting the best for all of our children."

Contributed by Emily Roden and the ReadyRosie team

Learn More...

ReadyRosie www.readyrosie.com

Chapter 12

Sharing Media Literacy Approaches with Parents and Families

Faith Rogow and Cyndy Scheibe

Katie's mother was surprised when her five-year-old refused her usual morning bowl of Fruity Pebbles. Katie explained, "Yesterday we learned in school that just because something has fruit in the name doesn't mean it really has fruit in it. And guess what? Fruity Pebbles doesn't have any fruit in it, and it's got a lot of sugar just like candy. I want Cheerios instead." Her mother happily complied. Then, a few weeks later, Katie requested Fruity Pebbles again. Her mother responded, "I thought you didn't want Fruity Pebbles anymore because it doesn't really have fruit in it?" to which Katie replied, "I shouldn't have told you about that!" But then she asked for the Cheerios.

This story was shared with Cyndy by Katie's mother. It's a great illustration of the "trickle-up effect"—children introducing their families to media literacy lessons they learn from teachers and child care providers. Fostering a trickle-up effect is one of three strategies we'll suggest as ways for early childhood professionals to help families become media literate:

1 fostering a trickle-up effect;
2 providing families with follow-up tips that help adults reinforce the media literacy lessons you teach; and
3 helping families distinguish between "media management" and "media literacy" and offering strategies for both.

Fostering a Trickle-up Effect

There are variations in the practice of media literacy education, and not all are equally likely to produce a trickle-up effect.

Katie's teacher had been trained in constructivist and inquiry-based media literacy approaches by Project Look Sharp (which Cyndy directs and Faith advises). The goal of this method is to develop "the habits of inquiry and skills of expression" needed to be a lifelong learner, effective communicator, critical and creative thinker, and active citizen in today's world (adapted from NAMLE, 2007). More than helping children become digitally literate in the

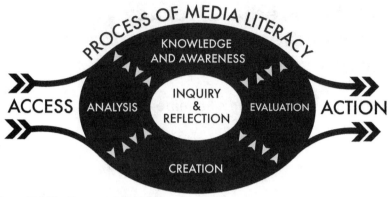

Figure 12.1 The Process of Media Literacy
(Courtesy of Faith Rogow)

sense of knowing how to use technology well, it is about helping children gain all the benefits of being literate in a digital world. The media literacy lessons we use throughout the chapter to illustrate this method were designed by Project Look Sharp to teach about nutrition and consumer education in pre-K and early elementary grades.

As Figure 12.1 shows, media literacy education links mastery of technology (a component of *access*) to *analysis, evaluation,* and *creation* of children's own media messages. These key skills are tied to *knowledge and awareness* as well as an assumption that children should be encouraged to put what they know into *action*. And at the core? *Inquiry* and *reflection*.

Media Literacy Definitions and Concepts

"Analysis" is defined as decoding media messages in order to think critically about them. "Evaluation" is making informed, reasoned judgments about the value or utility of media messages for specific purposes. (For additional details, see Scheibe and Rogow, 2012, p. 19–20.)

It's not uncommon for those who are new to media literacy education to think that these competencies are too sophisticated for young children, but teachers rarely feel that way after using the methods. To understand what constructivist and inquiry-based media literacy education looks like in practice, consider these features of the lessons that Katie experienced.

Curriculum Integration

Rather than being introduced as a stand-alone topic, media literacy was woven into the regular nutrition curriculum. The goals of the preexisting curriculum included identifying different food groups and the ways that proportional eating from each food group contribute to good health. The media literacy lessons were designed to support those goals.

Curriculum Linked to Children's Lived Experience

Because constructivist methods build on what children already know, one of the things that teachers using media literacy do is to ask children to think about where their current ideas come from ("Where did you learn that?")—a metacognitive practice that helps children build awareness of how they know what they know. It demonstrates to children that sources are important to pay attention to, even in cases where children are too young to provide accurate answers.

Advertising and food packaging are major sources for children's ideas about nutritional messages, so it was easy for Katie's teacher to link analysis of these media "texts" to the core curriculum. And because ads and food packages are a familiar part of children's lives, teachers often report that youngsters are more attentive to lessons using these media examples than when the lesson focuses only on simple food groups and nutritional information. Even better, children have frequent opportunities to take what they've learned and apply it at home.

Media Literacy Definitions and Concepts

We use the term texts to mean any media example—a song, ad, T-shirt, toy package, video clip, photograph, social media profile, and the like—as well as traditional printed forms of media such as books. Using text reminds us that all media are worthy of analysis and reflection.

In teaching with media literacy, we recommend focusing on media that children have already experienced. This allays parental concerns about exposing children to media they don't approve of, and it helps to avoid a "boomerang effect" where the distraction and appeal of something new overrides children's ability to think critically about it.

Discovery Through Questions and Clues

To explore the media texts, the teacher engaged children in constructivist media analysis—a technique pioneered by Project Look Sharp. Rather than telling children what the messages are, leaders of a constructivist analysis help children discover the messages for themselves by asking questions and probing for evidence.

The style of inquiry, analysis, and evaluation we are describing meets many of the ELA Common Core Anchor Standards, especially for close reading and identifying document-based evidence. It also exemplifies the inquiry skills described in the NCSS College, Career, and Civic Life Framework (C3) Social Studies Standards

KEY QUESTIONS TO ASK WHEN ANALYZING MEDIA MESSAGES
Adaptations for Early Childhood Education

USING THIS GRID - Media literate people routinely ASK QUESTIONS IN EVERY CATEGORY - the middle column - as they navigate the media world. Occasionally a category will not apply to a particular message, but in general, sophisticated "close reading" requires exploring the full range of issues covered by the ten categories. • The specific questions listed here are suggestions; adapt them or add your own to match your learning goals and children's developmental level. • Encourage children to recognize that many questions will have more than one answer (which is why the categories are in plural form). • To help children develop the habit of giving evidence- based answers, nearly every question should be followed with a probe for evidence: HOW DO YOU KNOW? WHAT MAKES YOU SAY THAT? • Help children expand their thinking by asking questions like WHAT ELSE DO YOU NOTICE? • And remember that the ultimate goal is for children to learn to ask questions for themselves.

		SAMPLE QUESTIONS
AUTHORS & AUDIENCES	**AUTHORSHIP**	Who created this? or Who made up this story?
	PURPOSES	What does this want me to do? Who are they talking to? or Who is this for?
	ECONOMICS	Who paid for this? Who makes money from it?
	EFFECTS	What does the storyteller want me to remember? Is this good for me or people like me? Is it good for people who aren't like me?
	RESPONSES	How does this make me feel? What could I do about [insert topic or message]? What else do I want to know and how could I find out?
MESSAGES & MEANINGS	**CONTENT**	What does this want me to think (or think about)? What is this? What does this tell me about [insert topic]?
	TECHNIQUES	What do they want me to notice? How do they get me to notice what they want?
	INTERPRETATIONS	What might someone think about this who is [insert a type of person, e.g., older than me, from a farm, a teacher, a pet owner, etc.]?
REPRESENTATIONS & REALITY	**CONTEXT**	When was this made? Is it from a long time ago or now?
	CREDIBILITY	How do they know [what they are saying is true]? What is the evidence? Can I trust this source to tell me the truth about this topic? Is this fact, opinion, a little of both, or neither?

Adapted in 2013 by Faith Rogow, InsightersEducation.com, from NAMLE's Core Principles for Media Literacy Education, April 2007, www.NAMLE.net/coreprinciples.

Licensed under a Creative Commons Attribution – NoDerivs 3.0 Unported License. Reproduction for educational use is encouraged.

Figure 12.2 Key Questions to Ask When Analyzing Media Messages
(Courtesy of Faith Rogow)

as well as the observation, questioning, and analysis skills included in the Next Generation Science Standards (see Learn More… for links to these resources).

This method recognizes that media—including product packaging such as cereal boxes—are forms of communication. We analyze and evaluate what those forms are saying to us by asking media literacy questions. Categories and examples of these key questions are listed in Figure 12.2 (Rogow, 2015, p. 97); the specific questions a teacher chooses always depend on the goals of the lesson, children's ages, their prior knowledge, and the media example itself.

As part of examining cereal boxes, a teacher might ask, "What sorts of foods have lots of sugar?" and "How could you tell whether this cereal has a lot of sugar?" Perhaps she would invite children to compare two different boxes (one sugary choice typically marketed to children and one healthier choice typically marketed to adults) and ask, "What do you notice about these boxes? What's the same and what's different? Which do you think has the most sugar?" These opening questions are nearly always followed with additional probes: "What makes you think that?" or "What else do you notice?" For the youngest children, this is a developmentally appropriate way of asking, "What's your evidence?" By ages 7 and 8, we suggest introducing *evidence* as an essential vocabulary word.

In the Project Look Sharp lesson, children were also taught some specific clues they could look for on the cereal box:

- sparkles usually means there is a lot of sugar;
- the word "frosted" means "covered with sugar";
- "honey" in the name of a cereal (and/or shown on the box) usually means it contains a lot of sugar; and
- using words such as *fruity* or *fruit-flavored* or even showing a picture of fruit doesn't mean there is actual fruit inside the box; it might only taste like fruit, and it probably has a lot of added sugar.

Media Literacy Definitions and Concepts

We use the word *clues* as a developmentally appropriate way to talk about the techniques that media makers use to convey their messages. Clues are taught in very much the same way that you might introduce the meaning of new vocabulary words before asking children to read a book.

Discussing the word *fruit* and what it means is especially important for young children, since they usually know that it's important to eat a lot of fruit, but they are likely to think that fruit-flavored cereals, candy, soda, and gum all count as fruit. As pre-readers, they don't recognize manipulated spellings (such as "froot" instead of "fruit"), and they (like some adults) are likely to be fooled by the product's name and images shown on the package. As one confident youngster reminded the Look Sharp researcher who asked her how much fruit was in Froot Loops, "A *lot* of fruit—it's called *Fruit* Loops. Duuuh!"

Even pre-readers can be taught that you can find out what is in a food or beverage by looking at the side panel of the package, and then asking a grown-up to read the list of ingredients to them while listening for words that indicate sugar or fruit. But teaching children to spot clues for themselves—on the food package or in advertising—is empowering in a way that simply telling them what to think about a particular cereal is not. Here's why:

- Categorizing information is a very fluid process for young children, so they don't always apply what they've learned about one thing to another, even if the things are similar. So, for example, if you use a box of Honeycomb cereal as you explain that cereals with added sugar aren't healthy, they may apply the message to Honeycomb but won't necessarily apply it to a cereal called Honey Nut Cheerios (especially if regular Cheerios is identified as a healthy option!). But if you teach them that "honey" is always a clue, they are learning to apply that knowledge to everything.
- Clues are tools. As such they don't imply value judgments that might put a child in conflict with a parent or guardian (e.g., "Your parents have been buying you cereal that's bad for you"). Instead, children can bring home new information and skills they've learned ("Ooh, ooh, did you know that there's no fruit in Froot Loops?"). And, as anyone knows who has ever experienced the tug of "Mama, mama (or daddy, daddy), look what I can do!", children are often eager to show off new skills. When parents reward that eagerness with attention, we get the sort of trickle-up effect experienced by Katie's mother.

Media Literacy Definitions and Concepts

To recognize the diverse family circumstances in which children are raised, we occasionally include terms such as *guardian*. However, to avoid writing that becomes too cumbersome to read, we sometimes only use the word *parent*. Every time we use the word *parent*, we mean anyone acting in a parental role in relation to a child.

Skill Building, Not Guilt Trips

The purpose of the lesson is to give children skills and knowledge that they can apply to all sorts of media messages, not convince them that they should stop eating their favorite foods. That clarity of purpose is important because it changes what and how you teach.

At no point did Katie's teacher ever say "Fruity Pebbles are bad for you; you shouldn't eat them." Instead, her focus on skills and knowledge, combined with media literacy education's explicit encouragement to put what you learn into action, led Katie to question her cereal choice. If her teacher had told Katie what to do ("Don't eat Fruity Pebbles"), Katie might have complied, if only to please her teacher, but she wouldn't really have learned very much about nutrition or about the ways that cereal is marketed. Teaching Katie to use clues and think critically is likely to produce the desired result of healthier eating but without putting the teacher in the condescending position of making choices for someone else's family.

We contend that media literacy interventions based on achieving specific changes in behavior (such as avoiding unhealthy foods or not wanting an advertised toy) are, at best, unpredictable. Even adults don't always act rationally. How many times have you grabbed a chocolate chip cookie rather than an apple at a staff meeting, even though you knew it wasn't the healthiest choice? So why would it be reasonable to expect consistency from young children? If the goal of the lesson is to teach children nutritional information and how to gather the information needed to make good decisions, but we evaluate only the actual food choices they make, then we end up assessing the wrong thing.

In this case, research on whether Katie had stopped eating Fruity Pebbles would have shown short-term success but long-term failure because Katie eventually asked to eat the sugar-laced cereal again—so researchers would have reasonably concluded that the media literacy lesson wasn't effective. But just because Katie asked to eat the sugared cereal she loved didn't mean she didn't learn the media literacy or nutrition lessons. In fact, she demonstrated that she knew that the cereal didn't have actual fruit, that it was like eating candy, and that candy should be eaten only occasionally. She just wanted that cereal anyway, and when she was reminded of what she had learned, she made a healthier choice.

Making, Not Just Consuming Media

In another of the Look Sharp lessons, students engage in a constructivist analysis of the "complete breakfast shot" (Figure 12.3) that appears in nearly every TV commercial for cereals marketed to children accompanied by a voice-over saying "[Cereal name] is part of this complete (or good) breakfast." During the analysis, children notice things such as the size of the

Figure 12.3 The Complete Breakfast Shot
(Courtesy of Faith Rogow)

bowl (which is much bigger than a normal serving), and they identify the healthy foods in the picture (milk, orange juice, fruit, wheat toast).

With a bit of guidance, they see that you could take the healthy foods and put anything next to them and say, "This _____ is part of this good breakfast." You can prompt them to fill in the blank with their own options (the sillier, the better: "this smelly sock" or "this toy school bus") and take pictures of the result. Making their own versions solidifies comprehension of the misleading nature of the complete breakfast shot. The memorable nature of the activity results in children's recognizing the shot in every cereal ad they see from that point on.

The benefits of engaging children in media production activities extend far beyond the nutrition aspect of the lesson. There is no better way than making media messages of their own to help children understand the core media literacy principle that "all media are constructed" (i.e., people made this and they made choices about what to include that were linked to their goals for making it). And if children create media messages to share with their families—or make media together with their families—adults are reminded of that principle, too.

Media Literacy Definitions and Concepts

> There is no better way than making media messages of their own to help children understand the core media literacy principle that "all media are constructed" (i.e., people made this and they made choices about what to include that were linked to their goals for making it).

As children begin to see themselves as media makers and communicators, you can use their growing skills to connect with families and to help children and family members connect to one another. For example, teachers can create class Twitter accounts or blogs that they can use to create tweets or posts about what they have been learning (e.g., "There's no fruit in Froot Loops! You can find out by having a grown-up read you the ingredients listed on the box!"); their followers might include their parents, grandparents, other classes in their school, or anyone else in their lives. New digital technologies make this sharing with families much easier than ever before.

Teachers with access to digital cameras might introduce children to photography, providing hands-on opportunities to learn how to use the camera and engage in the decision-making process involved in taking pictures for particular purposes. After a bit of in-class practice, teachers can send cameras home (or invite parents to use their phones provided they have a way to save the pictures in a way that can be shared and printed) so children and families together can make customized, illustrated alphabet books (these are things in my home and neighborhood that begin with the letter…). Then invite children to compare their own pictures with the illustrations that appear in other alphabet apps, books, or posters they see and talk about the similarities and differences.

And print out the photos to make individual books that children can show off to grandparents or share with classmates, friends, or younger siblings.

Or let children record and edit (and, where needed, translate) family histories or make a "day in the life of..." documentary of a family member or pet. Then show the children's productions as part of a family night. Or show parents and their children how to make art with digital tools or create joint tweets to describe a special event. There are myriad ways to craft production activities that encourage interaction between children and their families and provide a link between school and home. (See Chapter 2 by Sharon Thompson Hirschy; Chapter 3 by Jeremy Boyle, Melissa Butler, and Junlei Li; and Chapter 15 by Cen Campbell and Amy Koester for more ideas about the value of children using digital tools to become media creators.) The greater the diversity of activities, the better the chances that children will learn that there is so much more they can do with digital technologies than play games or watch videos.

Importantly, let families know that media production isn't just about knowing how to use the equipment. Children benefit most when they are allowed to make decisions about what to include. When you assign a media-making activity, remind parents about the importance of letting children be in charge. Send along tips—based on the strategies you have practiced in class—to help children plan and frame shots. Tips should also include suggested questions that can help parents engage children in conversations about picture choice and the needs of the intended ("target") audience (e.g., "What were you trying to say?" or "Why did you choose that shot?" or "What would be a good way to show that...?" or "Would your *abuela* think that was funny?").

Suggesting Follow-up Opportunities

Educators know that it is good practice to keep families posted on what they and the children do during the day. That's relatively easy when you're engaging in activities that parents immediately recognize (e.g., growing a plant from a seed or learning to add simple numbers). But if you tell parents "We've been doing media literacy," a parent may not know what that means or how to build on media literacy skills at home.

That's why Project Look Sharp's nutrition lessons include a booklet for families (available at www.projectlooksharp.org) with suggestions for ways to help children practice at home what they've been learning in class about food. In addition to explanations of lessons and media literacy, the booklet includes simple charts that children can use to judge how much juice is in a beverage (after finding the percentage of juice listed on the package) and how much sugar is in the food or beverage (after finding where that is listed on the package; Figure 12.4).

A personal experience underscored just how powerful this sort of resource can be. On a visit to the home of a friend whose daughter had, many months earlier, been part of a class that had used Look Sharp's nutrition lessons, the

How Much Fruit?

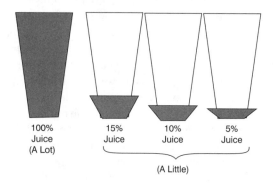

100%
Juice
(A Lot)

15%
Juice

10%
Juice

5%
Juice

(A Little)

How Much Sugar?

Find out how many grams of SUGAR is in one serving of the food or drink by looking on the package. It will give a number with the letter "g" for grams. Then find that number on the chart below to see if that is A LOT of sugar or only A LITTLE bit of sugar.

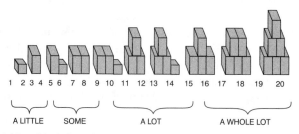

1 2 3 4 5 6 7 8 9 10 11 12 13 14 15 16 17 18 19 20

A LITTLE   SOME   A LOT   A WHOLE LOT

Figure 12.4 How Much Sugar?
(Courtesy of Faith Rogow)

mother proudly showed Cyndy tattered copies of these charts taped to the inside of a kitchen cabinet door. This family was still using the charts to spark conversations about advertising and grocery store purchases. When we facilitate these kinds of family conversations, the habit can last for years.

Media Management and Media Literacy

Parents are vital as children's first teachers, but we can't ask them to pass along skills they don't have. Because media literacy isn't yet routinely taught in schools—especially in the United States—parents aren't likely to practice much media literate inquiry or reflection themselves. So if we expect children to become media literate, those of us with the benefit of education in media literacy, technology, and child development need to assist families to fill in the gaps. We need to be media literacy mentors.

One good starting point is to help families recognize the difference between "media management" and "media literacy." When we recommend that parents create rules for use of electronic media (e.g., time limits or no phones or tablets at meals), we are recommending media management strategies. Management is an essential and central parental responsibility, but it doesn't help children develop "habits of inquiry" or "skills of expression," so it doesn't contribute much to children's becoming media-literate.

TRY THIS

At your next gathering with families, ask parents or guardians to imagine their child as an adult and make a list of what they hope that adult's major character attributes will be (e.g., honest, kind, hard-working). Then invite parents to use their list to evaluate the media that their children use. Do the media that their children spend a lot of time with reinforce the things on the list or contradict them? If it's the former, it's probably a good choice for the family. If it's the latter, they're making their job as a parent more difficult (and parenting is hard enough!).

Rather than abandon talking about media management strategies with families, we can share in ways that incorporate media literacy. For example, when recommending media, include an explanation of what it is you think is valuable. That way parents can begin to know what to look for themselves. And if you recommend ratings sites, be sure the sites include explanations. We're fond of the ratings provided by Common Sense Media and by Warren Buckleitner at the Children's Technology Review.

The idea is to do with parents what we do with children. We don't just tell children what to think, we help them learn to think for themselves. What a child takes away from a media interaction is determined by a range of factors anyway: No app or game or video will be the right (or wrong) choice for every child. So it's never simply about telling parents which media to use and which to avoid.

Instead, consider helping parents learn to determine value messages in media by suggesting questions they can ask. For example, families might look at a video or app game and ask:

What actions are rewarded?

Rewards are typically points or things that provide an advantage as you continue the game, but in games for young children, a reward might be something as simple as a funny sound or action on screen.

If there are human characters in the game, is there a character that resembles your child? If so, what does that character do (e.g., is he or she a hero or a villain)?

If players can customize an avatar, what choices are possible and what's embedded as so normal that it can't be changed?

What skin or hair colors, eye shapes, and body types are included or absent? Can a girl avatar sport a short haircut or a boy avatar choose a ponytail? Do all characters walk independently or do some use assist devices such as crutches or a wheelchair? How do the available choices limit the ways your child thinks about her or his physical self and individual potential? How do the available choices influence the way they perceive the potential of others?

Does the game offer problem-solving opportunities?

If so, are you comfortable with your child solving problems the way the game does? Are there opportunities for cooperation?

Media Literacy: Encouraging Children's Questions

Managing and selecting media are central to parents' function as media gatekeepers, especially for young children, but media are everywhere 24/7, and we are not. So we can't just be media managers; we all have to help children build the skills they need to navigate for themselves. We want them to hear our voices and our questions in their heads and then add their own.

Dozens of books and articles have been written encouraging parents to "co-view" and talk with their children about what's on screen. But that advice doesn't help if parents don't know how to start the conversation. We recommend that they start with questions.

Elsewhere we've provided detailed descriptions of the sorts of questions that help people think deeply about media messages and reflect on the media they make (Scheibe & Rogow, 2012; Rogow, 2015). Early childhood professionals can play a pivotal role as media mentors by learning the relevant categories of questions and then helping families turn them into developmentally appropriate prompts that can be woven into conversations over meals, while viewing or playing with media, during a long commute, while getting a haircut, or on a trip to the grocery store. Some examples might include the following:

- What does this want me to do? Why would they want me to do that? (authorship and purpose)
- Is that true? How could I find out? (credibility and investigation)
- How do they know that? (source/whose knowledge or experience is valued and whose is not)
- I wonder why none of the good guys (or all of the good guys) look like me? (value messages/whose experiences are represented and whose are missing)
- Why did they make the box that color? (production techniques and value messages)
- Is it okay to post this picture online, even if the people in the picture don't like it or haven't given me permission? (reflection)

Importantly, these are questions that a parent, grandparent, or guardian can ask, and the benefits of the questions or the ensuing conversation aren't dependent on everyone in a family speaking in English. Our colleague Karen Nemeth (a contributing author in this book) has suggested translating a few frequently asked questions into languages used by families in your educational setting or community and using those questions in classroom analysis of media. That way, children learning English can participate in classroom discussions and also teach the questions to their families.

Conclusion

It is rare to find an early childhood professional who doesn't have at least some concerns about media in children's lives, and with good reason. Media are influential shapers of ideas, behaviors, and culture. We should all be paying attention.

The question is what to do with our concerns. After several decades of grappling with that question, we find that the most effective answers are drawn from models of education for literacy and critical thinking.

It is not by accident that there are no theories of literacy education in which we protect children from bad books and then assume this will transform them into proficient readers. We don't expect children to develop fluency, comprehension, or analysis skills just because we make good book choices for them, even when our selections are developmentally appropriate, well-written and beautifully illustrated, free of stereotypes, and filled with wonderful messages. We surround children with high-quality literature and informational texts and then teach them how to read, analyze, write, and select books for themselves.

The same is true for media literacy. If we expect young children to gain the habits of inquiry and skills of expression that make one media-literate, media management is a logical starting point, but it can't be the end game. So we model how to ask questions and thoughtfully reflect on the media we use and create, and then we facilitate and celebrate children's efforts to follow our lead. When children begin to ask their own questions—and find their own answers—we are often amazed by their creativity and insight and ability to transform families' lives in sustained and sustaining ways. We think you will be, too. Trickle-up is powerful.

Helpful Hints for Media Mentors

- Parents are vital as children's first teachers; we can't ask them to pass along skills they don't have.
- There is a difference between *media management* (making rules about media use and selecting appropriate options) and *media literacy* (having the habits of inquiry and skills of expression needed to thrive in a digital world).
- Media are everywhere 24/7, and we are not. So we can't just be media managers; we all have to help children build the skills they need to navigate for themselves.

- Helping children develop media literacy skills, rather than telling them what to think about media, can produce a trickle-up effect that benefits the entire family.
- There is no better way than making media messages of their own to help children understand the core media literacy principle that "all media are constructed" (i.e., people made this and they made choices about what to include that were linked to their goals for making it).

When children begin to ask their own questions—and find their own answers—we are often amazed by their creativity and insight and ability to transform families' lives in sustained and sustaining ways.

References

National Association for Media Literacy Education (NAMLE). (2007 November). *Core principles of media literacy education in the United States.* Retrieved June 2013 from http://namle.net/core-principles

Rogow, F. (2015). Media literacy in early childhood education: Inquiry-based technology education. In C. Donohue (Ed.), *Technology and digital media in the early years: Tools for teaching and learning.* New York: Routledge and Washington, DC: NAEYC, 91–103

Scheibe C., & Rogow F. (2012). *The teacher's guide to media literacy: Critical thinking in a multimedia world.* Thousand Oaks, CA: Corwin

Resources

- Children's Technology Review http://childrenstech.com
- Common Sense Media www.commonsensemedia.org
- Insighters Educational Consulting, www.insighterseducation.com
- NAMLE, National Association for Media Literacy Education www.NAMLE.net
- Project Look Sharp www.projectlooksharp.org

Learn More...

- ELA Common Core Anchor Standards www.corestandards.org/ELA-Literacy/CCRA/R/
- NCSS College, Career, and Civic Life Framework (C3) Social Studies Standards http://socialstudies.org/c3
- Next Generation Science Standards www.nextgenscience.org/next-generation-science-standards
- Rogow, F. (2015). Media literacy in early childhood education: Inquiry-based technology integration. In C. Donohue (Ed.), *Technology and digital media in the early years: Tools for teaching and learning.* New York: Routledge; Washington, DC: NAEYC, 91–103.
- *The teacher's guide to media literacy: Critical thinking in a multimedia world.* Cyndy Scheibe & Faith Rogow (2012).

Spotlight On Engagement

Comienza en Casa: Family Engagement That Starts at Home

In Maine, there is an innovative family engagement program, Comienza en Casa|It Starts at Home, that serves migrant families. The family engagement strategies include using iPads at home to help parents play an active role in their children's learning. There is a common thread about the importance of relationships in the stories parents share. Edith Flores, a parent participant, said, "I need to cook, clean, feed my kids, be sure they are safe. I was missing a lot of… this relationship, my kid having a relationship with me."

Every month, the home visitor would arrive and ask how the suggested early learning activities, offered on-screen and off-screen, had worked out, requesting feedback from both parents. Edith and her husband worked together to figure out how to involve their preschool child, who had his own ideas of what he wanted to do and how he wanted to do it. They were getting to know their child better and understanding what he was thinking, seeing that he was a careful observer of the world around him and appreciating his big heart, imagination, and abilities as a creative storyteller.

They figured out ways to use e-books to help their son enjoy stories. "Technology is something I am not aware of too much. With Comienza en Casa that was the first time we handled an iPad in the house… The way we choose our books for stories, I let them choose. I learned if I choose the book it was something that I wanted, it was me, not them and they would be not as into it. So when the e-books came on the iPad, I let him choose." For reading e-books, he liked Mom, and for storytelling, Dad, so both parents worked together to create a rich story experience.

One e-book their son enjoyed was "A Frog Thing," which was on their iPad in English with an additional narrator option in Spanish (created by working with a Spanish-speaking volunteer in the community who recorded the Spanish version). While their older son enjoyed hearing stories read in Spanish, their younger son wanted to hear the e-book in English and wanted his Mom to use the option that would allow her to read it to him. Edith speaks English but wanted to be sure her pronunciation was correct and to become more familiar with vocabulary words in the story that were new to her as well. She would go through the e-book first, to be sure she mastered the words before sharing the story with her son.

When Dad, the storyteller, was asked to get involved with the e-book activity, he said, "You know better than me, it's in English." His wife was quick to point out, "*Unhunh*, you can switch it. It's in Spanish, too." So Dad could listen to the e-book in Spanish and retell it. Their son wanted to hear his Dad and didn't care if he changed the story—he just wanted to hear more about the frog. "What if the frog did this, what if the frog did that? What do you think will happen, Dad?" So they would read the story together, and Dad would explain or add a little to the story: Their son always wanted to go beyond what was written and learn more about the frog.

Their son also enjoyed using the iPad to take photos. Edith realized that for every photo he took, there was a story behind it that provided insights into what her child was thinking and feeling. The explanation that his stuffed animals, Toro and Tiger, were hugging, because they never get along since Toro thinks he is bigger and stronger, helped his parents realize their son was working through some issues related to emotions. When she wondered why he took three pictures of the same plant, he replied "Oh, Mom, I took this photo last week and then I took a photo another week and you see this leaf? It grew!" Edith realized, "I am learning my child pays attention to my plants, something I didn't even think about." Sometimes he would take photos when they didn't realize it and later comment. "I really like it when Dad is with us sitting down and watching a movie."

Her son always liked to tell stories. When asked to reflect on his digital storytelling experiences, Edith said she was hesitant to introduce one of the apps, Puppet Pals, because she thought it would be hard for him, but he loved it! He would take photos of different people to use as characters and make them move and talk. He might ask his dad or visiting grandma to get involved, helping tell his stories. When using the app Doodlecast, he created many drawings and stories including one where he thanked staff involved with Comienza en Casa, being sure to name and thank everyone involved. Edith was surprised and impressed with his thoughtfulness, naming everyone. Reviewing the digital story gift he created helped her to get to know her child better.

When asked for her reflections about technology use and family engagement now that her son is in elementary school, Edith highlights the importance of parents getting involved in helping their children learn. "As a migrant farm worker with English as a second language, sometimes we think our kids' education will be taken care of at school. Whatever they teach him in school, whatever they say, that's what's right. … The reality is, education starts at home no matter what the language is." The kinds of technology activities they tried at home she believes could be used in school to provide children with different ways to learn, express their ideas, and feelings. This might help teachers better understand a child's background and what is important to him or her. If the teacher is open to parent suggestions like this, it could help strengthen early education at home and in school.

Contributed by Bonnie Blagojevic & Edith Flores

Learn More…

- Comienza en Casa | It Starts at Home www.manomaine.org/programs/mep/comienzaencasa
- Doodlecast, zinc Roe design www.zincroe.com/portfolio/show/doodlecast_pro
- Puppet Pals, Polished Play www.polishedplay.com/apps/puppet-pals.html

Chapter 13

Family Engagement Strategies for All Languages and Cultures

Amaya Garcia and Karen Nemeth

Introduction: Reflections on Family Engagement for All

As you begin this chapter, take a moment to think about these questions and your responses:

1 What are the biggest challenges you face in connecting with families who speak languages other than English?
2 What assets could families of dual language learners bring to your program if you were better able to communicate and interact with them?
3 What are the particular needs of families that speak different languages to prepare them to be effective media mentors for their families and communities?

Parent engagement is a good thing. It is a topic found in many leading education publications, classroom assessments, quality ratings, and state policies. When the parents speak languages other than English, however, parent engagement becomes more challenging and, simultaneously, more important. Parents have the home language experience and resources that are needed to build effective early childhood programs for young dual language learners so their involvement is crucial (Barrueco, Smith, & Stephens, 2015). Supporting their involvement is complicated by many different languages spoken by families of young children in the United States—as many as 350 different languages (Ryan, 2013). With that kind of diversity, the role of technology in organizing and responding to the needs of dual language learners (DLLs) and their families cannot be denied. In this chapter, we discuss why this is so important and share examples of programs, initiatives, and resources to help.

There are four main functions of parent engagement to be considered when planning to work with diverse families:

1 sending comprehensible information to families about their child and about school events and requirements;

2   understanding communications from families;
3   supporting families in their role as their child's first and most important educator; and
4   including families as active members of the school community and the community at large.

The presence of different languages among the families and staff of the school makes each one of these functions more complicated. Each one of these functions can benefit from the support of digital resources that help to bridge language gaps. At each step, there is a place for modeling positive and appropriate ways to use technology.

In addition to these key factors, three other considerations must be included in the discussion of supporting parent engagement for families of DLLs:

- the existence of a "digital use divide" whereby families with lower incomes, lower maternal education levels, and lower levels of English proficiency may have less access to usable technology and digital resources and access to a broadband Internet connection;
- the critical need to involve families in extending education by supporting home language learning at literacy at home; and
- giving families the information they need to make informed choices and guide their child's use of digital media.

Keep in mind that the families with the lowest English proficiency or the rarest language may be the most difficult to reach in all seven of these areas, and yet they are likely to be the ones who need support the most.

The time has come to shift thinking from attempting to reach some families to taking responsibility to find a way to reach each and every child and family. There are many great tools and stories from the field about how those tools are being used. We will organize them according to the functions we described in the beginning of the chapter.

The time has come to shift thinking from attempting to reach some families to taking responsibility to find a way to reach each and every child and family.

Sending Comprehensible Information to Families About Their Child and About School Events and Requirements

The Head Start Parent, Family and Community Engagement Framework Framework (National Center on Parent, Family and Community Engagement, 2011) describes the importance of sharing information with families about their child's learning as well as their emotional and social development. Schools that succeed in this endeavor start by asking families what mode of communication they prefer and what language they'd like to receive. Qualified translators and interpreters can certainly help, but care must be taken to consider the literacy levels and dialects of the families. Services such as readability-score.com and read-able.com can help ensure the vocabulary and grammar are accessible to all. Some families prefer to receive information in writing or via email so that they can go over the information several times or get help to understand it. Other families prefer the briefest possible information—such as text messages. Others rely on the spoken word when reading text is not as easy for them.

Remind.com is a system that allows teachers and families to communicate via text messages without revealing their personal phone numbers. The school can send texts to large groups or individuals. They can use the system to remind families about important deadlines or send suggestions for home literacy activities in different languages. Similarly, ClassDojo is a free app that allows teachers to send text messages, photos, and important updates. Not only is ClassDojo widely used (by about 3 million teachers), but users have also translated the app into more than 40 languages (Hess, 2015). Voxer, or other voice-recording systems, allow spoken messages to be disseminated easily, and bilingual staff or volunteers can help with the different languages needed. Many programs and school districts post videos showing the layout of the building as well as procedures such as dismissal or fire drills so newcomer families have an immediate experience of confidence that they know what school will be like and they can help their child understand as well (Haynes, 2013). Now that Google Translate uses the camera on tablets and handheld devices to show translated print instantly on the screen, providing tablets for families might be the next logical step.

Understanding Communications From Families

True rapport with families depends as much on understanding what the families say as it does on sending out understandable information. The NAEYC and Fred Rogers Center Joint Position Statement reminds us that "...parents and families can use technology to ask questions, seek advice, share information about their child, and feel more engaged in the program and their child's experiences there" (2012, p. 7). We would add that provisions for the languages of the families must be made to ensure this works for all of the families.

It is important to engage with families as soon as possible to get the relationship off to a good start. The key is to focus on two-way communication that builds relationships. Many programs seek to begin this relationship by asking families to fill in a written "home language survey," but those are only the first step in getting to know a child and his or her family. Beyond asking what languages are spoken in the home, try asking about family celebrations, or activities the family enjoys doing together. Inviting families to submit photos is a great use of technology to build relationships and help classroom teachers create valuable classroom materials. Home visits are another way to help build stronger connections with families.

Family Engagement Strategies

Many public schools in Washington, DC have begun making home visits a standard practice for all early childhood education programs. Through a partnership with the Flamboyan Foundation, teachers in these schools receive training on how to build trusting relationships with families, stipends for working extra hours, and funds for interpretation services.

(Bhat & Reed, 2014)

A growing number of preschool and early primary teachers ask families to send in recordings of how they say a few key "survival" words in their language. If they call them in or send a video of how they say things such as "Hello, my name is…," "yes," "no," "eat," "drink," "hurt," "rest," "clean up," and "your mom will be here soon": teachers can use the words to make a young child feel safe and comfortable on their first day of school. The audio recording will help the teacher learn to say those keywords and build a strong relationship with the child, and the teacher can develop confidence about picking up a new language. Families also get the first impression that each of their languages is considered important in the classroom and beyond (Nemeth, 2014).

Teachers can protect their private time while still making themselves more available to answer questions from families. Use of email, text messages, or Voxer voice messages will allow families to contact the teacher and allow the teacher to save these until he or she is ready to review and respond.

Supporting Families in Their Role as Their Child's First and Most Important Educator

As the relationship with the child and family is being built, opportunities for engaging with DLL parents as true educational partners will arise. This is of the utmost importance for one particular reason. Children who are learning English while still in the formative years of learning their home language must receive support for continued learning and use of their home language in order to provide ample connections between prior knowledge and new knowledge in both languages (Castro, García, & Markos, 2013; Espinosa, 2013).

With so many different languages appearing in today's early childhood education settings, it is not possible to expect that schools will have the resources and staff ready to fully support all languages. That places a greater share of the educational responsibility on the parents to continue at home.

This is not a luxury—it is a necessity. Systems must be put into place to ensure that families know what to do and that they have the tools to do it. If it is difficult to find print books in all of the languages, send home tablets with digital books or story apps in the needed languages. Even this is not always possible, but class-made digital books using VoiceThread software, or storytelling apps such as Puppet Pals, Draw and Tell, or My Story allow teachers, parents, and children to collaborate on creating fiction and nonfiction books and videos that can include written or print words or voice narrations—making any language possible.

ReadyRosie is a parent engagement resource that has been mentioned frequently in this book. ReadyRosie provides partner school districts and early childhood education centers with a tool for providing parents with access to strategies and practices they can engage in to support their child's learning at home and in school. Parents receive a daily video (in English or Spanish) and are encouraged to do the activity with their child. Videos such as those created by ReadyRosie.com provide high-quality, easy-to-understand demonstrations of strategies for reading and discussing books with children and trying other learning activities at home.

Spanish has been a component of ReadyRosie from the start. Candis Grover, director of Literacy and Spanish Development at ReadyRosie, shared that the program emphasized with linguistically diverse families is the role that the home language plays in helping children be better prepared for school (Garcia, 2015a).

> The message has not been communicated across the country of the importance of home language and the power of these parents in their homes to just talk with their kids about the things they are so knowledgeable about and that will build a strong foundation for your child [shared Grover].

ReadyRosie transmits this message via tips such as "Did you know that speaking Spanish at home and playing with your child in Spanish at home will help them learn English once they enter school?"

Family Engagement Strategies

> Parents who useReady Rosie find the videos to be entertaining and helpful for their child's learning and development. In the words of one Spanish-speaking parent, "*Gracias por cada una de los videos. Nos han ayudado mucho y mi hija a aprendido cosa nuevas al mismo tiempo que nos divertimos./Thank you for each one of the videos. They have helped a lot and my daughter has learned new things all while we were being entertained.*" An evaluation of ReadyRosie is underway with 60 families to assess whether the program has an impact on

parent behavior. Initial results are promising: One mother demonstrated significant growth in the number of words and sentences she spoke to her child after just 3 weeks of exposure to the videos

(Garcia, 2015a)

Sorting, curating, and recommending digital media tools for home use can be extremely helpful for families so they don't waste valuable time and money on items that have little value. Common Sense Media has reviews and ratings for multiple types of media sources (apps, movies, television, etc.) and has resources available in English and Spanish to help parents navigate the ever-expanding media market. Teachers with Apps includes ratings of educational apps that are all field-tested by students and teachers. Be careful about resources in different languages that may have poor-quality translations. Ask parents or volunteers to help you make the best choices about what tools to recommend to families.

Schools can also help families work on developing their English skills while supporting the home languages. Providing developmentally appropriate bilingual reading materials, introduction to the local library, and even appropriate movies with subtitles can help. *High Five Bilingüe* magazine, for example, provides early literacy activities in English and Spanish—and free audio recordings in each language are available on the Highlights website supporting learning for adults and children together.

When messages are provided in English, make sure to use simple, consistent wording that will help families begin to connect with the new language. Where possible, include English in the same document that contains the home language for each family. Some programs offer classes in English as a second language for parents. Opening up the school computer labs for classes and access for services such as job searches and researching citizenship questions not only can strengthen the family, it also helps to build that school–family relationship. An example was piloted by Zoila Tazi, Amanda M. Gunning, and Meghan E. Marrero for English- and Spanish-speaking families of a kindergarten program. They successfully engaged families as co-teachers by offering a STEM learning program after school with activities in both languages (Tazi, Gunning, & Marrero, 2015).

Over time, you may learn that the parent has experienced trauma or has a limited formal education that makes him or her feel intimidated or unsure about participating with educational activities. Or, she or he may come from a culture where families are expected to allow the schools to handle education without much contact from the parents. Under these circumstances, the innovative and interesting ways schools use technology to reach out may help to overcome some of these limitations and get families to engage as educational partners. Knowing more about a parent's background can help teachers find literacy materials that are a good match for each family's needs, such as wordless books and Toca Boca apps that support conversation, interaction, and concept learning with little dependence on oral language or literacy.

Abriendo Puertas is a parent education program aimed at enhancing Latinos' parenting practices to support multiple areas of their children's development and on increasing parent's leadership and advocacy skills. The curriculum is structured around 10 sessions that focus on issues such as positive discipline practices, children's language development, and parents' role in the process, reading and choosing appropriate books, and leadership/advocacy strategies (Garcia, 2015b). All of the lessons are culturally relevant and delivered entirely in Spanish.

A 2014 evaluation of Abriendo Puertas conducted by Child Trends found that parents who participated in the program were more likely to engage in educational activities at home, read to their child, report having learned effective communication and discipline strategies, and believe that the example they set at home matters (Moore et al., 2014). And in the words of one parent, "This class is making us aware that kids are learning. I didn't used to talk to my children, but if you talk to them you motivate them and they learn. My son is 9 months, and when I say words to him, he starts repeating. Sometimes we think they are too young. It's very important to talk to them" (Moore et al., 2014, pp. 46–47).

Including Families as Active Members of the School Community and the Community at Large

When family engagement really works, it goes well beyond inviting families to attend school events. True engagement is found in authentic, individual, mutually beneficial relationships between members of the school community and the members of each child's family. When families of DLLs feel welcomed and respected, they have a great deal to offer to enrich and enliven the school and community. They bring the unique assets of each member of their family as well as their combined experiences, rich cultural traditions, and language resources. Engaging families as active members of the school community can enhance the social and educational experiences of their own children as well as all of the other children, families, and staff. Using technology to keep families informed in their own languages is a start. Providing opportunities for family members to participate, volunteer, and contribute to school activities by offering language matching, video invitations, a translatable website, and software such as Google Translate or iTranslate can help.

When family engagement really works, it goes well beyond inviting families to attend school events. True engagement is found in authentic, individual, mutually beneficial relationships between members of the school community and the members of each child's family.

Families can provide help to the school using technology resources. For example, they may be recorded reading stories or singing songs in their native language that can be shared with the children. They might type classroom labels in their language that can be printed out at school. They can contribute video and digital photos of their home and home and community for class projects.

Family Engagement Strategies

In one New York preschool program, the teacher asked families to send in digital photos of what their child ate for dinner. The teacher printed some of the photos to make a personalized class book that connected to each child's home and culture, then she printed more pictures, cut them out, and laminated them to use as pretend foods in the dramatic play area.

When planning events and services for families, it is important to ask them what they want or need. If some events are planned and you notice some families missing, it is important to go a step further and reach out to those families individually. No family engagement plan can be considered a success if it includes only some of the families. Technology can help. Some schools now use the Twitter accessory, Periscope, to capture videos of key school meetings to share with families that can't attend. Try allowing families to participate in parent–teacher conferences via video chat. This can also make it possible for family members who live in different countries to participate.

Family engagement experiences at school can prepare parents for more active roles in the community at large. Just as children need social connections to thrive in early education, families need connections with peers in their community to break down the isolation caused by language and culture barriers. The Head Start Parent, Family, and Community Engagement Framework lists family and community engagement as an important outcome. The PFCE Framework even recommends that programs should encourage and support families becoming advocates and leaders in their community (National Center on Parent, Family, and Community Engagement, 2011). This can come from strong beginnings at the school or program level.

Family Engagement Strategies

At Earl Boyles Elementary School in Portland, Oregon, the parent group *Padres Unidos/Parents United* has given families the opportunity to plan activities for the entire school community (including preparing food for teacher appreciation day and coordinating school celebrations), to learn about resources in the community, and to develop advocacy and leadership skills (Williams & Garcia, 2015). For example, a few parents testified in front of the Oregon state legislature in support of pending pre-K legislation and had opportunities to present at the 2015 National Family and Community Engagement conference. Many of the parents are native Spanish speakers and so meetings are completely bilingual—switching between English and Spanish—and translation is provided for all parents.

The Digital Use Divide for Families

There is a "digital use divide" whereby families with lower incomes, lower maternal education levels, and lower levels of English proficiency may have less access to usable technology and digital resources. Data from the Pew Hispanic Center show that even though the number of Latino families going online and that have access to a cell phone has been steadily increasing, there are important differences in access within different groups of Latinos (Lopez, Gonzalez-Barrera, & Patten, 2013). Latinos who primarily speak Spanish are less likely to use the Internet or own a cell phone. Programs must consider these differences in access and use when planning for the use of technology as a tool for parent engagement.

In early 2015, the Joan Ganz Cooney Center at Sesame Workshop released a series of reports that examined Latino families' use of digital media. A report authored by June Lee and Brigid Barron used survey data to explore differences in access and use among Latino families. Lee and Barron (2015) found that "higher educational attainment, higher family income, being native born, and being English-dominant or bilingual were consistently related to higher rates of technology adoption" (p. 7). Moreover, Spanish-dominant households were more likely to rely on smartphones for Internet access. These findings have important implications for how programs use technology to support parent engagement. Programs might consider conducting an informal survey to gauge families' level of access to technology and comfort using digital resources and tools.

Similarly, immigrants are less likely to have access to a home computer and Internet than those who are native-born. A 2006 study by researchers at the University of California, Santa Cruz, found that 60 percent of the native-born population has Internet access compared to 48 percent of the immigrant population. Comparisons between immigrants also show important differences in access to a home computer and Internet; for example, 77 percent of immigrants from India have access to both a computer and internet at home while only 20 percent of immigrants from Honduras do. Additionally, differences in access were present even when controlling for income; "even within income groups, immigrants are less likely than natives to access technology at home" (Fairlie et al., 2006).

Culture also has a role to play in how families use technology. In another report from the Cooney Center, authors Bruce Fuller, José Ramón Lizárraga, and James H. Gray note that our views on the purpose and use of digital technologies is socially constructed. They cite findings from a study that found that Latino parents placed stricter limits on their children's Internet and computer use than White parents, in part due to fears that these technologies "isolated their youngsters, promoting individualistic values and lax personal discipline" (Fuller, Lizárraga, & Gray, 2015, p. 25).

Relatedly, researchers Vikki Katz, Michael H. Levine, and Carmen Gonzalez studied the impact that technology use has on family relationships and found that "Parents' own tech-related attitudes directly affect how children use technology to complete assignments and to pursue their own interests" (Katz, Levine, & Gonzalez, 2015, p. 1). Taken together, it's clear that educators must communicate with parents about why and how technology is being used to support not only their involvement in the classroom but also their child's learning.

In many ways, the families that are most likely to be considered "have nots" are exactly the families that need more advantages than families considered to be the "haves." The NAEYC and Fred Rogers Center Joint Position Statement (2012) mentions on p. 4, "early childhood educators have an opportunity to provide leadership in assuring equitable access to technology tools and interactive media experiences for the children, parents, and families in their care." To be most effective, that leadership must take into account ways to reach all families.

Critical Home Language Literacy Practices

As discussed earlier in the chapter, the role of parent engagement has an added dimension when working with families of DLLs. With the critical need to support growing language and literacy in the home language, good connections with families take on even greater importance. Research has highlighted cultural differences in home literacy practices. For example, Latino families are less likely to read to their preschool-aged children than White families and have far fewer children's books in their homes (Sanchez, 2015). This means that building that important partnership to support home literacy must do more than reminding parents to read to their children. Schools and programs have to unite to present a strong message for families about the importance of supporting the home language and the importance of actively practicing early literacy skills at home. Sharing these messages on different media and in different languages can help to make sure families are being reached.

Programs such as Ready 4K!, developed by Ben York and Susanna Loeb (2014) at Stanford University, use text messaging to send parents tips and strategies for supporting their child's literacy development. The program was piloted in pre-K programs in the San Francisco Unified School District with a diverse group of Hispanic, Chinese, and African-American families. Text messages—which parents could elect to receive in English, Spanish, or

Chinese—were sent three times a week and included *Facts, Tips,* and *Growth*; for example:

- **FACT:** Beginning word sounds are essential for reading. You can help your child learn to read by saying the beginning sound of words. "Read" starts w/"rrr."
- **TIP:** Say two words to your child that start with the same sound, such as happy and healthy. Ask: can you hear the "hhh" sound in happy and healthy?
- **GROWTH:** By saying beginning word sounds, such as "ttt" in taco and tomato, you're preparing your child 4K. Now, have your child make the "ttt" sound.

York and Loeb's evaluation of the program found that parents who received these text messages engaged in more literacy-based activities with their children at home and were more involved in their child's school. Their children also benefitted from the program as demonstrated by increased alphabet knowledge and letter sounds.

Text messages could prove particularly useful when trying to engage diverse families for three reasons: the wide use and availability of cell phones, low cost, and preponderance of texting. York and Loeb note that 80 percent of families had unlimited texting plans and that their intervention cost less than $1 per family.

Digital and Media Literacy

The NAEYC and Fred Rogers Center Joint Position Statement (2012) makes this key point on page 9: "Digital literacy is essential to guiding early childhood educators and parents in the selection, use, integration, and evaluation of technology and interactive media." Surely, if this is considered essential, then every effort must be made to communicate this guidance via multiple languages and media so that it effectively reaches each and every family.

The Tech Goes Home initiative, developed by Open Air Boston, provides parents with strategies on how to engage and participate with their child while they use educational apps or the computer (Berdik, 2015). The program is offered at schools, where parents participate in 15 hours of training on topics such as creating an email account or accessing their child's grades online, and also has an early childhood program that helps parents build their computer literacy skills and children learn skills essential to ensuring they start school kindergarten ready (Technology Goes Home, 2015). Parents who complete the program are offered the opportunity to buy either a computer or tablet for $50.

Key Messages from the Joint Position Statement

Technology and media literacy are essential for the adults who work with young children. The prevalence of technology and media in the daily lives of young children and their families—in their learning and in their work—will continue to increase and expand in more ways than we can predict.

NAEYC & Fred Rogers Center (2012), p. 9

A unique challenge about serving as a media mentor for families that speak different languages is that you need to advise families about selecting appropriate, high-quality resources when you are not able to fully review those resources. Schools often run into this conundrum when they are being urged to offer learning materials in the home languages of the children, yet there may be so few in each language that they don't know whether it is better to risk using something that is not top quality or to end up with nothing because the standards were so high. There is no easy answer to this puzzle. The compromise is to try to do the best on both sides and fill in with class made or family made materials.

Helpful Hints for Media Mentors

Early childhood educators can be media mentors for children who are DLLs, and they can also mentor families to be informed consumers of media well beyond their child's time in the early education program. Technology and digital media are tools that can help both the educators and the families as they work together to ensure bright futures for young children. The following recommendations will support effective practices for working with families from all languages and cultures:

- use technology and digital resources to communicate effectively with families who speak different languages and to ensure two-way connections with each family;
- use technology and digital resources to support families in their role as the child's first educator by giving families information about early learning and about making wise technology choices for and with their children; and
- prepare families to use technology and digital resources to strengthen their participation in school and in the community as digital citizens and as advocates.

Working across language and culture barriers takes more time and more effort, but the benefits will be measurable, lasting, and rewarding for all involved.

Early childhood educators can be media mentors for children who are DLLs, and they can also mentor families to be informed consumers of media well beyond their child's time in the early education program.

References

Barrueco, S., Smith, S., & Stephens, S. A. (2015). *Supporting parent engagement in linguistically diverse families to promote young children's learning: Implications for early care and education policy.* New York: Child Care & Early Education Research Connections.

Berdik, C. (2015). The best screen time. *Slate.* July 23, 2015.

Bhat, S., and Reed, J. (2014). *Unlocking opportunities: Services that help poor children succeed in the classroom. Part 2: Parent engagement services.* Washington, DC: DC Fiscal Policy Institute.

Castro, D. C., García, E. E., & Markos, A. M. (2013). *Dual language learners: Research informing policy.* Chapel Hill, NC: The University of North Carolina, Frank Porter Graham Child Development Institute, Center for Early Care and Education—Dual Language Learners.

Espinosa, L. (2013). *PreK–3rd—Challenging common myths about dual language learners: An update to the seminal 2008 report.* Washington, DC: Foundation for Child Development.

Fairlie, R. W., London, R. A., Rosner, R., & Pastor, M. (2006). *Crossing the divide: Immigrant youth and digital disparity in California.* Santa Cruz, CA: Center for Justice, Tolerance and Community, University of California Santa Cruz, p. 19.

Fuller, B., Lizárraga, J. R., & Gray, J. H. (2015). *Digital media and Latino families: New channels for learning, parenting, and local organizing.* New York: The Joan Ganz Cooney Center at Sesame Workshop. Winter 2015, p. 25.

Garcia, A. (2015a). Interview with Candis Grover, September 10, 2015.

Garcia, A. (2015b). Opening the door to parent engagement. *New America: Ed Central,* April 28, 2015.

Haynes, J. (2013). *Getting started with English language learners: How educators can meet the challenge.* Washington, DC: Association for Supervision and Curriculum Development.

Hess, R. (2015, September 30). Straight-up conversation: ClassDojo's Sam Chaudhary. *Education Week* [Web log post]. Retrieved from http://blogs.edweek.org/edweek/rick_hess_straight_up/2015/09/straight_up_conversation_classdojos_sam_chaudhary.html

Katz, V. S., Levine, M. H., & Gonzalez, C. (2015, September 16). Family partnerships are key to digital equity. *Education Week* [Web log post]. Retrieved from http://www.edweek.org/ew/articles/2015/09/16/family-partnerships-are-key-to-digital-equity.html

Lee, J., & Barron, B. (2015). *Aprendiendo en Casa: Media as a resource for learning among Hispanic-Latino families.* New York: The Joan Ganz Cooney Center at Sesame Workshop, p.7.

Lopez, M. H., Gonzalez-Barrera, A., & Patten, E. (2013). *Closing the digital divide: Latinos and technology adoption.* Washington, DC: Pew Hispanic Center.

Moore, K. A., Caal, S., Lawner, E., Rojas, A., & Walker, K. (2014). *Abriendo Puertas/ Opening Doors parenting program: Summary report of program implementation and impacts.* Bethesda, MD: Child Trends.

National Association for the Education of Young Children & Fred Rogers Center for Early Learning and Children's Media at Saint Vincent College. (2012). *Technology and interactive media as tools in early childhood programs serving children from birth through age 8.* Washington, DC: NAEYC; Latrobe, PA: Fred Rogers Center for Early Learning and Children's Media at Saint Vincent College.

National Center on Parent, Family, and Community Engagement. (2011). *The Head Start parent, family, and community engagement framework.* Washington, DC: National Center on Parent, Family and Community Engagement

Nemeth, K. (Ed.) (2014). *Young dual language learners: A guide for PreK—3 leaders.* Philadelphia, PA: Caslon Publishing.

Ryan, C. (2013). *Language use in the United States: 2011.* Washington, DC: American Community Census Reports, U.S. Census Bureau.

Sanchez, I. (2015). *Zooming in: A close look at literacy practices in low-income Latino homes.* Washington, DC: New America.

Tazi, Z., Gunning, A. M., & Marrero, M. E. (2015). Engaging parents as co-teachers. *Educational Leadership, 72*(6). Retrieved from http://www.ascd.org/publications/ educational-leadership/mar15/vol72/num06/Engaging-Parents-as-Coteachers. aspx

Technology Goes Home (retrieved September 15, 2015). www.techgoeshome. org/#!overview/c1539

Williams, C. P., & Garcia, A. (2015). *A voice for all: Oregon's David Douglas School District builds a better PreK–3rd system for dual language learners.* Washington, DC: New America.

York, B. N., & Loeb, S. (2014). One step at a time: The effects of an early literacy text messaging program for parents of preschoolers. NBER Working Paper No. 20659 (November 2014), p.13.

Resources

- ClassDojo www.classdojo.com
- Common Sense Media www.commonsensemedia.org/
- Common Sense Media, Latino www.commonsensemedia.org/Latino
- Draw and Tell, Duck Duck Moose www.duckduckmoose.com/ educational-iphone-itouch-apps-for-kids/draw-and-tell/
- Ed Central, New America www.edcentral.org/
- Google Translate https://translate.google.com
- *High Five Bilingüe Magazine* https://store.highlights.com/high-five-bilingual-magazine-for-kids
- Joan Ganz Cooney Center at Sesame Workshop www. joanganzcooneycenter.org/
- My Story www.mystoryapp.org
- Puppet Pals www.polishedplay.com/apps/puppet-pals-2.html

- Readability www.readability-score.com
- ReadyRosie www.readyrosie.com
- Remind.com www.remind.com
- Teachers with Apps www.teacherswithapps.com
- Toca Boca www.tocaboca.com
- Voice Thread www.voicethread.com
- Voxer www.voxer.com

Learn More...

- Barrueco, S., Smith, S., & Stephens, S. A. (2015). *Supporting parent engagement in linguistically diverse families to promote young children's learning: Implications for early care and education policy.* Child Care & Early Education Research Connections. www.researchconnections.org/childcare/resources/30185/pdf
- Connell, S. L., Kirkpatrick, E., Lauricella, A. R., & Wartella, E. (2013). *Media, technology and reading in Hispanic families.* National Center for Families Learning. http://web5.soc.northwestern.edu/cmhd/wp-content/uploads/2014/08/NWU.MediaTechReading.Hispanic.FINAL2014.pdf
- Fuller, B., Lizárraga, J. R., & Gray, J. H. (2015). *Digital media and Latino families: New channels for learning, parenting, and local organizing.* New York: The Joan Ganz Cooney Center at Sesame Workshop. www.joanganzcooneycenter.org/wp-content/uploads/2015/02/jgcc_digitalmediaandlatinofamilies.pdf
- Garcia, A. (2015). *Differences in Hispanic-Latino families' access to and use of educational media.* Washington, DC: New America. www.edcentral.org/differentaccess/
- Garcia, A. (2015). *Navigating the "Empirical Darkness" of impacts of digital media on Hispanic-Latino families.* Washington, DC: New America. www.edcentral.org/media-hispanic-latinos/
- Nemeth, K. (2009). *Many languages, one classroom: Teaching dual and English language learners.* Lewisville, NC: Gryphon House. www.gryphonhouse.com/books/details/many_languages_one_classroom
- Nemeth, K. (Ed.) (2014). *Young dual language learners: A guide for PreK–3 leaders,* Philadelphia: Caslon Publishing. www.caslonpublishing.com/titles/14/young-dual-language-learners/
- Nemeth, K. (2015). Technology to support dual language learners. In C. Donohue (Ed.), *Technology and digital media in the early years: Tools for teaching and learning.* New York: Routledge; Washington, DC: NAEYC.
- Simon, F. S., & Nemeth, K. (2012). *Digital decisions: Choosing the right technology tools for early childhood education.* Lewisville, NC: Gryphon House. www.gryphonhouse.com/books/details/digital_decisions

Spotlight On Engagement

Tech and Family Engagement Tips from Comienza en Casa

Parents of migrant preschool and kindergarten children participating in Comienza en Casa | It Starts at Home, a home-based family engagement program in Maine, learned to use a variety of tech tools and iPads to help support their young children's early learning. Through their experience in the program, parents gained insights into what aspects of the technology use they found to be most valuable. How can technology be used to engage families? Here are 10 tips based on a conversation among the home visitor/program coordinator and three parents involved in the program.

1 **Gather information.** Don't make assumptions about home tech use. A quick survey or conversation can help you find out what tech is being used at home, how it's being used, and whether Internet access is available.

2 **Document and share.** Invite family members to document activities at home using technology. When children share this digital documentation from home with their class, teachers, program staff, and peers gain additional insights.

3 **Share favorite apps.** Finding high-quality, age-appropriate educational apps is a challenge. Share the apps you use in your classroom with families. Provide tips on how to evaluate apps and ask families to share their favorites.

4 **Open new communication pathways.** People like to receive information in different ways. Group texting services such as Remind can make everyone's life easier by sending reminders about parent–teacher conferences or an upcoming field trip right to a parent's mobile phone. Messaging services with voice and photo, for families who have smartphones, can help reach families with low literacy levels or those with a preference for verbal communication.

5 **Model and discuss appropriate tech use.** During family nights, open house, or registration time, have simple, hands-on activities that model appropriate tech use. Increasingly parents purchase devices because they believe they have educational value but are unsure how to use them in beneficial ways to help their child learn. Show innovative activities families can try at home, such as digital storytelling using one of several free apps that allow children to draw, import photos, and/or record audio or video to create stories. Share information about media diet, Internet safety, and other high-interest topics related to tech use.

6 **Use video to model.** Create your own videos on the fly with a smartphone or use a service such as ReadyRosie, which has a large library of high-quality videos in English and Spanish. Families are able to view the videos repeatedly and return to vocabulary that might be new.

7 **Meet families where they are**. Tech literacy and experience will vary, so plan on providing different levels of support. Look for community partners such as the local library or adult education centers that can help facilitate a family night when families can sign up for a texting service or email account, get help finding local Internet access sites, and learn about other services that can help them take advantage of tech-related school services.

8 **Share information digitally**. There are a variety of ways schools and programs share information digitally, such as classroom blogs, Facebook, and Google drive. Providing a digital copy means parents don't have to worry about losing track of papers. They can always go back and look up information as they need it.

9 **Invest in people, not only devices.** Invest in developing relationships and building capacity. Professional development opportunities for teachers, technical support for stakeholders, and digital literacy workshops for families should be prioritized in budget planning. One iPad being used in an intentional way may have a greater impact than many iPads in a classroom where teachers have not received the appropriate training.

10 **Promote a community of learners.** Help facilitate a learning community wherein parents learn with and from other parents and community members. Together, identify issues such as device management or media diet and search for solutions, tutorials, and ways to share information so that all families feel they can use technology to help their child learn.

Contributed by Ana Blagojevic, Patricia Garcia,
Adriana Paniagua, and Juana Vazquez

These tips originally appeared in Teaching Young Children magazine published by NAEYC.

Chapter 14

Universal Design for Learning and Assistive Technology

Ensuring Every Child Belongs

Pamela Brillante

Belonging. What a simple word to describe such a multifaceted concept. Belonging is much more than just being present. In his hierarchy of needs, Abraham Maslow (1970) identified belongingness as one of the basic needs of all people. When unmet, the need for belonging, much like the need for food and safety, motivates people to action. Belonging is interactive and meaningful; it implies being welcome and accepted for whom you are. Early childhood is a time for belonging, a time when children start to want to be *a part* of the world around them, not *apart* from the world around them.

All too often, young children with disabilities have a difficult time belonging and making connections to the people and places in their everyday lives. Some aspects of a disability may even make participating in everyday routines and activities of childhood downright impossible. The presence of a disability should not be the defining factor to meeting the need for belonging in a person's life. The Individuals with Disabilities Education Act (2004) supports that concept, explaining in part, "Disability is a natural part of the human experience and in no way diminishes the right of individuals to participate in or contribute to society" (p.117).

Early childhood is a time for belonging, a time when children start to want to be a part *of the world around them, not* apart *from the world around them.*

What adults do to help young children with disabilities develop feelings of belonging has a lot to do with how we make them part of the community, how we level the playing field for them. Taking a closer look at how we structure the physical and social environments as well as use the available technology around us in order to give children access and ways to participate is the answer.

Technology has changed the way we do almost everything, including educating young children. Young children see and interact with the technology that surrounds them on a daily basis, and they are not afraid (Simon & Nemeth, 2012). Educators have begun to recognize the power technology can have to support children with disabilities in the early childhood classroom when done in developmentally appropriate ways (Parette & Blum, 2015). Done correctly, technology can be a tool that can support young children with disabilities as they interact, communicate, and play with and learn from peers (National Association for the Education of Young Children and the Fred Rogers Center, 2012a). Technology can break down barriers.

In 2012, The National Association for the Education of Young Children and the Fred Rogers Center for Early Learning and Children's Media at Saint Vincent College issued a joint position statement on the use of interactive technology with all young children. This joint statement clearly focuses on the concept of technology as a tool that is not meant to replace any part of the developmentally appropriate practices that work with young children, but when used appropriately and intentionally, interactive technology can be a very positive addition to the life of any child, including children with disabilities (2012a). The Key Messages document introducing the position statement states the following.

Key Messages from the Joint Position Statement

There are many ways that technology can extend opportunities for learning and development—helping to better meet the needs of individual children (e.g., assistive technologies that improve children's ability to learn, move, communicate, and create); supporting enhanced communication with families (e.g., digital portfolios documenting children's progress); and providing children new opportunities for exploration and mastery (e.g., making a book of scanned images of children's artwork and dictations).

NAEYC & Fred Rogers Center (2012), pp. 1–2

In other words, we can add technology to the developmentally appropriate practices we already use in order for schools and families to help all children, including children with disabilities who may need to use assistive technology or have other supports to belong.

Inclusion as the Starting Point

By taking a closer look at the issues surrounding access, participation, and support for young children with disabilities within typical routines and activities of childhood, we will find the key that will unlock quality-inclusive experiences that foster belonging for all children (Division for Early Childhood & National Association for the Education of Young Children, 2009).

Access is of primary importance, and an environment that claims to be accepting of all children must be free from physical barriers. Barriers found in the physical environment speak volumes about the philosophical acceptance of individuals with disabilities and the lack of consideration of their needs. Looking at access also means eliminating a "one-size-fits-all model" of expectations at home and of learning and development in schools. Eliminating the one-size-fits-all model takes into account different variables such as background knowledge, language experience, and developmental readiness. Every child, including children who are excelling at different skills and students who are struggling, will benefit from removing the one-size-fits-all model. Looking at access is the first step in looking at quality-inclusive practice.

Participation is more than just a physical presence; engagement with a peer, an adult, or some kind of material is required to make participation meaningful. The goal of inclusive practices is to make sure that every child can participate in every routine and activity; so it is up to the adults to design the interventions as well as develop the needed supports that the child requires to be as independent as possible. Physical presence is only the first step in fostering a sense of belonging for every child. To move toward meaningful participation, genuine engagement is critical.

Broad supports in place are essential in order to develop quality-inclusive programs. For children, supports can come in the form of the specially designed techniques and instruction that are designed by specialists in other areas including speech pathology, occupational therapy, or physical therapy.

Supports such as picture schedules and labels on play centers support not only the child with an expressive language delay communicate with adults or peers, but it is also a support for a child who is not a native-language speaker. The picture schedule can be individualized for one child or used by the whole class. Special education supports and services that are designed for a specific child do not have to be taught in isolation; teaching those supports must be embedded across the child's entire day in order for them to become a natural part of the child's routines (Jung, 2003).

Supports can also come in the form of technology. According to the joint position statement from NAEYC and the Fred Rogers Center (2012a), "Technology can be a tool to augment sensory input or reduce distractions. It can provide support for cognitive processing or enhancing memory and recall" (p. 9).

Supports for the professional refer to the communication and collaboration among the specialized professionals and teams working with children with disabilities and their families. These systems of supports are essential if we strive for the child to develop some level of independence. This sounds straightforward and simple enough; however, it has not always been successfully implemented in practice. Therefore, the impetus is for all professionals to work together to embed the specially designed techniques and instruction across the day. The goal is for the child to be able to be engaged in all activities with the least amount of intrusion from adults as possible.

This is a delicate balance, with the needs of the student being the primary guide. So the question emerges: What is the key that will unlock quality early childhood inclusive practices that foster belonging for all children?

Rethinking Inclusive Practices: Universal Design

The key to true inclusion is universal design. Universal design is about people, all people. The concept of universal design originally comes from the field of architecture, a plan to think about how spaces or materials will be used by a variety of people (Meyer, Rose, & Gordon, 2013). The concept proactively designs these spaces and materials as user-friendly as possible. Universal designs are varied and flexible, designed to benefit as many people with and without disabilities as possible. The principles of universal design can be used in many different ways.

Universal Design for Learning

In the 1990s, the Center for Applied Special Technology (CAST) took the concept of universal design and adapted it for use in schools, developing the principles of universal design for learning (UDL; Meyer et al., 2013). This development came as there was a realization that schools, and education as a whole, needed to be redesigned to accommodate the varied needs and learning styles of many different students, from gifted students to students with disabilities (South-Western Cengage Learning, 2010). The concept of UDL is founded on the idea that the *ways of learning* must be different for different people, but the larger concepts and constructs should be the same for most children (Meyer et al., 2013). This is true for early childhood programs as well, what we know about developmentally appropriate practices and constructively learning through play, as well as the need for children to be engaged with adults, peers, and materials are the same for all children, including children with the most significant disabilities (Meyer et al., 2013).

The concept of UDL is founded on the idea that the ways of learning *must be different for different people, but the larger concepts and constructs should be the same for most children.*

These different ways of learning that students need to access as well the different ways these students are able to demonstrate their knowledge are described below in the core principles of UDL.

The three core principals of universal design for learning are

1   multiple means of representation
2   multiple means of action and expression, and
3   multiple means of engagement

(Meyer et al., 2013)

Multiple Means of Representation

This principle describes the multiple ways that content or the "what" of learning can be presented so all students will learn (Meyer et al., 2013). This principle talks about changing the ways you are teaching and presenting the concepts that need to be learned to the class. Presenting content in varied and flexible ways is a core principle of UDL. Frequently the varied and flexible ways are a matter of student choice based upon learning needs and preferences.

Think of using all five of your senses to learn about an object. We can explore the object with all of our senses, and categorize what we are seeing, hearing, smelling, touching, and tasting into different groups. Each of our five senses will add different information that will bring meaning to the object and, using several of our senses together, we can develop a more comprehensive understanding about this object. Adding multiple means of representations brings different dimensions into our learning.

Allowing exploration for each of our senses is not feasible for every learning situation, but we can change what we do in order to allow children to use *more* of their senses. Instead of just limiting things to what children can hear or see, providing access to real objects that children can manipulate in order to add learning from the sense of touch, smell, or even taste will provide more depth to their understanding. For example, reading a book at story time is usually just an auditory and visual experience. You can add tactile experiences by having multiple copies of the book and allowing children to hold their own copy and turn the pages themselves as you read. Using felt board activities to recreate the story also gives children a tactile experience interacting with the story.

Some young children need to learn using multiple senses in order to develop a basic understanding. Other young children prefer to have material presented to them in one specific way, but that way may be a way different from that of everyone else. No child should be denied the opportunity to learn in the way that makes the most sense to him or her.

No child should be denied the opportunity to learn in the way that makes the most sense to him or her.

Thinking about multiple means of representation is also a wonderful way to reach students who are not native English speakers. Research shows that young learners will develop stronger language skills when we make sure the quality of language we use with them is elaborate and diverse (Carey, 2013). Teachers can take language learning and content learning out of isolation by adding key vocabulary in the children's home language and linking their real-life experiences and concrete materials that are familiar to them within classroom activities. This deepens the connections dual language learners make with the English language as well as the content knowledge

(Nemeth, 2014). Adding multiple means of representation to the child's day will develop what CAST describes as "resourceful, knowledgeable learners" (Center for Applied Special Technology, 2011).

Multiple Means of Action and Expression

This UDL principle describes the multiple ways that children demonstrate what they know and can do. We can proactively design different ways and methods children may respond and participate as a way to get an accurate measure of their understanding and knowledge. This is also a way to develop independence in young children by giving them multiple options for action and expression so that they set their own goals and monitor their own progress (Bertling, Darrah, Lyon, & Jackson, n.d.). Having multiple ways for children to actively participate in routines and activities as independently as possible will also help develop executive function skills. Executive function skills help young children learn how to plan what they are going to do and organize themselves in order to get started on, and complete. tasks and routines (Bertling et al., n.d.).

Parents can get to know how children express their ideas, feelings, and preferences, and teachers can proactively design authentic assessments with "real-world" products as a way to understand what children know. Sometimes adults need to provide additional supports to help children express themselves at their current stage, but those additional supports can be systematically decreased as the children become independent. For example, the adult can add supports to materials such as small knobs to puzzle pieces to make them easier to use or give the children a bingo marker so they can independently make their choices known when planning for play or sharing what they did play with during recall.

The Gift of Time

Time is another factor when thinking about allowing children to participate in activities and routines as independently as possible. Many children need more time to process information and perform routine tasks. As they complete these tasks over and over, the amount of time needed will probably be reduced, but the gift of time is not always easy to provide. Can the activity or routine be adapted so that some time is saved but the child is still completing it independently? Have the adults built in enough time for students to be able to participate and complete the activity as well as express their knowledge and feelings? This will develop what CAST describes as "goal-directed learners" (CAST, 2011).

Multiple Means of Engagement

This principle describes the multiple ways we can engage children in the process of learning, or the "why" the students are learning (CAST, 2011). Tapping into children's interest as well as providing them choices will engage them and increase their motivation to learn. One of the things we know about young children is that experiential background and relevance to their own lives are some of the most powerful interest motivators. As children increase the amount of time they are engaged with their environment (adults, peers, and materials) in developmentally and contextually appropriate ways, the more their depth of knowledge increases (McWilliam & Casey, 2008; Bertling et al., n.d.).

Parents can add more choices and autonomy within routines at home such as giving children a selection of different clothes they could wear and having them choose which one they want that day. Young children can be given simple job charts that they need to complete including household chores such as feeding a pet or putting away toys. They can even work on pre-academic skills at home such as sorting the socks in the clean laundry and putting those socks on the bed of the person they belong to.

Teachers can proactively design activities and routines that give students more choices and more autonomy within the classroom by looking at their activities with a more critical eye. Teachers must ensure that an activity is not designed for only one group of students with similar abilities and learning styles but for all children. Teachers can design and facilitate long-term projects where multiple levels of complexity are present and different parts of the project can accommodate the needs of many different children. Long-term projects such as growing an indoor or an outdoor garden or even caring for a class pet can have different levels of complexity built in. Adding multiple means of engagement to the child's routines will develop what CAST describes as "purposeful, motivated learners" (CAST, 2011).

The Role of Technology and Assistive Technology in UDL

Technology has changed the way we do most things in our society. Families and young children have access to different kinds of technologies at many different times during the day. Advances in technology come along quickly, and it is a very exciting time to think about the power that technology—and assistive technology (AT) in particular—can have to help young children with disabilities become more independent and actively participate at home and in the early childhood classrooms (Campbell et al., 2006).

According to the Individuals with Disabilities Education Act of 2004, AT is defined as "any item, piece of equipment, or product system whether acquired commercially off the shelf, modified, or customized, that is used to increase, maintain, or improve functional capabilities of individuals with disabilities (Individuals with Disabilities Education Act, 2004).

The definition of AT in the law is extremely broad by design, taking into consideration the constantly evolving nature of technology. The broadness of the definition gives some flexibility to make individualized decisions about the appropriate AT devices for their students. As a result of this broad definition, AT tools can be very low-tech, such as Velcro or a pencil grip, or they can be very high-tech, such as computerized wheelchairs and augmentative communication devices. What is considered an AT device is inclusive of many different objects, and some may not even look like technology to most people.

Low-Tech and High-Tech Solutions

Low-tech AT devices work without any power source and almost anything, including things that are made by the parents, therapists, and teachers can be considered low-tech AT. Inset puzzles with knobs that make it easier for a child with motor disabilities to put the puzzle together independently can be considered low-tech AT. A paper clip put on the top of the page on a child's storybook to make the pages easier to turn themselves is even considered low-tech AT.

High-tech AT devices have sources of power and may be more complex to work. There is also a broad range of what is considered a high-tech AT device. On one end of the spectrum would be sophisticated computer hardware or software that help individuals with disabilities communicate, all the way to the other end of the spectrum to basic tape recorders and battery-operated toys. High-tech devices do not have to be expensive, but they often are.

Assistive Technology Across the Environments

The goal of all AT devices is to give children a way to actively and fully participate in all aspects of their day as independently as possible. There are many different ways AT devices can be used by a child across many different environments. These ways include, but are not limited to, academic and learning aids; aids for daily living, augmentative communication, computer access and instruction; recreation and leisure aids; as well as seating and positioning aids.

The goal of all AT devices is to give children a way to actively and fully participate in all aspects of their day as independently as possible.

Academic and Learning Aids

Modified early childhood classroom tools such as different scissors to make cutting easier and different writing instruments to make writing easier for children with fine-motor deficits and disabilities are common adaptations found in early childhood classrooms. Children's story books can be adapted to make them easier to hold or turn pages independently, and toys with batteries can be adapted to be used with a large button as an on/off switch.

Aids for Daily Living

Tools and adaptations that can help children feed, dress, bathe, and use the toilet as independently as possible are also considered AT. Tools such as Velcro to make clothing attach easier; cups with lids or large bases that will not easily tip over; and non-slip material added to the bottom of the shower or tub and on the floor of the bathroom to prevent slips on wet surfaces are common adaptations and AT for children with mobility issues.

Augmentative Communication

Having different ways to communicate with peers and adults is essential for many children with disabilities. Small pictures or photos kept in a notebook or around the room can be used as a picture exchange communication system (PECS). Using these PECS symbols, a child gives the picture of a desired item or action to an adult or peer as a way to express wants and needs to the other person (Bondy & Frost, n.d.). PECS symbols can be either low-tech pictures downloaded from a computer or photos that are familiar to the child or used within high-tech augmentative communication devices. PECS can also be used to provide a way for children to communicate both expressively and receptively.

Computer Access and Instruction

Giving children access to different types of technology is the first step in introducing higher-tech AT tools. How children access the computer can be changed by adding such tools as touch screens, switches, or alternate keyboards, but is it important to give children different ways to use a computer independently.

Recreation and Leisure Aids

Adapted gross-motor play equipment such as adapted bikes and wheelchair swings and things such as bowling ball ramps and bumpers make it easier for children to participate in sports and play with peers.

Seating and Positioning

Children many need multiple choices for seating in the family room and in the classroom in order to be on the same visual level as everyone else and make participating in activities routines easier for them. Seating aids may be low-tech AT devices such pillows and bolsters all the way to higher-tech AT devices such as adapted computerized wheelchairs that can change heights.

As with any technology, AT is not a solution but an intervention, a way of using a specific material, device, or piece of equipment as a way to allow the child to participate more independently, and be more fully engaged in activities at home and at school. While technology is not a cure-all, and we know it should not replace traditional early childhood education and activities, technology hardware and software may be a key to unlocking the potential for many young children with disabilities.

Working with Families

Teachers and other early childhood professionals can help to provide support to families in order to make the rest of the child's day as universally designed as school is. We need to work together to strengthen the home–school connection in order to best meet the needs of the child, the parents, and the family. Here are some ideas on how to do that.

- **Talk to them!** Parents of young children with disabilities cannot rely on the children to give or share information with the school, so teachers need to make sure the lines of communication are open. Strategize with the families when either of you has issues, concerns, and especially success stories. Discuss what the best form of communication is for them and chat away. Open and honest communication will make everyone's job easier.
- **Be open to ideas and suggestions.** Parents may have found a new piece of technology or app that you are not aware of yet. Parents and other caregivers see the child in very different situations and circumstances than teachers do. They also have a lifelong investment in their child, so they are always on the lookout for new and exciting things that may help them. Help build these new finds into your daily routines.
- **Never discount the child's abilities.** Watch how a child naturally tries to participate or complete a task or routine independently and build off of that. See how they use technology and the environment to their advantage. Watching the children will give you many of the tools you need to make their environment universally accessible in order for them to participate and be as independent as possible. Teach the parents to watch the children at home and discuss with them how to redesign their environments.
- **Let them be.** Watch that well-intentioned caregivers and support staff do not over-support or help children do things that they can already do themselves or have the potential to do, given the right instruction and circumstances. Let the children make mistakes and get a little frustrated without swooping in to do something for them. Scaffold your supports: Let them fail sometimes, and see how they can develop their own way of being independent. Do not set the stage for learned helplessness.
- **Help build friendships.** Nourish budding friendships in the classroom, and then help connect the children outside of school. Letting both sets of parents know when children form friendships at school can be an impetus for play dates on weekends and in the

summer. Parents of children with disabilities may need reminders that their child does belong in your classroom, and that they belong with other parents of children the same age.

Taking Steps Toward a UDL Frame of Mind

UDL is about being proactive instead of reactive with regard to designing and redesigning environments as well as instruction. Using technology can level the playing field for many children, including children with disabilities, and can be used to help children be active instead of passive members of their families, their classrooms, and their communities. Using the core principles of UDL as a model, we can change our own ways of thinking as we help parents and early childhood professionals accommodate for the needs of a child with a disability. One child may access and engage in play or in a routine differently than other children, and that is okay. *In no way does that mean we need to lower our expectations.*

Helpful Hints for Media Mentors

- **Physical participation is only the first step in fostering a sense of belonging for every child.** Look at your routines and embed opportunities for participation and engagement with peers within daily routines and open-ended activities.
- **Embrace technology.** Empower the parents to understand how children learn and how technology can be a part of that. Help them know that when used appropriately, technology can support and empower the child to learn, participate and belong. Explore both high-tech and low-tech solutions when designing supports for inclusion, and make sure those supports are also used at home.
- **Look at the room through the child's eyes.** Look at the permanent structure of the environment and how moveable furniture can create or inhibit access and participation. Move your furniture if you need to, and have parents do the same thing at home.
- **Use the technology you have.** Almost all of the newer technologies have some accessibility features built in. You do not need something new; you can change the visual, auditory, and input features to make it easier for a child to use. Discuss with parents the technology they have and how to change those features so it is appropriate for their child.

References

Bertling, J., Darrah, M., Lyon, D., & Jackson, S. (n.d.). *Early childhood building blocks: Universal design for learning in early childhood inclusive classrooms.* Resources for Early Childhood. Retrieved from http://rec.ohiorc.org/orc_documents/orc/recv2/briefs/pdf/0018.pdf

Bondy, A. S., & Frost, L. (n.d.). *What is PECS? Picture exchange communication system.* Pyramid Educational Consultants. Retrieved from http://www.pecsusa.com/pecs.php

Campbell, P. H., Milbourne, S., Dugan, L. M., & Wilcox, M. J. (2006). A review of evidence on practices for teaching young children to use assistive technology devices. *Topics in Early Childhood Special Education, 26*(1), 3–13.

Carey, B. (2013). SES differences in language processing skills and vocabulary are evident at 18 months. *Developmental Science 16*(2), 234–248.

Center for Applied Special Technology. (2011). *Universal design for learning guidelines version 2.0.* Wakefield, MA: Author.

Division for Early Childhood and National Association for the Education of Young Children. (2009). *Early childhood inclusion: A joint position statement of the Division for Early Childhood (DEC) and the National Association for the Education of Young Children (NAEYC).* Chapel Hill, NC: The University of North Carolina, FPG Child Development Institute.

Individuals with Disabilities Education Act, 20 U.S.C. § 1400 (2004).

Jung, L. (2003). More is better: Maximizing natural learning opportunities. *Young Exceptional Children 6*(3), 21–26. DOI:10.1177/109625060300600303

Maslow, A. (1970). *Motivation and personality* (2nd ed.). New York,: Harper & Row.

McWilliam, R., & Casey, A. (2008). *Engagement of every child in the preschool classroom.* Baltimore, MD: Brookes.

Meyer, A., Rose, D. H., & Gordon, D. (2013). *Universal design for learning: Theory and practice.* Wakefield, MA: CAST Inc.

National Association for the Education of Young Children and Fred Rogers Center for Early Learning and Children's Media at Saint Vincent College. (2012a). *Joint position statement on technology and interactive media in early childhood programs: Technology and interactive media as tools in early childhood programs serving children from birth through age 8.* Washington, DC: NAEYC; Latrobe, PA: Fred Rogers Center for Early Learning and Children's Media at Saint Vincent College.

National Association for the Education of Young Children and the Fred Rogers Center for Early Learning and Children's Media at Saint Vincent College. (2012b). *Key messages of the NAEYC/Fred Rogers Center position statement on technology and interactive media in early childhood programs.* Washington, DC: NAEYC; Latrobe, PA: Fred Rogers Center for Early Learning and Children's Media at Saint Vincent College.

Nemeth, K. (2014). *Young dual language learners: A guide for preK–3 leaders.* Philadelphia, PA: Caslon Publishing.

Parette, H. P., & Blum, C. (2015). Including all young children in technology-supported curriculum: A UDL technology integration framework for 21st century classrooms. In C. Donohue (Ed.), *Technology and digital media in the early years* (pp. 128–149). New York: Routledge and Washington DC: NAEYC.

Simon, F., & Nemeth, K. (2012). *Digital decisions: Choosing the right technology tools for early childhood education.* Lewisville, NC: Gryphon House.

South-Western Cengage Learning. (2010). *Diverse populations and learning styles.* Boston, MA: Authors.

Resources

- AAC Intervention www.aacintervention.com
- American Academy of Pediatrics, Policy statement: Children, adolescents, and the media http://pediatrics.aappublications.org/content/early/2013/10/24/peds.2013-2656

- Building the Legacy: IDEA 2004, Ed.gov http://idea.ed.gov
- CAST (Center for Applied Special Technology) www.cast.org
- Center for Creative Play www.center4creativeplay.org
- Enabling Devices/Toys for Special Children www.enablingdevices.com
- KITE (Kids Included through Technology are Enriched) www.pacer.org/stc/kite/
- Let's Play! The University of Buffalo http://letsplay.buffalo.edu/
- National Center on Universal Design for Learning, UDL Guidelines www.udlcenter.org/research/researchevidence
- Pacer Center www.pacer.org
- Tots-n-Tech Research Institute http://tnt.asu.edu/

Learn More...

- *A Parent's Guide to Universal Design for Learning (UDL).* A Parent Advocacy Brief from the National Center for Learning Disabilities www.cpacinc.org/wpcontent/uploads/2009/12/ParentsGuidetoUDL.pdf
- *Parents Guide to Assistive Technology.* Great Schools E-ssential Guide www.greatschools.org/pdfs/e_guide_at.pdf?date=3-13-06&status=new
- *Toy Guide for Differently-Abled Kids.* Toys R Us, Inc. www.toysrus.com/shop/index.jsp?categoryId=3261680
- UDL at a Glance Video. National Center on Universal Design for Learning www.udlcenter.org/resource_library/videos/udlcenter/udl#video0
- Tool Kit on Universal Design for Learning. US Department of Education, Office of Special Education Programs: Ideas that Work series www.osepideasthatwork.org/UDL/intro.asp
- Right from the start: Universal design for preschool. Stockall, N.S., Dennis, L., & Miller, M. *Teaching Exceptional Children, 45*(1), pp. 10–17.
- Together from the start: Preschoolers with disabilities in inclusive settings. Brillante, P., & Vaughan, L. (2009). *Common Ground, 3*(1), pp. 7–9.
- Supporting dual language learners with challenging behaviors. Nemeth, K., & Brillante, P. (2014). In M. Dombrink-Green & H. Bohart (Eds.) *Spotlight on Young Children: Supporting Dual Language Learners.* Washington, DC: NAEYC
- How should we address first and second language supports in the special education plan? Brillante, P. (2014). In K. Nemeth (Ed.) *Young Dual Language Learners: A Guide for Prek–3 Leaders.* Philadelphia, PA: Caslon Publishing.
- Using AT toolkits to develop early writing skills with preschoolers. Parette, P., Stoner, J., Watts, E., & Wojcik, B. W. (2006). In technology, reading, and learning difficulties world conference, San Francisco, CA.

Chapter 15

Children's Librarians as Media Mentors

Cen Campbell and Amy Koester

The number of children and families who use digital media is growing, and children require mediated and guided experiences with digital media for the experiences to translate into positive and productive digital literacy skills. Libraries have the capacity to support families with all their literacy needs, traditional and digital, including needs as they arise. Librarians and youth services staff support children and their families in their decisions and practice around media use.

(Campbell, Haines, Koester & Stoltz, 2015, p. 1)

On March 11, 2015, the board of the Association for Library Service to Children (ALSC) adopted a white paper titled *Media Mentorship in Libraries Serving Youth* (Campbell, Haines, Koester, & Stoltz, 2015). ALSC, a division of the American Library Association (ALA), is a professional organization dedicated to supporting, developing, and enhancing excellent library service to children ages birth to 14 in public, school, and other library settings. The adoption of this white paper by a library organization with a mission to serve children and their families was a benchmark in the continual evolution of thought around what it means to serve those populations in the digital age. While the ALSC previously included a technology component in their *Competencies for Librarians Serving Children in Public Libraries* (ALSC, 2009), the invention of the iPad and the recent proliferation of other formats of digital media for children has significantly changed the way that children's librarians provide services to their communities.

The white paper, as a formal resource for youth librarianship, provides children's librarians with two important perspectives for their practice. First, the white paper provides the vocabulary with which practitioners can discuss and advocate for youth library services that encompass the entire spectrum of media developed for children. Second, it reaffirms that while our specific practices may change as the media landscape expands and evolves, our fundamental role of serving children and families remains our mission and trademark. Since the formal adoption of the white paper, libraries across the country have shared their own experiences with media mentorship, including their specifically designed programs and services as well as patron responses to these programs. This chapter provides context for the children's librarians' role as media mentor within the larger conversation about digital-age family engagement and early childhood educators as media mentors, followed by a discussion of current practice in media mentorship as well as examples of media mentorship in practice in libraries.

The Library and Its Services to Children

Libraries serving youths, including public, school, and special libraries, share a number of core values and major initiatives, and it is useful to understand this context to see how media mentorship has evolved from longstanding library service models and motivations. Libraries, in particular public and school libraries, have asserted themselves in a number of key areas.

Access, Collections, and Programming

Libraries are committed to equity of access. This tenet asserts that all people, "regardless of age, education, ethnicity, language, income, physical limitations or geographic barriers," have access to the information they need in print and electronic formats (American Library Association, n.d.). A commitment to access includes a commitment to the freedom to read without fear of censorship, including format-based censorship.

With regard to content made available by the library for the communities they serve, the *Library Bill of Rights* (American Library Association, 1996) affirms that all libraries provide materials for the "interest, information, and enlightenment of all people of the community the library serves"; such materials should not be excluded from library collections because of the background or viewpoint of the author or because of the views expressed within the work. It is the library's responsibility to provide collections that represent all points of view on topics, in both print and digital formats, and reflecting cultural diversity (Naidoo, 2014). While libraries are committed to offering these broad, uncensored collections, the profession does regularly recognize materials that are exemplary for a particular audience or in a particular field. The annual Youth Media Awards constitute the majority of awards for youth-focused materials and are awarded through national committees within the American Library Association. Many state organizations, as well as some libraries and consortia, also recognize outstanding media for youths through their own awards.

Finally, libraries believe in cultural and community programming as a core service. Programming for youths may include audiences from newborns through teenagers, and common program types include story times; book clubs; reading programs; science, technology, engineering, arts, and math programs; craft and game events; performances; and demonstrations. Libraries are continually adapting these traditional program types to meet new needs and audiences both in the library space and out in the community.

Early Literacy

Libraries are committed to developing and fostering literacy in all members of the communities they serve. A particular core focus is early literacy, or the promotion of the skills a young child needs to develop in order to start school prepared to learn to read. Every Child Ready to Read First Edition, a parent education initiative and collaboration between ALSC and the Public Library Association (PLA), was released in 2000 to provide the resources to integrate research and evidence-based practices on childhood reading development into the programs for young children offered by public libraries around the country.

The emphasis of Every Child Ready to Read First Edition was the definition and development in young children of six early literacy skills:

1 phonological awareness;
2 vocabulary development;
3 narrative skills;
4 letter knowledge;
5 print awareness; and
6 print motivation.

In 2011, after a substantial evaluation of the initiative and a review of research that had been published in the decade since its inception, Every Child Ready to Read Second Edition was released by ALSC and PLA (see www. everychildreadytoread.org). This revised edition incorporated findings by Neuman and Celano (2010), which determined that parents respond best to suggestions for how they can support their children's early literacy development. As such, Every Child Ready to Read Second Edition promotes the use of five main practices that contribute to the development of early literacy skills:

1 talking
2 singing
3 reading
4 writing, and
5 playing.

These tangible suggestions for parents are indicative of one of the firmly held philosophical underpinnings that children's librarians espouse in all their dealings with families: that parents are their child's first and best teacher and that what they need most is to be supported in that role. In that vein, story times are designed to encourage parental involvement with their children, whether it be shaking egg shakers, sharing a book together, or talking about their trip to the grocery store. Story times, while they serve officially to support the development of the skills that children will eventually need when the time comes for them to read independently, ultimately center around the relationship between children and their caregivers. Much of the early work on young children and new media in libraries centered around the incorporation of new digital formats into early literacy programs such as story times, and the Every Child Ready to Read model of talking, singing, reading, writing, and playing to support parent engagement formed the basis for recommendations around healthy media use with young children. These early learning practices, with the integration of new media, incorporated the notion of "joint media engagement" as defined in the by the Joan Ganz Cooney Center in *The New Coviewing: Designing for Learning through Joint Media Engagement* (Takeuchi & Stevens, 2011), with special attention to the facts that books are an earlier form of media and that some of the same book co-reading techniques can be applied to new forms of media as well.

Spotlight on Media Mentorship

The practice of interacting with media together allows the experience itself, as well as the content of the media, to resonate more deeply with the child using it.

Campbell, Haines, Koester, & Stoltz, 2015, p. 4

Young Children, New Media, and Libraries: A Survey

In advance of the writing of the white paper *Media Mentorship in Libraries Serving Youth,* ALSC collaborated with the iSchool at the University of Washington and LittleeLit.com to survey the library field with regard to current use of and practice with new media in library services for youths. The survey was made available to library practitioners across the United States; 415 responses were recorded at the end of the survey period in August 2014. The survey found more prevalent media usage in libraries than anecdotal information had led the survey authors to expect. Seventy-one percent of respondents indicated using new media in some capacity in their programming aimed at young children. Around 40 percent of respondents noted using such technology in story time settings, and another 31 percent noted using it in other programs. Additionally, 41 percent responded that they offer devices for use by young children and their families in the library. Yet despite this rather prevalent use of new media technologies in library services and programs for children, only 22 percent of survey respondents indicated that they provide mentoring of any kind (Mills, Romeijn-Stout, Campbell, & Koester, 2015).

The Young Children, New Media, and Libraries survey found evidence that while a majority of libraries are currently utilizing new media in their spaces and programs—and that 58 percent of surveyed libraries anticipate increasing such use in the future (Mills, Romeijn-Stout, Campbell, & Koester, 2015)—a smaller minority are extending those offerings into mentorship. In other words, libraries are providing the hardware without the support. Children and families might be able to see and use this technology in the library, but by and large they were not getting the guidance to do so in the most appropriate, productive, and educational ways possible. This finding served as an invitation of sorts to the white paper co-authors: it invited the theoretical and practical exploration of what it means to support children and families in their literacy in a multi-format age.

The White Paper: Media Mentorship in Libraries Serving Youth

As information professionals who are attuned to what is happening in our communities and around the world, librarians are able to know certain things: that children and families are using digital media in high and increasing numbers (Rideout, 2013); that content developers have created, and are marketing to children, a plethora of digital content and media; and that experts in child health and education are weighing in on best use and appropriateness of this technology with children. But these three observed factors are not overlapping; what we see, instead of three major forces in children and digital media intersecting and informing one another to create the most productive, positive practices possible, is a jumble of the good and the less good; the informed and the uninformed; and parents who need support in making the best decisions and doing the best things for their children. Libraries serve these families, and these families require a guide. Or, as Lisa Guernsey so clearly stated in her TEDx talk, they require a "media mentor" (2014).

Librarians have always served as guides and mentors to families with young children. Librarians are the supporters and champions of the literacy lives of the children we serve, regardless of the format in question. That is what librarians do, full stop. At its core, the white paper *Media Mentorship in Libraries Serving Youth* does nothing more than affirm this vital role of the librarian:

> It is a fundamental responsibility of youth services staff to meet the needs of children and their families with regard to both access to and support of digital media, and to prioritize the development of our own knowledge of these areas so that we might best serve our communities.
>
> (Campbell, Haines, Koester, & Stoltz, 2015, p. 1)

The white paper emphasizes that the role of the librarian is unequivocally vital and that the role applies to all situations in which the children we serve are learning and engaging with media of any kind.

Spotlight on Media Mentorship

It is a fundamental responsibility of youth services staff to meet the needs of children and their families with regard to both access to and support of digital media and to prioritize the development of our own knowledge of these areas so that we might best serve our communities

Campbell, Haines, Koester, & Stoltz, 2015, p. 1

The white paper cites research that shows that "children require mediated and guided experiences with digital media for the experiences to translate into positive and productive digital literacy skills" (Campbell, Haines, Koester, & Stoltz 2015, p. 2). This fact mirrors what librarians have known for decades about creating and sharing experience with children to support their literacy development: one of our core values. These experiences also presuppose a need for "services and collections that support the development of digital literacy" (Campbell, Haines, Koester, & Stoltz, 2015, p. 2), a need that also fits within our professional mission to support literacy in all its facets.

The commitment to media mentorship in librarians is articulated in the white paper with four key positions.

Spotlight on Media Mentorship

The Commitment to Media Mentorship:

1 Every library has librarians and other staff serving youths who embrace their role as media mentors for their community.
2 Media mentors support children and families in their media use and decisions.
3 Library schools provide resources and training to support future librarians and youth services practitioners in serving as media mentors.
4 Professional development for current librarians and youth services practitioners include formal training and informal support for serving as media mentors.

Campbell, Haines, Koester, & Stoltz, 2015, p. 7

Key to this book is the second position: that media mentorship is a supportive role for children's and families' media use and practice. It is the media mentor's role to be aware of research, resources, and recommendations that pertain to children's media use and then to share that knowledge to meet a family's stated or implied needs. The role of media mentor is an objective one, in which families will be given the resources they request and will be able to make their own decisions about how to use those resources in their media-use decisions and habits.

It is the media mentor's role to be aware of research, resources, and recommendations that pertain to children's media use and then to share that knowledge to meet a family's stated or implied needs.

With the white paper, ALSC and the larger profession are stating that by embracing our role as media mentors for youth and families—that is, by knowing the media landscape and the research about it and by helping families to have access to that knowledge through library experiences—we and our libraries are continuing to fulfill our longstanding mission to support and meet the needs of those whom we serve.

Spotlight on Media Mentorship

Media mentors actively engage with children and families interacting with digital media provided within the library context, both guiding children through positive and efficient uses of the technology and modeling for caregivers how they can support their children's digital literacy development outside of the library.

Campbell, Haines, Koester, & Stoltz, 2015, p. 8

Media Mentorship in Practice: Examples From Libraries

Both before the release of the white paper and since, libraries have been serving as media mentors in their communities in a number of ways. There are as many ways to act as media mentors as there are unique communities served by libraries, as each community will require mentorship that is responsive to their needs and expectations. Librarians have shared stories and best practices related to:

- incorporating digital media into story times;
- app play and advisory in programs;
- messages specific to caregivers of young children;
- devices for in-library use; and
- curated lists of content and other technology.

Incorporating Digital Media into Story Times

According to Claudia Haines, an Alaska children's librarian, the media mentorship benefits of using technology in story times is straightforward: "The idea is to include digital media as part of the storytime [sic] toolkit and expand what we can use to foster early literacy in a program that reaches a wide variety of kids and families." Through intentional use in story times, technology becomes another tool to support the early literacy development in children. Haines considers use of all available tools to be showing "the many faces of early literacy."

Awnali Mills, a Virginia librarian, incorporates digital media into her story times so that she can emphasize the potential benefits of the technology to the parents in attendance:

> I support parent/caregiver engagement with young kids and tech through my storytimes [sic]. I use book apps, game apps, and the iPad to enrich my storytimes. By demonstrating good apps in an educational setting, I show parents and caregivers that tablets are great for enhancing learning.

Parents leave these programs having witnessed positive, educational, and developmentally appropriate ways in which to use a range of digital media options in order to support their children's learning—and equipping caregivers to support their children's learning is a primary goal of story time.

App Play and Advisory in Programs

Many libraries offer opportunities for children and their caregivers to engage in app play within program settings beyond story times. In a number of such programs, including examples from Michigan and Illinois, the program provides each child/caregiver pair in attendance with an iPad (or similar device) with specific pre-loaded content as they enter the program space. Throughout the program, the children and caregivers are able to explore the curated apps on the devices together. In these examples, a librarian provides tips and recommendations to the children and caregivers throughout the program as they try and test the technology together.

Other programmatic uses serve more of a formal advisory function before opening the space for play and exploration. Programs in California, Wisconsin, and Massachusetts take this format, providing caregivers with recommendations of high-quality apps based on a central theme or target age range. These programs also offer tips for positive media habits alongside app recommendations. Massachusetts librarian Clara Hendricks offers programs on raising "app-y" children, where she provides parents with assistance and guidance in using technology with their children, as she describes in the box on p. 237.

Spotlight on Media Mentorship

Parents seem anxious about all of the different advice and recommendations out there, and all of the different media available for their children. Through these programs, they develop ideas about how to choose media for children that develop pre-reading and other skills, [as well as] an understanding of the most appropriate ways to introduce touch-screen technology into their children's lives. Teaching parents of young children about joint engagement, how to select apps, and ways to incorporate technology into their lives helps develop a healthy relationship with technology from a young age.

Such programs allow caregivers to be better equipped to use the best possible information about media and children in order to make personal, important decisions about media use in their own families.

Messages Specific to Caregivers of Young Children

Some libraries are seamlessly integrating caregiver-directed media mentorship into programs through the crafting and sharing of recommendations-based messages in their programs. This method is an iteration of an Every Child Ready to Read–inspired practice of peppering a story time with informational asides in order to equip parents with positive ways to promote early literacy skills in their children through shared activities. In the same vein, media mentorship messages equip parents with information and suggestions for positive media use and practices.

Amy Koester, one of this chapter's co-authors, made a point of offering such caregiver messages in every technology-infused children's program at her former library in Missouri. The goal was for a one-to-one tech use-to-message ratio—that every instance of using digital technology be accompanied by relevant messages to the children's caregivers. In story times, after using an app to share pictures of zoo animals through a National Geographic Society app such as Look & Learn: Animals Vol. 1, an accompanying message might state:

> You can use technology to expose children to animals, places, and other things that they can't see in their everyday lives. Help your child to use this content to learn more about things they're interested in, and make sure you explore along with them to talk about what you learn and see.

While these types of media mentorship messages may be proactive—that is, providing caregivers with information and recommendations without being directly asked for it—librarians are also using them as opportunities to respond to stated caregiver concerns. Sharon Lanasa, a Maryland librarian, shares an example in the box on p. 238.

Spotlight on Media Mentorship

Parents are often concerned about exposing their very young children to screens of any kind, and I use reliable and authoritative information…to assure parents that the most important component of screen time with young [children] is to make it engaging, purposeful, and an enjoyable shared experience between adult and child. The relationship is the thing.

Such responsive messages can go a long way toward helping caregivers make the best choices for their children using research-based practices and recommendations rather than alarmist worries that tend to be propagated about the news media and on social media.

Library staff who are new to media mentorship find the process of crafting caregiver messages to be energizing. At an Arizona training led by Carissa Christner and Anne Hicks, the trainees were asked to create simple media use tips they could share with parents in their programs. Trainees offered messages such as "Treat it like a book, and together, take a look!" and "Tablet time is talking time!" both of which reinforce the importance of joint media engagement when children use digital technology. The relative ease of creating such positive and encouraging messages for parents out of the wealth of research and recommendations on media and children had led to more and more libraries adopting this method of media mentorship.

Devices for In-Library Use

Libraries offer their patrons a number of options for using different technologies in the library itself. One such option is mounting iPads or other tablet devices in child-accessible spaces in the library. The library is able to determine what types of content are available on the devices for children to use; substantial thought goes into that decision, as with any collection development decision that a library or librarian makes. At one Alaska library, these mounted devices are set up to display a single app—changing to another app is not an option. Claudia Haines explains the philosophy behind this decision: "One app a week allows kids to explore an app. Instead of kids getting sucked into the device, they explore the content and then move on to something else when they are done with the content." This strategy for offering device use allows children to experience the app and its content in small chunks of time alongside their other experiences at the library.

Other libraries opt to offer devices curated with a range of app options, with children able to select the apps they want to use on any given visit. The curation of such devices is deliberate, with certain apps being offered with specific rationale. Michigan librarian Emily Hudak explains the philosophy at her library in the box on p. 239.

Spotlight on Media Mentorship

Our library has 3 early literacy iPad stations. These iPads are loaded with various educational apps geared to the under-5 crowd. The apps are divided into category folders such as Concepts (this includes apps that focus on colors, shapes, ABCs, etc.), Creative Play (apps that allow children more freedom to do what they want), Fairy Tales, Storybooks, etc. We try to choose apps with a strong educational value that are also relatively low cost and free of ads and in-app purchases. We want to show parents the great apps that are out there so they don't have to muddle through the App Store looking for them.

Such collection plans for in-library devices emphasize the benefits of device availability not only to children for whom content is intended but for their caregivers as well.

Libraries also offer computers and proprietary devices for patron use in the library. According to Claudia Haines, why these devices are chosen and how they are made available for use is determined by as much intentionality as with tablets. Computer and device stations may be equipped with two headsets to encourage children and adults to interact and explore together. Such stations may be accompanied by signage that explains the benefits of joint media engagement. Additionally, the orientation of the space in which devices are available often takes into account the social potential of technology use. By offering the devices in a communal space, children end up playing parallel or with one another; says Haines, "It gets kids who need social skill development out of hiding when they have to play together in the same room."

Curated Lists of Content and Other Technology

Librarians have a longstanding reputation as experts in print content, and many libraries now offer a digital technology counterpart to this traditional service. More and more libraries are offering curated lists—be they verbal, on paper, or digitally available—to aid their patrons in finding high-quality, developmentally appropriate, recommended content for use with children. An example of an in-person, customized, curated list comes from a library in New York: they offer their patrons an app recommendation service in which a patron can request apps for a particular age or on a certain topic while in the library, with a librarian creating a tailored list of relevant resources.

Many other libraries offer more general recommendations in the form of brochures and handouts; librarians in Alaska and Wisconsin emphasize that these print lists are regularly updated with new content and to address new audiences. Plenty of libraries have also taken to social media to curate lists of apps, in particular with Pinterest. Libraries in California report sharing the names of apps they use in programs with attendees, then follow up by pinning those apps to their library recommendation boards so that others may see what is available.

More recently, librarians have also begun to share their technology curation and recommendation expertise outside of the library itself. California librarian AnneMarie Hurtado wrote an article on apps and children for the free publication *LA Parent* (2014); knowing this article would reach a wider audience than she could on her own at her library, she took the opportunity to give parents tips about what to look for in finding high-quality apps as well as providing them with a list of recommended apps. Carissa Christner, a Wisconsin librarian, has also been invited to appear on the local evening news to share information and recommendations about using apps with children. This connection stemmed from the librarian's engaging app-visory programs for families at her library; she will now be able to reach a larger, broader population by sharing her expertise on television.

Reactions From Parents and Caregivers

How do parents and caregivers react to librarians' serving as media mentors? While no formal studies have been undertaken, librarians have shared their personal experiences with families whom they have mentored in some capacity. At the app recommendation end of the media mentorship spectrum, caregivers have indicated how much they appreciate the opportunity to preview and/or try out an app in the library before purchasing it for themselves. Recommending the best possible resources serves not only to allow parents to make the best decisions for their families but to avoid spending money unnecessarily as well. A Michigan librarian echoes caregivers' appreciation of app recommendations in her report that families begin downloading select apps she uses with children in her programs before the program has concluded. The Mission Viejo Library in California reported the following from a grant report based around a digital storytelling initiative:

Spotlight on Media Mentorship

One of our focuses during the parent education programs and our early literacy classes was to emphasize to parents the importance of joint engagement around technology and how technology can be another tool for building relationships. We were very happy to get comments and stories from parents that demonstrated that they took this to heart. One mom, talking about Tablet Time, said, "It's a great class! We really enjoy coming. It's very helpful to preview apps before buying and to get new ideas for ways to play with my daughter." Another mom said, "All four weeks were fabulous. We loaded our iPad with lots of cool stuff and love doing it together." A dad told us, "This class was amazing. I spent quality time with my daughter learning about apps for our tablet I had no idea were available." Those were exactly the kind of stories we wanted to hear: "ways to play WITH my daughter"; "love doing it TOGETHER"; "quality time WITH my daughter."

One Alaska librarian received a shout out from a patron on Facebook regarding the media mentorship she and her daughter received at the library. The patron shared her pride and excitement at her child's using an app she learned about at the library to create her own stories. The patron expressed thanks alongside sharing a screen grab of her daughter's creation, providing visual evidence of one possible impact of media mentorship. This parent knows she can look to the library for recommendations of technology that can promote her daughter's creativity in developmentally-appropriate ways.

The impact of media mentorship can be broad and meaningful. When one Wisconsin library asked caregivers who attend one of their programs how the library has affected their family's use of technology, they received the following enthusiastic response:

Spotlight on Media Mentorship

Tremendously! Eighty [percent] of the apps I download for my children are recommendations of the library. Discussions with my librarian have helped me curate my iPad to a place of learning, discovery and creativity. I now have a very high standard of the quality of app I will allow on my devices. I try to engage with them on the device at least 1/3 the time they play (the rest I want them to have the freedom to explore on their own). Additional library discussions have helped me to be a better role model with how I use (or don't use) electronic devices in my life.

In one short survey response, a caregiver illustrates many of the myriad ways that media mentorship can impact a family for the better. The family now knows where to look for recommended content, and they know how to identify high-quality content on their own. The family actively practices joint media engagement. Additionally, the caregivers in the family are aware of how their own media use and decisions affect their children's practice. Through having access to media mentors at this library, the parents of this family are now empowered to act as role models to their children, who in turn benefit from having access to the best content and engagement possible.

Conclusion

While the phrase *media mentorship* has just recently been launched in the library profession, the concept of supporting families is not a new one. Many librarians are enthusiastically taking on the role of media mentor. Often, the only shift in taking on this role is the application of traditional librarian skills to new formats as they emerge as well as making authoritative resources readily available to the community. There are, however, still concerns about the appropriateness of media use by young children, both in the library and elsewhere, and some libraries simply do not have the budget, staff time, or infrastructure to serve this role in their communities yet. Community partnerships with non-profit organizations, early childhood educators, caregivers, content developers, and others can sometimes help to serve the need for media mentorship for families with young children. While there are some well-developed media mentorship programs in place in public and school libraries, there is always a need for feedback and collaboration with community members. As such, the authors of this chapter extend an open invitation to early childhood educators, families, and everyone else who cares about and for young children to reach out to their local libraries and ask about what collections, services, and programs they offer to support families to make healthy media decisions.

Helpful Hits from Librarians for Educators as Media Mentors

- Contact your local children's librarian and ask for suggestions for high-quality, age-appropriate digital media for the age group you serve. While many libraries have taken on the role of media mentorship, some could benefit from community partnership.
- Check out new media offerings at the library. There may be curated app collections, interactive books to download, iPads to check out, makerspaces, app recommendation lists, or other resources to help you. If there aren't any media mentor resources, ask for some! It's the librarian's mission to serve your information needs.
- Children's librarians specialize in locating and curating high-quality, age-appropriate media of all kinds for all ages. Ask for recommendations at the reference desk, either by phone, in-person, or online.
- Use some of the same techniques with new forms of media as you do with older forms of media like books: engagement with the child is paramount! Dialogic reading, pointing to words, asking "What do you think happens next?" can all take place with new forms of media.
- The best app (or any other format) for young children is one that supports the development of a relationship with another human being. Relationships comes first, technology comes second.
- Talk, sing, read, write, and play with young children, whether technology is involved or is not.

References

American Library Association. (n.d.) *Equity of access*. Retrieved from www.ala.org/advocacy/access/equityofaccess

American Library Association. (1996). *Library bill of rights*. Retrieved from www.ala.org/advocacy/intfreedom/librarybill

Association of Library Service to Children. (2009). *Competencies for librarians serving children in public libraries*. Chicago, IL: ALSC. Retrieved from www.ala.org/alsc/edcareeers/alsccorecomps

Campbell, C., Haines, C., Koester, A., & Stoltz, D. (2015). *Media mentorship in libraries serving youth*. Chicago, IL: ALSC. Retrieved from www.ala.org/alsc/mediamentorship

Guernsey, Lisa. (2014). How the iPad affects young children, and what we can do about it. *TEDxMidAtlantic* video, 13:14. Posted April 27, 2014. www.youtube.com/watch?v=P41_nyYY3Zg.

Hurtardo, A. M. (2014). *Finding great educational apps for your kids*. Los Angeles, CA: L. A. Parent. Retrieved from www.laparent.com/finding-great-educational-apps-kids/

Mills, J. E., Romeijn-Stout, E., Campbell, C., & Koester, A. (2015). Results from the Young Children, New Media, and Libraries Survey: What did we learn? *Children and Libraries 13*(2), 26–32, 35.

Naidoo, J. C. (2014). *The importance of diversity in library programs and material collections for children*. Chicago, IL: ALSC.

Neuman, S. B., & Celano, D. (2010). *An evaluation of Every Child Ready to Read: A parent education initiative*. Chicago, IL: ALA.

Rideout, V. J. 2013. *Zero to eight: Children's media use in America 2013*. Washington, DC: Common Sense Media.

Takeuchi, L., & Stevens, R. (2011). *The new coviewing: Designing for learning through joint media engagement*. New York, NY: Joan Ganz Cooney Center at Sesame Workshop. Retrieved from www.joanganzcooneycenter.org/publication/the-new-coviewing-designing-for-learning-through-joint-media-engagement/

Resources

- American Library Association (ALA) www.ala.org
- Association for Library Service to Children (ALSC) www.ala.org/alsc/
- Facebook www.facebook.com
- Institute of Museum and Library Services (IMLS) www.imls.gov
- Little eLit http://littleelit.com
- Pinterest www.pinterest.com
- Public Library Association (PLA) www.ala.org/pla/

Learn more...

- ALA Youth Media Awards www.ala.org/news/mediapresscenter/presskits/youthmediaawards/alayouthmediaawards

- Campbell, C., & Kluver, C. (2015). Access, content, and engagement: How children's librarians support early learning in the digital age. In C. Donohue (Ed.), *Technology and digital media in the early years: Tools for teaching and learning* (pp. 235–249). New York: Routledge and Washington, DC: National Association for the Education of young Children.
- *Competencies for librarians serving children in public libraries* www.ala.org/alsc/edcareeers/alsccorecomps
- *Every Child Ready to Read*® Second Edition www.everychildreadytoread.org
- *Equity of access*, ALA www.ala.org/advocacy/access/equityofaccess
- *Growing young minds: How museums and libraries create lifelong learning.* Institute of Museum and Library Services www.imls.gov/assets/1/AssetManager/GrowingYoungMinds.pdf
- *Library Bill of Rights* www.ala.org/advocacy/intfreedom/librarybill
- *Library services in the digital age.* Pew Research Center http://libraries.pewinternet.org/2013/01/22/library-services/
- *Look & Learn: Animals Vol. 1,* National Geographic Society https://itunes.apple.com/us/app/look-learn-animals-vol.-1/id525073512?mt=8&ign-mpt=uo%3D8
- *Media mentorship in libraries serving youth* www.ala.org/alsc/mediamentorship
- *Worlds apart: One city, two libraries, and ten years of watching inequality grow.* Susan B. Neuman and Donna C. Celano http://www.aft.org/pdfs/americaneducator/fall2012/Neuman.pdf
- *Young Children, New Media and Libraries Survey results* www.ala.org/alsc/sites/ala.org.alsc/files/content/YCNML%20Infographic_0.pdf
- *Young children, new media, and libraries: A guide for incorporating new media into library collections, services, and programs for families and children ages 0–5* http://littleelit.com/book/

Chapter 16

Public Media and Learning at Home

Engaging Families With Transmedia:
Case Studies and Stories From
EDC/SRI, WestEd, KBTC, and WGBH

Chip Donohue

Setting the Context

This chapter includes two case studies and a collection of stories that spotlight lessons learned and promising directions from an innovative transmedia approach to technology-mediated family engagement and learning using public media. The case studies have been drawn from the evaluations and impact studies of the Corporation for Public Broadcasting (CPB) and Public Broadcasting Service (PBS) 5-year U.S. Department of Education's (DOE) Ready to Learn (RTL) initiative. RTL has funded public television stations to develop new educational programs and learning tools that provide children with the fundamental skills needed for school readiness and school success in the twenty-first century. The transmedia approach explored strategies for connecting learning at home with learning in school and in early childhood programs—equipping and empowering parents as teachers and learners with their children.

The 2010–2015 RTL projects, "Expanded Learning Through Transmedia Content," explored how free digital media (existing and newly developed) from CPB/PBS could best support early learning at home for children, parents, and families living in lower-income, lower-resourced communities. The transmedia projects created new means of access and deeper levels of engagement with public media using digital devices, the Internet, and technology platforms including television, videos, websites, hand-held digital games, laptops computers, smartphones, tablets, and other multi-touch devices. Issues of access and equity and barriers to participation due to a digital use divide informed program design, development, and delivery.

Since 1994, the DOE RTL grant program has encouraged the use of educational television and newer digital media to promote early learning and school readiness, including a mandate to reach children in lower-income communities. In addition to creating television and other media products, the program promotes national distribution of the programming, effective educational uses of the resources, community-based engagement, and research on educational effectiveness. Results from the evaluations and impact studies form the basis of the case studies that follow. More information about the research and researchers can be found in the Resources and Learn More… sections at the end of the chapter.

As part of the RTL initiative, CPB and PBS funded 30 public media stations to support the early learning needs of children from low-income families through collaboration with local partners. Teaching and learning tools that were developed, implemented, and evaluated included: high-quality educational video; interactive games; apps; hands-on activities; classroom materials; parent–teacher resources; and activities to support community engagement. By implementing the RTL transmedia approach, these stations were able to "improve the math and literacy skills of children ages two to eight, empower families to be leaders in their children's academic success, and increase teachers' capacities for successfully using transmedia learning tools in a variety of educational settings" (CPB/PBS 2015).

To put the CPB/PBS RTL process, products, lessons learned, and evaluation of program effectiveness within the context of this book on digital-age family engagement, this chapter includes two case studies and two Spotlight on Engagement stories. The first case study, *Engaging Families with Transmedia Math Content*, was contributed by the team at WestEd and focuses on a model for parent engagement using PBS Kids Transmedia content. The second case study, *Digital Media and Learning at Home*, was contributed by the research team from Education Development Center and SRI International (EDC/SRI) and explores lessons learned from transmedia approaches to enhancing family engagement and early math achievement. Both cases explore successful strategies for using digital media specifically designed to support early learning and school readiness for young children and their families. Between the two case studies you'll find two Spotlight on Engagement stories from local PBS stations in Tacoma, Washington and Boston, Massachusetts that were participating sites in the CPB/PBS RTL initiative.

The case study and stories you are about to read were contributed by members of the research teams at WestEd and EDC/SRI and by station staff and participants at KBTC and WGBH and are based on the formative research and evidence of effectiveness described in detail in recent reports (McCarthy, Li, Tiu, Atienza, & Sexton, 2015; Pasnik et al., 2015). Pseudonyms were used for the children, parents, and families described in this chapter, but the stories, experiences, and quotations attributed to participants are authentic to connect the dots between family engagement and technology in the digital age.

Case Study 1: Engaging Families with Transmedia Math Content

Contributed by Betsy McCarthy, Sarah Atienza, Linlin Li, Ursula Sexton, and Michelle Tiu at WestEd

Introduction

Research tells us that family engagement in children's learning is an important element for systemic and sustained effects on academic outcomes for young children. A recent review of research, The *Impact of Family Involvement on the Education of Children Ages 3 to 8* (Van Voorhis, Maier, Epstein, Lloyd, & Leuong, 2013), concludes that three types of family engagement are strongly related to math achievement in young children:

1 parents' use of learning activities in the home;
2 school outreach to engage families; and
3 a supportive family environment, including a positive learning atmosphere and quality parent–child interactions.

As educators seek ways to include families in their children's math learning, many are considering how increased access to technology and digital media may help promote family engagement in learning, especially in low-income communities. Results from a recent study by WestEd (2015) suggest that increased access to technology and digital media can provide new opportunities for educators to support preschool families in positively influencing their children's math learning and in creating supportive learning environments outside of the classroom.

In the WestEd study, *Learning with PBS KIDS: A Study of Family Engagement and Early Mathematics Achievement* (McCarthy, Li, Tiu, Atienza, & Sexton, 2015), researchers followed up 153 children, ages 3 to 5 years, and their families in preschool and home settings over 9 weeks. Families were recruited from preschools in underserved communities. The intervention focused on two math concepts: numbers and operations, and shapes. Using videos, online games, and hands-on activities that include many children's favorite PBS KIDS characters—such as *Curious George, Peg+Cat,* and *The Cat in the Hat*—family members and children worked together on activities for 30 minutes per day for 4 days per week. Additionally, parents and guardians were encouraged to attend weekly meetings at their child's preschool.

For children and families in the intervention group preschools, the study found that:

- children's math scores on the rigorous Test of Early Mathematics Ability (TEMA-3) were on average 3 points higher—a statistically significant gain—than those for students in the comparison group over the study's duration; and

- parents' awareness of their children's math learning increased significantly, as did their use of strategies to support their children's learning; participation in the study motivated parents to set aside time each day to do math activities with their children.

Additionally, the study found that teachers from participating schools successfully facilitated parent meetings related to the intervention.

A Case Study of Family Engagement and Student Learning

At the same time as the larger study was being conducted, a representative sample of families was chosen to be the focus of a case study. The case study included data from a group of six families and resulted in a composite description of a family as they participate in a family engagement program (McCarthy, Sexton, Li, Tiu, & Atienza, in preparation). The following case description highlights how families used the family engagement program and how the engagement model led to changes in behavior and knowledge.

Spotlight on the Garcia Family

Maria Garcia, a rambunctious 4-year-old, lives in a suburban/rural community in Northern California with her father, Ernesto, and her mother, Juana. The family also includes Maria's brother, Roberto (6 years), and her grandmother, Abuela. The family lives in a small community housing condominium several blocks from Maria's state-funded preschool. Maria's parents both go to work each day. Ernesto and Juana work at local small businesses. The parents' combined annual income totals about $23,000. Maria's family typically speaks Spanish at home, but Ernesto, Juana, Maria, and Roberto frequently speak English outside of their home.

One morning, when Juana was dropping Maria off at her at preschool, she was haled by the school receptionist and handed an invitation for Maria and her family. The invitation said that her family was invited to take part in a family math-learning program. Participation would mean Juana and her husband (or another family member), would attend a 1-hour weekly parent meeting facilitated by her child's preschool teachers for 9 weeks. Juana read that her family would use a small laptop to access PBS KIDS math digital games and videos at home for the duration of the program. Juana brought the invitation home with her and shared it with Ernesto, Maria, Roberto, and Abuela. The family agreed that the program sounded interesting and exciting. They agreed to participate in the program.

At their first parent meeting, Juana and Ernesto sat around a table with other parents from Maria's preschool. Many tables full of other parents filled the room and there was an air of excitement as the group was greeted by the teacher facilitators. Next, parents were given a binder that detailed which digital games, videos, and hands-on activities to use with their child during each week of the program. Families were asked to interact with their children using program activities for 30 minutes per day, 4 days per week. Figure 16.1 shows a typical week of activities displayed in a parent binder. In Juana and Ernesto's binder, activities for Days 1 through 4 were displayed for each week of the program. Though some weeks differed, Day 1 usually involved using a hands-on activity; Day 2, an activity and a digital game; Day 3, digital games

Figure 16.1 Typical Weekly Plan In The Parent Binder
(Courtesy of WestEd)

and a video; and Day 4, interaction with all digital media presented during the week. The teacher facilitators explained that each week would focus on a specific math concept (e.g., counting). When Juana opened the laptop they would use for the study, she found that the screen looked just like the page in her parent binder. On the laptop, live links to games and videos were added, making it easy to jump to games and videos for Days 2 through 4. At this first parent meeting, and each meeting going forward, Juana and Ernesto experienced a similar routine. First, the parents at the meeting would spend time discussing the math-learning activities they had done with their children in the previous week. Next, teacher facilitators would introduce parents to the math concept, digital media, and hands-on activities for the coming week, and parents would be invited to try some of the activities.

At home during the next 9 weeks, the family found time—usually in the late afternoon—to work on program activities for about 30 minutes per day. One particularly fun week for Maria and Ernesto involved playing the digital game *Hide and Seek*, where players assist Curious George in counting and finding the digits and words for numbers 1 through 10. Activities also involved playing a matching game with number cards, whereby the player matches a card with dots with its corresponding word (e.g., card with 6 dots, the card with the number "Six"). Maria and Ernesto laughed at Curious George's antics as they worked through the digital game, all the way up to "10." They smiled, laughed, and encouraged each other during the matching game with cards. Later that week, Ernesto applied this concept outside of the digital game and had Maria independently count pieces of fruit at the market when they were shopping and name the numbers they saw in the store.

At the last parent meeting, Ernesto and Juana celebrated with other families in the program by sharing what they had learned during the program. Over the course of the program, Juana and Ernesto reported that participation in the program opened their eyes to new ways to support Maria's math learning. Not only did they report seeing Maria advance in her math learning over the course of the intervention, they said that they gained a new awareness of early mathematics, and new techniques for supporting Maria's learning. In addition, they reported that Abuela and Roberto participated in many aspects of the program. Specifically, the family mentioned that Maria grew in her math abilities, that the family grew more aware of Maria's math learning and how to support it, and that the high-quality content contributed to making the engagement program effective.

Maria's Parents Reported They Noticed Maria Learning Math

In focus groups and during table conversations at parent meetings, both Juana and Ernesto mentioned that they observed their daughter learning new mathematics content. Ernesto explained, "My daughter learned a lot.

She learned to add small numbers, less than ten. Before, she didn't know any adding. She now knows the numbers up to 12, and she also identifies shapes." Juana added, "In mathematics, it did help her a lot; not at the level I would like, but I am proud of her. She is still small, and I know she's going to be smart."

Interestingly, Juana also mentioned that she learned math right along with her daughter: "It also helped me, because I only studied up to 9th grade. Sometimes we don't know how to teach our kids. I also learned the names of the shapes." She mentioned that Maria's grandmother became more aware as well: "Sometimes Abuela would be there, watching, so she was also noticing what addition was."

The Family Grew in Awareness of Maria's Mathematics Learning

Juana and Ernesto mentioned their entire family became more aware of the early math that Maria was learning at preschool and at home. In a table discussion at a parent meeting, Juana and Ernesto both mentioned a precise assessment of Maria's knowledge of addition and geometric shapes. According to Ernesto, "She is learning how to add small numbers. If we put up two fingers and three fingers, she will count how many there are. She has trouble with 'take-away' subtraction. She struggles with that." Juana added information about Maria's knowledge of shapes, explaining, "She learned almost all the shapes except she still gets confused with hexagon, pentagon, and octagon. She only gets confused with those three, but she knows how to count the sides, she knows how many sides it has." Juana expressed surprise that Maria could learn mathematics during her preschool years.

> Sometimes I thought, "My kid's too little to know that." But, well she learned it, so it must not be that hard…This [program] makes you think that even though they're so young, their minds are growing and they're really smart and they catch onto everything, building on everything.

The Family Learned New Skills to Support Maria's Learning

In focus groups and table discussions, Juana and Ernesto mentioned that they learned new skills and strategies from the family engagement program that allowed them to enrich their learning interactions with Maria. Specific skills they mentioned included asking questions and deepening conversations about math with Maria; setting aside time each day to focus on learning; making learning interactions fun and positive; and integrating math learning throughout the day.

Asking Questions and Deepening the Conversations About Math

Ernesto said that the family engagement program helped him understand that by conversing with Maria and by talking about the math all around them, he could support her learning:

> It [the program] was good because it helped me to consciously think more about asking her questions, about counting and colors and shapes and stuff like that. Which I did before, but I didn't consciously do it as often as I would do now. Like, everyday objects that pass us by throughout the day.

He said that this type of everyday teaching was very different than how he learned math.

> It's a different way of learning. In our country [of origin] we had studies like one plus one, one plus two. We didn't have different activities or games. There we had to learn by repetition. It [the program] showed us how we can help our child everywhere. Our home is a school for our kids. If we go to the store, if we go to the park, we can say: "What color is the tree?" "What change [money] is there?" They [the teachers] provided lots of ideas to us. I really liked it.

Setting Aside Time Each Day to Focus on Learning

Juana and Ernesto both mentioned that they appreciated the structure of the family engagement program. They said that putting aside 30 minutes each day for 4 days per week was sometimes difficult, but they found ways to make it work, and they found they appreciated the time they spent with Maria focused on learning. According to Juana:

> The experience for us was positive. You do need to invest a little time, both parents, and kids, but working together, you can do anything. If you get organized, and you dedicate the time, you can do it; it doesn't matter if you can't do it every day, but if you're organized you can do the activities.

She said that the whole family enjoyed time learning together: "It [the program] gave us the chance to put other things aside and sit down with our child." They laughed remembering how Maria would remind them to sit with her each day to play the program's learning games and activities. "And she would remind us sometimes. 'Study Time' is what she calls it. She would grab the bag and bring it to where we were, and we would say, 'Okay, let's do it!'" Ernesto added:

Before the program, she didn't know how to count. I think it motivated her because sometimes she would say, "I want to do my homework." I would get home, and she would say, "What time are we doing homework today?" She would always wait to see what I would give her, and she would do it. Coloring, counting? I think it has helped her a lot, and helped me too because, I spent time with her, and sometimes we tend to think that we don't know or that we don't have time to listen to them. So it helped me a lot with her.

Ernesto said he thought having specific activities outlined for each week, similar to her older sibling's "homework," motivated the young Maria. "It motivated her. She felt like she had a responsibility like an adult. Like saying, 'I'm like my big brother, I have homework too.' So it would give her a little pride."

Making Learning Fun and Positive

Another aspect of the family engagement program was the focus on playfulness and positive affect. The characters and narrative arc of the games and the videos and activities that are used in the program are playful and engaging. In the Garcia family, these narratives set the stage for learning interactions filled with positive emotions and fun. Juana reported that their family increased their use of fun and playfulness during learning interactions with Maria. She said she realized that positive encouragement and adding an element of play to their interactions would motivate Maria to stay engaged in learning. Juana recounted a learning interaction she had with Maria while playing a digital game included in the program:

> I would act like I didn't know, and she would do it fine, and she would laugh at me because she'd say, "I beat you, you didn't know!" But I would let her win so that she could keep trying, and if she couldn't do something, she would say, "Mom…" and I would say, "You can. You know!" I told her, "If every person couldn't do anything then we would all be stuck. Keep trying." So she would try once again, and she would be able to do it, and she would smile.

Ernesto added that the program activities were fun and that both Maria and Roberto liked them.

> For me as well, the experience was very good because we noticed, even if it's a little while you're with them, they learn. She liked it—well both did since I have a girl and a boy—they would both do it, and they liked for me to be a part of it, to sit with them. It helped them both, and also

to me because, I was able to spend time with them, and I would also get happy to see that they were learning more.

Finding Ways to Integrate Math Learning Throughout the Day

During focus groups and table conversations, Juana and Ernesto frequently mentioned they were learning new ways to integrate math practices into their everyday activities with Maria. This suggests that Maria's parents were growing in their level of support for her math learning. In a conversation with other parents at her table Juana said, "When we are in the car I say, 'How many lights did we pass? How many with color? Without color?' And she will tell you." She added:

> We started counting everyday objects. When we go to the grocery store, I say, "Can you find me a thing of bananas that has five bananas on it, one for each of us?" She'll count the bananas and find the one for each of us.

High-Quality and Engaging Content Contributed to the Program

Juana and Ernesto frequently mentioned they appreciated the high-quality PBS KIDS content used in the engagement program. They mentioned that the characters and storylines were highly engaging and that they found the learning content was well designed and useful. They mentioned appreciating all types of content. In addition, they appreciated that the academic content and storylines were connected across different media, making the narratives continuous and engaging throughout. Ernesto mentioned that their family enjoyed all of the content in the program, including the digital games, videos and hand-on materials. "She learned to count better with a game, which went up to number 20. Definitely, the game was really very good and she liked the videos a lot." Juana added, "She liked the games, reading the books, the videos, hands-on activity, like the shapes that we brought home last time. She pretty much liked it all, and I did too!"

Benefits of Engagement

The Garcia family benefitted from the family engagement program. Not only did Maria grow significantly in her math ability, her family members grew in their capacity to support her. All indications suggest that Maria's family will continue to support her in coming years. According to Ernesto,

> It motivated me as a parent to get a little more focused on my daughter's education, to help her to learn more, to motivate her, not only in school, but telling her that learning isn't boring, but can be fun with characters that she likes.

Research-Backed Helpful Hints for Media Mentors

Parents, teachers, and caregivers can play the role of "media mentor" in young children's lives. As media mentors, trusted adults are responsible for guiding young children in appropriate use of technology, while also providing opportunities to engage and have fun with digital tools.

- The most important role parents, teachers, and caregivers play with technology use is to *be an active participant*! Discuss what is on the screen with young children. Use technology for exploring, learning, and having fun.
- Interactions with technology can lead to interesting conversations between adult and child and can boost language development.
- Model healthy technology use by placing limits on screen time and ensuring appropriate content.
- Older children can teach their younger siblings how to use technology and help them play successfully with digital devices. This is a great opportunity for siblings to connect over a shared interest— under adult supervision of course!

Choose Appropriate Technology and Digital Media

There are dozens of websites, devices, and tools that parents can use to supplement their child's literacy development using technology. Many of these resources are used similarly or the same as their non-digital counterparts. Technology can also offer children opportunities to be exposed to things that they would not otherwise have access to, such as images, songs, and stories from different parts of the world.

Websites

- Search for websites that are kid-friendly: pictures that are familiar, not much text, limited or no advertisements, and easy-to-find games.
- Look for websites that connect with children's favorite television, movie, or book characters; for example, PBSkids.org, Sproutonline.com, and Disneyjunior.com.
- Be mindful of children's personal safety: kid-friendly websites should never offer options to interact with adults via social media or require providing personal information.

Games and Apps

- Find games that match the abilities of your child and challenge him or her to use skills that they have acquired off-screen.

- Games that have multiple levels of increasing difficulty may keep a child motivated to continue practicing and developing mastery of certain skills.
- Look for clean and clear presentation—avoid games that have a lot of extra visual "noise" and overstimulation.
- Games that do not require reading, have easy-to-use controls, and spoken directions as well as visuals are most effective to play with young children.
- Games that provide feedback that reinforces the learning goals and lets the child know when they have made an error.
- Graphics that are inviting and fun without detracting from the game's educational intentions.

Devices

- Use devices that have special settings for children or are specifically formatted for use only by children; this will prevent youngsters from coming across information by accident or being unable to access the tools intended for their use.
- Use of any digital device by a child should always be done under adult supervision.

Videos

- Always preview online videos for appropriate content before sharing them with any children.
- Many popular children's educational television shows also have videos available online.
- Appropriate online videos for children will mirror those developed for traditional viewing; vocabulary that is easy to understand, kid-friendly topics, and clear story lines are some key characteristics to look for.

Trusted Sources

- Seek out trusted sources to learn about quality digital media and to get advice for using technology and digital media with young children.
- Talk to teachers and other adults for recommendations.
- Read online reviews of educational digital media.
- Bookmark favorite websites that recommend digital media for young children.

Spotlight on Engagement: KBTC in Tacoma, Washington

KBTC, the local PBS station in Tacoma, Washington, served as one of the demonstration sites through a project in Hilltop, one of the highest-need neighborhoods in the city. The student population at Hilltop's McCarver Elementary School is among the poorest in Tacoma, with high rates of homelessness, transience, and free and reduced-price lunches. In response to families' needs for additional support to help their children succeed, the Tacoma Housing Authority and Tacoma Public Schools created the McCarver Elementary Special Housing Project. The Project provides families with much-needed stability through housing, job training, and education, resulting in a better foundation for successful parenting and improved learning outcomes for children. KBTC joined the Project in 2011 to engage children, families, and educators with RTL transmedia math and literacy content and resources.

One of KBTC's most successful contributions to the Project was the creation of PBS KIDS Spring Break and Summer Camps, featuring RTL content, to serve kids during times when they would otherwise have no opportunities for academic enrichment. Students who attended the camp received two meals a day, positive interactions with adults, and fun and educational learning experiences with PBS KIDS games and activities. One such student was Tyler, then 7 years old, whose parents had struggled with homelessness since he was born. Tyler's mother Dawn knew, "Transitional housing is not the best place for kids."

Learning had always been difficult for Tyler. He was kicked out of kindergarten for disruptive behavior, and his father became accustomed to receiving calls from the school every day with reports of his son's problems. When Tyler enrolled in the PBS KIDS Spring Break Camp, everyone worried that he would be distracting to the teachers and other students and doubted that he would make any gains. But Tyler took to the games and activities that camp teachers were using. "The writing activities kept him engaged," says Dawn. "I also liked that there were themes for the activities and computer games." He was interested in learning and found a way to connect to the lessons his teachers were sharing.

Tyler and his family were also supported by the monthly parent engagement meetings that were held leading up to, and following, the Spring Break Camp. KBTC offered child engagement activities during these meetings, providing a fun and educational diversion for kids while their parents participate in mandated training activities. Dawn agrees: "Having KBTC there kept the kids involved in the program and kept parents involved with each other."

Dawn recognizes that there were many factors that helped the family on their path to stability and success. And the family's new attitude and approach to learning continued when regular classes resumed after camp. Soon after, Tyler received his first SOAR (Safe, On Task, Awesome Attitude, Respectful) Award from the school. By the end of the year, Tyler was named "Most Improved Student" at McCarver Elementary for transforming into an exceptional student.

Spotlight on Engagement: WGBH in Boston, Massachusetts

In their role as an RTL demonstration site, WGBH Educational Foundation partnered with Imajine That, an award-winning Massachusetts-based educational organization, to incorporate RTL digital learning tools into their family play spaces and extended day programs offered to at-risk children in Boston and Lawrence public schools. The WGBH Kids' Digital team customized hands-on trainings in media literacy, including navigating the digital landscape and identifying quality media. WGBH also introduced Imajine That staff to the RTL transmedia suites, deepening their understanding of the curricular underpinnings of the content so that they were well equipped to strategically incorporate them into their curricula. WGBH and Imajine That also raised awareness among parents, educators, and policymakers of the value of developmentally appropriate media in early childhood through community events and social media.

> We are all surrounded by media every day. We've learned to select the best apps to help us deposit our paychecks, navigate around a new city, shop, or just keep in touch with friends and relatives both near and far. However, when it comes to our children, many young parents confess that they don't know what's good and what's potentially harmful when it comes to tablet apps.
>
> Susan Leger Ferraro, Founder of Imajine That

Susan Leger Ferraro continued: "Through our partnership with WGBH, we knew we had a unique opportunity to help build parents' knowledge and confidence in selecting and playing apps with their children to help them learn and grow."

Imajine That and WGBH started by observing parents with their young children in the Imajine That family play space. While most parents hugged their children tight as they read books together, parents took a more stand-off approach when it came to tablet apps. Something prevented them from joining in the fun and the learning. Didn't they think that tablet apps could be shared? Were parents suffering from a bit of math anxiety themselves? It turned out to be a bit of both.

"As educators, we needed to learn for ourselves that tablet apps are for sharing and that math, just like science, is fun to explore," said Jess Brenes, VP of Operations at Imajine That. "Only then could we be good digital role models for our parents." So, the Imajinators (as Imajine That staff are called) set out to model joint media engagement and talk to parents about math explorations as opposed to math calculations. Over time, Imajinators saw a transformation in the confidence level of parents and how engaged they were with their children and technology. Gone are days when parents stood on the sidelines while their children played with apps. Now parents are focused on learning, for themselves and for their children. Parents reported that the combination of RTL apps and the hands-on activities made math more accessible and less intimidating for them to explore with their children. Parents also felt more knowledgeable about the characteristics of real learning apps so that they could discern between the good and the not-so-good, taking the lead in their own family's media literacy.

Case Study 2: Digital Media and Learning at Home

Contributed by Naomi Hupert, Shelley Pasnik, Savitha Moorthy, and Carlin Llorente of Education Development Center and SRI International

Why Use Free Digital Media to Support Early Learning at Home?

Much attention and concern have been directed toward the underwhelming academic progress of children living in communities with high levels of poverty and too little access to supports that can lead to educational achievement. As concern about reaching this population grows, educators, policymakers, and community leaders have turned their attention to children's earliest learning opportunities, including the home interactions between parents and young children before they reach school. Of course, reaching and engaging every family with young children is a mammoth task to undertake in any community, requiring extensive resources to support an enormous network of service providers. How then can we continue to explore effective and realistic efforts to support children's earliest learning experiences? One approach is to consider the possibilities afforded by technology, specifically digital media designed for young children and their families, whose purpose is to support learning across a broad range of content and skill areas. What follows is a description of one study of digital media, made and distributed by public media stations and meant to support young children's early math learning and what it found.

Supporting Parent–Child Experiences with PEG+CAT Early Math Concepts: Report to the CPB-PBS Ready To Learn Initiative is the long, formal name researchers at Education Development Center and SRI International (EDC/ SRI) gave to a study we conducted in Winter/Spring 2015. Informally and for the purposes of this case study we call it the *PEG+CAT* Home Study. It was a research project that explored how a media program designed to support math learning among 4-year-olds produced positive learning experiences and measurable gains for children and their parents. *PEG+CAT* is a multimedia animated PBS KIDS series produced by The Fred Rogers Company and available on local television stations across the country as well as on the PBS KIDS website where children and adults can access this content for free.

Purpose of the PEG+CAT Home Study

On behalf of CPB/PBS, we designed the study to answer an important question: how does time spent viewing and playing with educational, non-commercial media benefit young children's learning, especially those who are growing up in lower-income communities and typically have limited exposure to experiences that are oriented toward school-readiness skills?

Young children are in a unique position regarding digital content; their access is typically guided by adults who oversee viewing and access to devices, and their time with digital media is influenced by the expectations and beliefs of parents and caregivers. We designed a study that would attempt to answer this question while also considering the complexity of family life. Following a two-condition, randomized, controlled trial study design, we randomly assigned the nearly 200 families who participated into 1 of 2 groups:

1   The *PEG+CAT* group received a tablet and laptop computer to use for 12 weeks along with some information about how to talk about math with their child, and about how to support their child by sitting and watching or playing together.
2   The other group engaged with television and videos and played computer games as they normally would during the 12 weeks.

All of the families were living in lower-income communities and were predominantly Latino, Asian American, and African American.

Vision of Math Learning With Digital Media at Home

The ability to engage with and understand common mathematical concepts, such as percentages and quantities, can have a huge impact on one's life and well-being. Interpreting dosage for a medical prescription or calculating the cost of a purchase are potential challenges for adults who have limited math knowledge and skill. Ensuring that all adults have the essential mathematical skills and understanding needed to participate in all aspects of modern life requires laying a foundation of solid math experiences and skills early on. Recent research has indicated that early mathematics achievement is a highly accurate predictor of later academic achievement in all content areas, not just mathematics (Claessens, Duncan, & Engel, 2009). Yet beyond counting and other basics, adults are either unsure of the role that math can and should play in a young child's life or are not aware of how to integrate math learning in a way that is developmentally appropriate for young children in everyday settings. Providing parents with public programming as well as models of how they can support young children's math talk and math activities can help adults act on their desire to support learning. Similarly, the combination of parent-and-child co-viewing and well-designed and developmentally appropriate content produced for children can lead families to engage with a range of math concepts that they can discuss and practice in on-line and off-line home activities. This is the approach that our *PEG+CAT* study took to supporting early math learning so that every child could have exposure to early math skills, leaving them more prepared for later academic tasks.

Digital Media, Text Messages, and Other Supports to Encourage Math

Life in a home with one or more young children, we all know, can be chaotic, spontaneous, and well-intentioned but often does not follow best-laid plans. These are the realities of nearly all parents regardless of their work lives, whether members of a family do or do not live in the same home, or taking into account their children's particular personalities and needs. Taking these realities into consideration and building a research study based on families' challenges was one of our goals: if we want to learn about how families make use of digital media, then we must figure out how our study can to fit into families' real lives.

Based on several of our prior studies (Pasnik & Llorente, 2013; Penuel et al., 2012), we recognized that simply placing educational media in front of a child at home is no guarantee that she or he will understand the educational content. Support and guidance—what we call *adult mediation*—are necessary for a productive learning experience (McCarthy, Li, & Tiu, 2012). And the most productive experiences happen when adults understand the educational goals of the digital media and how to make those clear, connecting to young children's lives in ways that are developmentally appropriate.

For the *PEG+CAT* study, this meant thinking through all aspects of how families might engage with digital media, what supports they might need to make the most of a math-focused program, and how our staff of researchers could best support parent-and-child engagement with study activities in ways that were doable for family members yet structured enough for research.

We provided a range of activities that children and their parents in the *PEG+CAT* group could do using *PEG+CAT* resources. These included engaging with full episodes of the *PEG+CAT* program, shorter video clips, online games, a tablet-based app, and printable hands-on activities. All resources focused on math concepts that were integrated into stories involving Peg and her pet cat as they explored their world and encountered challenges requiring mathematical solutions. Math concepts included:

- recognizing, completing, and making patterns (e.g., a visual and auditory pattern: short, short, short, long);
- recognizing and labeling 2-D geometric shapes (triangle, rectangle) and 3-D geometric shapes (sphere, cube);
- ordinal numbers (first, second, third…) and counting (1, 2, 3…);
- measurable attributes (e.g., height or weight); and
- spatial relationships (e.g., between or under).

Researchers also provided short videos (approximately 6 minutes) for parents about math talk with young children, joint video viewing with young children, and supporting problem-solving strategies for young children linked to *PEG+CAT* videos and games.

Researchers used videos to give parents the chance to hear and see examples of how to support their child's engagement with the mathematics concepts using various digital media. This included covering topics such as what it means to talk with a young child about math, including the concepts and skills that are developmentally appropriate; and when and where math conversations could fit into parents and children's lives on a regular basis. For example, when watching the episode of the *Sparkling Sphere Problem* (see Figure 16.2), pause the video and ask your child if he or she knows the name of the shape that Ramone is inside of. Introduce the word *sphere* and point out its features (e.g., it has no straight lines) or help children identify other spheres, such as a ball or soap bubble. Or ask your child if he or she can notice differences and similarities between objects such as an apple or an orange: "What differences can you notice about their sizes, their weight, their shape, their color?"

Beyond technology and guidance described above, families participated in three in-person meetings (at the start, middle, and end of the study) where they could ask questions, review study resources, and share their experiences with the research team. At the first meeting, researchers asked families how they would like to be contacted with updates and reminders about study activities. A large majority of families opted to receive text message (other choices were phone calls and email messages) from the research team. Researchers divided up families into groups assigned to a researcher who sent out regular text

Tips for Math Talk - English

Figure 16.2 Ramone in a Sphere during the *Sparkling Sphere Problem*
(Courtesy of EDC/SRI)

reminders regarding different study activities. Families in the *PEG+CAT* group received two weekly texts, 1 at the beginning of the week providing a short tip (160 characters or less) about a math activity, and 1 reminder to complete a media use journal for researchers. Families in the other group received one weekly text reminding them to complete their media use journals. The majority of families reported the text messages they received as a part of the study to be helpful, practical, and useful, showing promise for the use of text messaging as a convenient and effective way to connect with families.

Researchers provided ongoing technical support, troubleshooting problems that arose with laptops and tablets. When a device was broken or (in one case) stolen, it was replaced within a week to ensure limited disruption to study activities. Nearly every family who attended our first study meeting continued to the end of the study period, and every participating family received either a laptop or tablet as a thank you for participating in the study and so that they could continue to access *PEG+CAT* as well as other media resources.

These additional supports—in-person meetings, text messages, and free resources—were meant to help us use the study to address three big questions: (1) how use of *PEG+CAT* resources influenced children's knowledge of target mathematics and social emotional skills; (2) how use of these resources influenced parent/caregiver attitudes and beliefs; and (3) how children and families engaged with selected *PEG+CAT* resources in their homes. The social emotional skills, also known as approaches to learning, include skills such as problem-solving, persistence, and cognitive flexibility.

How We Measured Kids' Math Learning and Changes Among Parents

Our research team collected children's assessment data, information from parents, and participating children's teachers and through back-end data collection tools embedded in the study website that housed all *PEG+CAT* resources. In order to collect data about children's math learning, researchers developed an assessment that aligned to the target math concepts covered in the *PEG+CAT* resources but did not align with the specific activities or tasks that the program introduced. Children who participated in this study completed a one-to-one researcher-designed assessment at the beginning and end of the study. Researchers also collected information about classroom teachers' perceptions of study participants' attitudes toward learning (such as persistence and problem solving) as well as information from parents about their math learning; comfort level supporting their child's math learning and using educational technology to support early learning (the parent survey); and about their use of digital media in their homes (the media diary). Finally, we used software to track family use of the study website and different *PEG+CAT* resources during the 12-week study.

Researchers conducted home visits to a small sample of participating families. These were made twice during the course of the study, and researchers spent time observing and talking with families (both children and their parents) about how they use media, when they use it, and what they choose to view or play on different devices.

What We Discovered About Early Math Learning—and Why Parents Are Essential

This study revealed several positive findings for both children and parents. First, we found that children in the *PEG+CAT* group learned more math than children in the other group. However, the gains were evident only in the areas of math that are not typically covered in preschool curricula: 3-D shapes, ordinal numbers, and spatial relationships. We also found that parents and caregivers in the *PEG+CAT* group were more likely to engage in joint (parent-and-child) technology use, such as joint video viewing and joint game play. In addition, parents and caregivers reported higher levels of confidence in being able to support their child with math learning after the study period than did parents and caregivers in the other group.

One example of joint engagement among children and parents was a 4-year-old we'll call Adrian and his mother, who we'll call Jessica, playing the *Chicken Dance Game*, a *PEG+CAT* game in which players help chickens complete their "really cool dance" pattern by choosing the dance step for the last chicken in the group. As they played, Adrian's mother consistently attempted to direct the conversation and support Adrian's game play by asking questions such as "What comes next?" and "Is that the right one?" Another example was "Ana" and her mother, "Sonia," while watching the *Big Dog Problem*, a *PEG+CAT* episode where a very big dog helps Peg and Cat become tall enough to reach a mailbox and mail important letters for Peg's mother. As they watched this episode, Sonia told Ana to pause the show on a number of occasions, each time saying, "Can you explain to me what was going on, because I didn't understand?" In a similar vein, a third parent, "Veronica," described how her son, "Carlo," had come to her after playing *Pizza Place*, a *PEG+CAT* online game in which Peg directs children to place a specific number of toppings on a pizza, saying, "Mommy come! I want you to eat one of the slices of pizza!" This opened up a dialogue between Veronica and Carlo about the game and how to play it.

At the end of the study, a majority (double the percentage at the start of the study) of parents and caregivers in the *PEG+CAT* group agreed that technology and media were tools for math learning. In particular, parents noted how the different media resources worked together to support children's learning and that the games offered a context for children to apply and practice math skills introduced by the video. For example, Jessica noted that:

When Adrian watches just the videos on his own, I don't think he's paying attention to the counting or the subtracting or measuring things they are doing, but when there is a game that goes along with it, then he's able to do it himself and understand it better.

Finally, a higher proportion of *PEG+CAT* group parents and caregivers reported engaging in problem-solving strategies with their children at the end of the study. In particular, more than three-fourths of them said they explored "what if" scenarios with their children (e.g., a problem-solving strategy that supports cognitive flexibility and generating new ideas). In the case of Ana and Sonia, Sonia turned the conversation toward real life at the conclusion of the *Big Dog Problem* episode and asked Ana how she would deal with Peg and Cat's problem and what she, Ana, would do if she had to reach something that was up high and out of reach. Ana told her mother they could use a ladder, stand up on a table or chair, or they could jump and "be big and reach." Ana and Sonia's example highlights how parents took up the strategies in the family support materials to turn Peg's "big problems" into opportunities for applying problem-solving strategies based on mathematical questions in everyday life.

We also found that familiar, beloved characters can model learning and problem-solving behavior for children. For example, Sonia reported that since watching *PEG+CAT*, Ana had begun to copy Peg's language and antics, often saying, "I have to think" and "I have to find a way," putting her finger to her forehead, and when she saw a mess she wanted to clean up, she would say that she was going to think of a solution. Similarly, Veronica explained how, since watching *PEG+CAT*, Carlo had begun to use Peg's strategies to deal with frustration. Each *PEG+CAT* episode begins with a problem Peg encounters, causing her to squeal, "I'm totally freaking out!" to which Cat responds by reminding Peg to count backward from 5 to calm down. Veronica noted that Carlo had begun to declare, "Mommy, I'm angry. I'm counting," and then count "1, 2, 3..." to relax. Veronica said Carlo learned this from *PEG+CAT* videos and, with her encouragement, had been using this strategy at home and at school. Likewise, Jessica said Adrian was learning about patience from *PEG+CAT*. Even though Jessica did not believe that Adrian knew how to apply Peg's counting-backward strategy to his own life, he often noticed Peg's frustration while watching the show and would point out that, "Peg needs to calm down."

Our observations also highlighted how adults are differently prepared to engage with children around media. For example, during a visit to one home, researchers watched as 4-year-old "Liliana" selected the *Penguin Problem* episode on her tablet while "Angela," her mother, stood beside her. Angela explained that she often watched Liliana view episodes or play games "because the worksheet said that an adult is supposed to be here to supervise the media." She was referring to a Parent Tip Sheet the study team had provided, which offered suggestions for how parents could interact with their children as they watched and played media together. In this example, it is clear that the information provided to parents about how to engage in co-viewing and how to support a child's engagement with the media is not modeled adequately. Additional opportunities for showing and modeling how interactions between adult and child during game play or video viewing would likely support parents who want to support their children's learning but require more information about how to do so.

While a majority of *PEG+CAT* group families reported that the resources were engaging and our research findings suggest that the study experience had a positive impact on both children's math learning and parents understanding of how to support using digital media and also on their own understanding of early math concepts, teachers did not report seeing any differences between children who were in the *PEG+CAT* group and those in the other group while they were at preschool. This suggests either that the approaches to learning that were presented in the *PEG+CAT* resources did not transfer to a more formal learning environment or that the instrument used to measure this was not adequate for this purpose.

Research-Backed Helpful Hints for Media Mentors

How might this study's findings be useful to educators working with parents, early learning professionals, and children? Our research shows the potential for digital media to support learning among children and families in ways that can contribute to later school readiness and that can also contribute to learning as a family activity. By supporting parents trying out new activities with their children, such as exploring new math concepts and ways of talking about math and problem solving, parents can develop more confidence in their ability to help their children learn and can open up new opportunities for their own engagement in their children's later school experiences. Below are some basic recommendations drawn from research, including this study, which have examined how digital media can be used to support early learning for young children and for the parents and other adults who care for young children:

- **Provide parents with models of how to interact with their children when viewing videos or playing games.** These models must be brief and explicit, and framed in a way that invites participation and modification rather than adherence to a specific approach or task.
- **Give parents sample language to use when asking children questions or engaging in discussion with them.** Despite wanting to support math learning, many adults have had limited experiences with math and are not familiar with ways to approach this topic with children.

Providing examples can help give adults a better understanding of what they are trying to achieve when they talk with their child about math.

- **Make learning goals clear and specific.** When parents know where a game or digital activity is heading, they are more able to help their child stay on track. Providing parents with information about what the goals of a particular media experience are, for example, PEG+CAT focuses on 3-D shapes, patterns, and so on, can help them focus on relevant aspects of what they are watching and can lead to discussions between parents and children that are more focused on the target content.

- **Encourage parents to try playing games as a way for them to model play for kids.** Children need modeling as much as parents do. Encourage adults to "talk aloud" as they play through a game, including talking through a mistake or wrong answer and how to recover from making a mistake. This can both provide children with information about how to approach and engage with digital media and provide an example of persisting even after providing a wrong answer.

- **Encourage a connection between on-screen and off-screen experiences.** Ask parents to connect what happens in a video or a game to real-life experiences to help children personally connect with the content; for example, Peg and Cat walking down stairs and counting third, second, first for each floor they reach. A parent can help a child recall when she was using ordinal numbers when they counted flights of stairs, bus stops, or passing stoplights on a recent trip around the neighborhood.

- **Help children focus on a game or activity's core learning goals.** Young children benefit from educational media most when adults help children know where to focus during joint viewing or joint play. For example, an adult can point out that a game's goal is to complete a pattern by filling in the missing piece when children might otherwise randomly click their way through a game or activity or miss the math goal of a video episode because they chose to dance to the music instead. Encouraging adults to guide children to the learning content of digital media, without interrupting children's engagement and play with these digital resources, will provide the structure and focus that young children need to benefit most from digital media experience.

References

Case Study 1: Engaging Families with Transmedia Math Content, WestEd

McCarthy, B., Li, L., Tiu, M., Atienza, S., & Sexton, U. (2015). *Learning with PBS KIDS: A study of family engagement and early mathematics achievement.* Retrieved from: www.wested.org/resources/learning-with-pbs-kids/

McCarthy, B., Sexton, U., Li, L., Tiu, M., & Atienza, S. (in preparation). A case study of family engagement and early mathematics achievement.

Van Voorhis, F. L., Maier, M. F., Epstein, J. L., Lloyd, C. M., & Leuong, T. (2013). *The impact of family involvement on the education of children ages 3 to 8: A focus on literacy and math achievement outcomes and social-emotional skills.* New York: MRDC.

Case Study 2: Digital Media and Learning at Home, EDC/SRI International

Claessens, A., Duncan, G. J., & Engel, M. (2009). Kindergarten skills and fifth-grade achievement: Evidence from the ECLS-K. *Economics of Education Review*, 28(4), 415–427.

McCarthy, B., Li, L., & Tiu, M. (2012). *PBS KIDS mathematics transmedia suites in preschool homes: A report to the CPB-PBS ready to learn initiative.* San Francisco, CA: WestEd.

Pasnik, S., & Llorente, C. (2013). *Preschool teachers can use a PBS KIDS transmedia curriculum supplement to support young children's mathematics learning: Results of a randomized controlled trial.* New York, & Menlo Park, CA: Education Development Center & SRI International.

Pasnik, S., Moorthy, S., Llorente, C., Hupert, N., Dominguez, X., & Silander, M. (2015). *Supporting parent–child experiences with PEG+CAT early math concepts: Report to the CPB-PBS Ready to Learn Initiative.* New York, & Menlo Park, CA: Education Development Center & SRI International.

Penuel, W. R., Bates, L., Gallagher, L. P., Pasnik, S., et al. (2012). Supplementing literacy instruction with a media-rich intervention: Results of a randomized controlled trial. *Early Childhood Research Quarterly*, 27(1), 115–127.

Resources

- *Learning with PBS KIDS: A Study of Family Engagement and Early Mathematics Achievement,* WestEd, 2015 www.wested.org/resources/learning-with-pbs-kids/
- *Supporting Parent–Child Experiences with PEG+CAT Early Math Concepts,* EDC/SRI, 2015 http://cct.edc.org/sites/cct.edc.org/files/ms-resources/edc-sri-rtl-peg-math-study-report-2015.pdf
- PBS Summative Evaluations/Impact Studies http://pbskids.org/lab/research/summative-evaluationsimpact-studies/

Learn More…

- Center for Children and Technology, EDC http://cct.edc.org
- Corporation for Public Broadcasting (CPB) www.cpb.org
- CPB, Findings from Ready to Learn: 2005–2010 www.cpb.org/rtl/
- Fred Rogers Company www.fredrogers.org
- Education Development Center (EDC) www.edc.org
- Imajine That www.imajinethat.com

- KBTC, Tacoma, WA www.kbtc.org
- PBS www.pbs.org
- PBS Kids http://pbskids.org
- *PEG+CAT* http://pbskids.org/peg/
- *PEG+CAT* Lab http://pbskids.org/lab/show/peg-cat/
- SRI International www.sri.com
- U.S. Department of Education, Ready to Learn http://www2.ed.gov/programs/rtltv/index.html
- WestEd www.wested.org
- WGBH, Boston, MA www.wgbh.org

Chapter 17

New Allies for the Digital Age

Building a Policy and Research Infrastructure to Support Media Mentorship

Lisa Guernsey and Michael H. Levine

Introduction

The need to help families and educators navigate the digital seas is clear.

Bright and compelling examples are coursing through the pages of this book, from the early childhood specialist in Fairfax, who opened the eyes of family child care providers, to early intervention programs that use text messages and video examples as nudges for parents.

These stories reinforce what we know from ecological systems theory as developed by the renowned developmental psychologist Urie Bronfenbrener. The theory contends that children's learning and development unfold in the context of the "nested" environment in which they live. There is no longer any doubt that that environment increasingly includes digital media and interactive communication tools (Takeuchi & Levine, 2014). The vast majority of American households, wealthy and low-income, are consuming and interacting with technologies everyday, from the always-on television to the laptop computer in the kitchen streaming YouTube videos, to the smartphone or tablet pinging with text messages and updates to new games. How children learn to grow and develop in this new media environment will depend greatly on how the adults in their lives use these various forms of media with them.

This is why figuring out how to guide and respond to the needs of those adults is a critical task for educators of the twenty-first century. This is not simply a matter of pushing messages at parents and telling them to get smart about how they use media. Today's parents need new resources, not a guilt trip. Imagine if, at the dawn of the twentieth century, parents had simply been told to educate their children without the presence of a growing network of public schools and libraries. They would have thrown up their hands in exasperation. Only the families with income to pay tuition for tutors or private schools would have been able to do anything about it.

The concept of media mentors, touched upon by many writers throughout this book, grows out of this need for new guidance. Media mentors, and the infrastructure to support them, will need to be integrated into public education and public library systems to give all families opportunities for new learning. And those systems will need to adapt to serve children at very young ages. As science has shown the importance of nurturing children's health and development starting at birth, whole new fields of professionals— from home visitors to early intervention specialists to preschool teachers— have become important forces in young children's lives and the lives of their parents. Now it is time to both upgrade the skills of these professionals and envision new professional roles to help families understand and become savvy users of the digital media and interactive communication tools that are part of children's nested environments.

Building this new force will not happen overnight. It will take planning and visioning, not to mention years of evaluating, reassessing, tweaking, and improving, to create a modern infrastructure for training these professionals and to mold public policies to support them. To get started, we propose the introduction of a new policy and research strategy and a series of aligned actions. We suggest here that to ensure families have resources to make smart decisions about the adoption of new communications' technologies, we will need to create a big tent and develop a mobilization strategy built on equity and civil rights. We also suggest 2 tactics to produce gains within the next 5 years: Inject media mentorship into the national conversation about the early childhood workforce and embark on a national program of iterative research and development. We are still in the early days of understanding how best to apply research. By making media mentorship a priority on the national agenda, we will be able to study, refine, adapt, and invest new resources in programs that will help prepare all children to learn in a digital age.

Now it is time to both upgrade the skills of these professionals and envision new professional roles to help families understand and become savvy users of the digital media and interactive communication tools that are part of children's nested environments.

Create a Big Tent

It could be argued that one reason early childhood services have not expanded rapidly for all children is that stakeholders had a difficult time seeing themselves as part of a greater whole. In the late 1960s and early 1970s, advocates rallied for a "big coalition" to support legislation that would have greatly expanded child development programs and services on a national scale, but it was vetoed by President Nixon in 1971. Since then, most of the past 45 years have been focused on building particular programs and their funding streams (think Head Start or the Child Care Development Block Grant) instead of on building and supporting a corps of professionals across settings. Early childhood leaders tended to put their energies into protecting distinct programs instead of seeing themselves as part of a broader field that needs training and support. Spend any time on Capitol Hill or with policy leaders in local and state communities and you will hear stories of in-fighting that led to stalled legislation and politicians opting to put their energies elsewhere.

In the past decade, these divisions have softened as governors have organized "integrated services" plans and "children's cabinets" and as organizations such as Educare and myriad school districts and community-based organizations have shown the power of partnering and blending funding streams. The Obama administration and state governments have built grant programs to motivate the pursuit of cooperative efforts, and the U.S. Department of Health and Human Services and the U.S. Department of Education have created an inter-agency policy board for tackling shared issues. By working across sectors and creating partnerships in the same way, we can ensure that media mentorship for young children and families does not become a "boutique" program that exists only in a few locations around the country.

Already the library community has provided leadership to give us a strong start. In 2015, the Association for Library Services to Children (ALSC), which is a division of the American Library Association, produced a white paper, "Media Mentorship in Libraries Serving Youth." The paper argues that taking a mentorship approach to serving children and families is strongly aligned with the competencies spelled out in ASLC's competencies statement, which lists skills librarians are already supposed to have, such as offering convenient access to resources, listening to families, and "continually developing skills pertaining to technology and related tools" (Campbell, Haines, Koester, & Stolz, 2015, p. 1). The authors wrote, "There is precedent for libraries creating and tailoring programming and services to best meet the needs of the children and families they serve, and this relatively newer need for digital literacy is no different." (Campbell et al., 2015, p. 2)

In 2015, the board of directors for ALSC adopted the white paper as a call to action for its members. As the paper said,

> It is the responsibility of library training programs, including library schools and formal professional development opportunities, to prepare future and current librarians and youth services practitioners to serve as media mentors. It is the responsibility of supervisors, administrators, and professional associations to support practitioners in this capacity.
>
> (Campbell et al., 2015, p. 1).

Leaders in the library community, including Cen Campbell and Amy Koester, who wrote Chapter 15 of this book "Children's Librarians as Media Mentors," which includes many stories of libarians in the role of media mentors) are now putting together strategies for enabling librarians to truly fulfill those responsibilities. A survey in 2014 of libraries across the country showed that only 22 percent were providing mentoring services to families (Mills, Romeijn-Stout, Campbell, & Koester, 2015). This "relatively small number of libraries," the chapter's authors write, points to "the area primed for growth."

Library leaders, however, are only one connection point for families with young children seeking advice and resources. Every day, specialists across different service areas in early childhood are also encountering families with the need for information and guidance about how to adopt new technologies and engage with their children around digital media in positive ways. Is there a way to create networks of mentorship training that could help professionals in the fields of early intervention and health as well as early learning and development?

Consider the case of Stacey Landberg, an early interventionist who runs a speech therapy practice in Los Angeles. A big part of her job involves visiting the homes of low-income families and giving parents guidance on how to help promote language development in their infants and toddlers, some of whom have been diagnosed with autism. A few years ago, Landberg started noticing that parents often ask about apps and media to help their children and yet at the same time many of them have the television running all day in the background, a practice that research has shown to interfere with children's play patterns and verbal interactions with their parents (Kirkorian, Pempek, Murphy, Schmidt, & Anderson, 2009; Lapierre, Piotrowski, & Linebarger, 2012).

Electronic media, she said, "is a part of every family's life, and it is a topic that we need to have a conversation with them about," but interventionists need strategies for working with families in a non-judgmental way. It isn't right, she said, "if we are going in and asking them to turn off their TVs and not talking to them about why." She also wanted to know how to guide parents to use well-designed apps and other media to promote speech development, but she found a dearth of materials for children younger than age 3.

Frustrated by a lack of resources and seeing a need to provide better guidance to families, Landberg did her own research. She came across the notion of media mentorship and contacted the Los Angeles Public Library hoping to find a mentor who could help her work with families. When she discovered that the library was new to the idea of media mentors but was interested in figuring out what it would take to put together a program, she contacted one of us (Lisa) to find out whether certifications or trainings might exist and learned that the concept is relatively new. "I feel that our field should be part of this conversation," she told us. "It will be exciting to see these programs take off."

Another group of professionals who could be guided by mentors, or learn to become mentors themselves, are teachers and other professionals in early learning programs. Home visitors, parenting educators, child care providers (in family-based programs or centers), and classroom-based pre-K and K–3 teachers are often, and should be, trusted sources of information for parents. Many of these professionals get bits and pieces of guidance from professional associations such as the National Association for the Education of Young Children, but they may not have direct training in working with families in ways that address the exact questions and concerns they have. These professionals may not yet have the skills to, in the words of many smart family-engagement experts, "meet them where they are."

Our lack of a field-building strategy may unintentionally be contributing to a bigger national challenge: the weak performance of our children, especially from low-income backgrounds, in literacy, math, science, and other academic subjects. We urgently need to examine the potential and opportunity costs associated with the time currently spent by our young children with media. Imagine the possibilities if librarians, early childhood specialists, schools, and the early learning community could work together to create pathways toward media mentorship. Taking a "big tent" approach would not only help to bring these groups closer together, it could lend weight to the cause while helping to build new standards and professionalism across sectors. And the nature of this networked age—with communications technologies allowing for real-time chat across thousands of miles—could help to foster it.

The common need across the field to gain more practical information, guidance, and support is a great opportunity to build a new action coalition. A media mentoring initiative (Michael has referred in other writing to a "digital teacher corps": Levine & Gee, 2011) could start with a convening laying out who will do what and distilling the kinds of competencies that will be needed. A coalition of organizations and higher-education institutions could take the lead in developing a certification process. Schools of library and information science and schools of education could create shared-degree programs, for example. And libraries, early childhood centers, early intervention programs, and school districts could join arms in their communities to create shared positions and new job descriptions.

Strike a Chord for Equity and Diversity

For too long, concerns about technology in early childhood have been relegated to overheated debates about screen time, typically touched off by upper-middle-class or highly educated parents who come from a culture that prizes the avoidance of television and digital entertainment. The debates often do not encompass the full diversity of families in the United States. They do not help to answer questions from immigrant families who look to media of all kinds to help acclimate their children to a new culture, nor do they speak to low-income parents who want their children to gain technology skills so they don't feel lost at school and can have a better chance of acquiring a job someday.

Also for too long, the dialogue on how families use and engage with media has happened in a universe separate from the growing calls for equity in children's learning opportunities in their early years. As we argue in *Tap, Click,*

Read: Growing Readers in a World of Screens (Guernsey & Levine, 2015), these two issues need to be addressed together. Children in low-income families and underserved neighborhoods rarely have access to the same level of mentorship and adult guidance that is available to their more well-to-do peers. Children learn by observing how adults around them use apps and software and how they talk about television shows, and children learn even more when those adults engage them in conversation while they are watching or playing together. They also learn better when the cultural resonance of the content they are reading is clear and compelling; too often, media developers and practitioners have lagged behind family needs in designing literacy programs and products that recognize America's growing diversity. The early literacy field has largely succeeded in helping to spread the message that children need reading partners and that children learn best when adults pause while reading and ask them questions about what stories they hear. Now it is time for those same messages to be carried into the realm of digital media.

Literacy scores alone should cause us to feel real urgency here. More than two-thirds of fourth graders do not fully comprehend what they read—or, in the lingo of the National Assessment of Educational Progress, they are not "proficient." Reading at merely a "basic" level does not help a child to stay at grade level and enable mastery of a subject or skill. These struggling students fall behind, year after year, and many of them do not graduate from high school at all. These students and their parents need intensive interventions and support throughout their school day and in their informal environments to help them achieve parity with their peers. Among the tools that could address this problem are programs that help families find digital media that could help them learn to read and gain skills in using that media with their children.

To illustrate, an edition of the widely respected journal *The Future of Children* devoted to literacy included this observation:

> Innovative technology applications show promise for supporting the development of advanced reading skills that students need to master discipline-specific knowledge areas and that may be particularly challenging for students from low socioeconomic backgrounds and non-English-speaking homes. Self-paced tutorials have led to gains in self-questioning, error detection, inference, summarization, and concept-mapping skills and strategies to enhance readers' use of reading strategies and comprehension of texts.
>
> (Biancarosa & Griffiths, 2012)

Media mentorship must also be culturally sensitive and competent if we wish to be responsive to America's diverse learners. As recent research conducted by the Joan Ganz Cooney Center and the scholar Vikki Katz establish, low-income Hispanic-Latino families and recent immigrants have different interpretations and uses of media and technology assets that are available for both home and school use (Rideout, 2014; Lee & Barron, 2015; Katz, 2014; Katz & Levine, 2015). Too often, professional practices, media offerings, and public policies are not well designed to take advantage of natural strengths in these homes.

What has resulted from a lack of attention to both equity considerations and a lack of nuanced cultural knowledge has been referred to as "digital participation gaps." Scholars such as Susan Neuman and Henry Jenkins have documented that a lack of media mentoring and supports can lead to new inequities between well-resourced and low-income communities (Neuman & Celano, 2012, Jenkins, Purushotma, Weigel, Clinton, & Robison, 2009).

Table 17.1 Media Mentors as Part of Broader Reform

Media Mentors as Part of Broader Reforms

Rethinking Early and Elementary Education Policies and Family Engagement Policies

We see media mentorship and the strategy and tactics described in this chapter as part of a larger array of policy changes that are needed to modernize approaches to supporting families and improving early education from birth through age 8. Three papers provide complimentary frameworks for moving policies forward. Below are those resources and a sampling of key recommendations within each.

Take a Giant Step (Barron, et al., 2011). A blueprint for teaching young children in a digital age included several recommendations that might better prepare media mentors for our digital age. Among the most important were...

- Recruit, prepare, and retain principals and preschool directors who understand and practice the use of new technologies to promote teaching and learning.
- Examine all financial and human resources committed for the training of teachers of young children to determine if program quality priorities can be improved through new forms of technology integration.
- Identify a place in every community where teachers and parents can receive support, mentoring, and resources for the productive use of technology.
- Create public–private partnerships to support new forms of design and a new distribution system to enable digital innovation in the classroom.

Envisioning a Digital Age Architecture for Early Education (Guernsey, 2014). A framework to guide policy discussions on where technology fits in early childhood. The five pillars were:

- Aim high in determining standards for tech-integrated instruction.

- Boost the workforce through new training and preparation programs.
- Tap hidden assets in public media and public libraries.
- Connect teachers and families to information and to each other.
- Investigate and conduct independent research on what works.

Tap, Click, Read: Growing Readers in a World of Screens (Guernsey & Levine, 2015). The final chapter of this book provides a roadmap to achieving stronger literacy outcomes for all children. It outlined four main areas needing action:

- **Build a coherent pathway** for the birth-through-8 years, starting with paid leave and extending up through pre-K and elementary school with new teaching strategies and family partnerships.
- **Advance digital equity** through investment in free or low-cost Internet access and a revitalized public media capacity.
- **Create connected teachers, schools, and communities** through ed-school reforms, library programs, and professional development systems. (Media mentorship should be a key driver here.)
- **Engage the diversity of families in America:** Mine cultural capital and recognize families' assets linguistically and in how they work with and support their children's development.

Two Steps to Take Now

Every good strategy needs good tactics for successful execution. Making and sustaining the changes described in this chapter will require improvements and reforms to policies at the federal, state, and local level, but today's public and policymakers may not yet see the urgency we describe here, nor realize why it is imperative to build an infrastructure of human capital to help guide and support families as they use and engage with new technologies. Certainly a great deal of broader awareness-building is needed to reform early education in general, and we see media mentors as part of that broader campaign (Table 17.1). However, there are also concrete steps that education and family-engagement leaders can take to create momentum for growing a corps of media mentors across the country. Below we offer two steps to take now.

Inject Media Mentorship into the Dialogue on Improving the Workforce

In April 2015, the Institute of Medicine and the National Academy of Science published an influential volume that laid out the scientific case for improving the early childhood workforce and provided recommendations on how to do it. The volume, *Transforming the Workforce for Children From Birth through Age 8: A Unifying Foundation* is a "consensus report," meaning that it reflects the consensus of a 19-member committee of researchers, practitioners, and policy experts vetted and appointed by the academy. The report lays out

13 recommendations that require the engagement of nearly every organization involved in the care, development, and cognitive and social learning of young children, from health professionals to principals in elementary schools. A chapter on child development and early learning provides a comprehensive report of how children build literacy and language, math, and social-emotional skills, and descriptions of the significance of digital media are embedded throughout. The implications of media and technology are also highlighted in a section describing how little training many teachers have to adequately address technology use in classrooms and with families.

One conclusion from the report is that competency statements and documents from professional organizations and states—the documents that help guide professional learning and licensure programs—need to be updated. As the report states:

> Areas likely in need of enhancement in many existing statements include teaching subject-matter–specific content, addressing stress and adversity, fostering socioemotional development, promoting general learning competencies, working with dual language learners, and *integrating technology into curricula.*
> (Allen & Kelly, 2015) [emphasis added]

The emphasis on integrating technology into curricula is welcome, but once you consider the potential role of media mentors, curriculum enhancement is just one of many areas where the workforce needs assistance with technology. Each of the other competencies listed above—from teaching content to working with dual-language learners—can also be augmented through the intentional use of communications tools and digital media, particularly when adults and children use those tools together. The challenge is in providing members of the workforce with enough training and practice to do so. That need for help with technology also comes through in surveys of teachers of older students. A report from the LEAD Commission, a bipartisan group designed to support the U.S. Department of Education and the Federal Communications Commission, showed that 82 percent of teachers said they are not receiving the necessary training to use technology to its fullest potential in the classroom (LEAD Commission, 2013).

In other words, as much as media mentors are needed for families, they are also needed for teachers. And once taught, those teachers can then pass down those skills to parents, helping them to gain a better understanding of how to use technology effectively and when to avoid it; how to become more selective about the apps, games, and e-books that are offered to children; and how to encourage adults, children, and their peers to use media as an opportunity to talk and learn together.

...as much as media mentors are needed for families, they are also needed for teachers.

The *Transforming the Workforce* report is already guiding the National Association for the Education of Young Children and several influential philanthropies. As organizations across the country act upon the recommendations in this report, leaders in media mentorship and family engagement will need to be at the table. The recommendations have implications for education schools, professional development systems, and certification and licensure programs. As these stakeholders begin to make reforms, they should consider integrating proposals for media mentorship and building a digital teacher corps into their work. Imagine, for example, what might be possible if all prospective pre-K–3 teachers took courses that embedded trainings on using media with children and if their clinical experiences included working with master teachers to help young students become creators and communicators using new tools. Imagine what might be possible for would-be library professionals if new career paths combined the art of curation, the new science of instructional technology, and the expertise in working with families to support children's learning.

In addition to the focus on improving the workforce generally, national education discussions have been revolving around two big challenges: How to ensure students are strong readers by third grade and how to motivate young students to excel in the fields of science, technology, engineering, and math (STEM). Equipping librarians and early educators as media mentors could open a new channel for improving outcomes in literacy and STEM. Done well, media mentorship can help strengthen STEM and literacy learning experiences in the home, can assist teachers in harnessing digital media to improve student engagement in these content areas, and can help parents gain confidence in using new tools to connect with teachers, see video models, and become partners in helping young children with guided reading, hands-on science projects, online math games, and more. Connecting these dots will be key to helping policymakers and the public see these connections between investing in mentorship and propelling literacy and STEM outcomes.

In short, given the continued focus on early childhood, the push for better literacy rates, and the new attention paid to STEM in the early years, momentum will continue to build for improving the workforce for young children. Discussions are already happening around the country on how to bring professionalization to child care and early learning settings and how to ensure better collaboration with health and mental health professionals as well as with leaders in school districts. Public libraries and public media producers and stations are not always top-of-mind in early childhood circles, but they should make efforts to join these discussions and play a guiding role in transforming the way technology is considered among teachers and parents.

Experiment and Build a Research Base

Projects are popping up around the country, but very few are being rigorously evaluated and tested to determine whether they work. Researchers should design more studies to determine the key ingredients of effective media mentorship. One case to consider: Some early childhood centers in Boston have the benefit of a program called Tech Goes Home, in which librarians train teachers and administrators to lead classes of parents. The idea is to raise parents' awareness of whether their children are—or are not—learning from various games, TV shows, and apps they play with every day and to show parents what joint engagement looks like. "Parents are encouraged to ask their kids questions about what they're doing and learning as they work on the computers," wrote Chris Berdik, in a *Slate* article about the program. "The goal is to bring technology to the pre-K crowd *and* help bridge the digital divide" (Berdik, 2015), but is that goal being met? Are teachers able to raise parents' awareness? Have families changed some of their routines because of the program? Are children learning more than they would have before?

Answering these questions will be critical to garnering support for programs that are designed to promote intentional and scientifically based media mentorship. Data will need to be assembled on which interventions work and why the costs are worth it. Bringing mentorship to teachers and families will require trainings, certification systems, and new materials and devices, not to mention the costs of running new weekly story time programs, coaching teachers, or creating maker spaces for children and families.

Some librarians have already learned the lesson of the importance of collecting data to justify investments in their programs. In 2008, when the National Early Literacy Panel (NELP) released its findings on how to support children's early literacy skills, librarians were upset to discover that the impact of libraries and their story time programs were not mentioned. As library researchers later explained, "Regardless of their emphasis on early literacy focused programs, libraries were left out of the NELP report because of the lack of empirical research examining the early literacy outcomes of their programs" (Campana et al., forthcoming).

To rectify that omission, those same researchers, led by scholars at the iSchool at the University of Washington, embarked on a study to determine whether story times made a difference and if so, why. In the first year of research, they examined 120 story times in libraries across the state of Washington, observing approximately 1,440 children ranging in age from birth to 5 years. Finding a significant impact of these programs was a challenge: Story times do not follow a prescribed curriculum sequence, and children attend irregularly. Still, the researchers—with the help of nearly two dozen graduate students—visited scores of story times and used scientific observation tools to take field notes and record video, keeping track of librarian's behaviors and the responses and behaviors of the children who attended. After analyzing the results, researchers found a "strong positive" correlation between librarians' literacy-oriented activities and children's abilities to perform literacy-oriented tasks. "When story time providers offer early literacy content," the researchers found, "corresponding early literacy behaviors can be observed in the children" (Campana et al., forthcoming).

It is not only library programs that will need to examine their effectiveness. Initiatives have emerged around the country that are using digital media and other tech tools to promote early literacy. In a multi-year project at New America and the Cooney Center, our teams have gained information on more than 30 programs in libraries, early childhood centers, schools, and home visiting programs that are harnessing technology in new ways. (For more on this project, called Integrating Technology in Early Literacy, see atlas.newamerica. org.) Not all of these programs are about media mentorship: Some of them are about using technology to reach parents with messages about literacy in general, not specifically messages about *using media* to promote literacy or being selective in one's media choices. But as these initiatives take shape and technology becomes further integrated into early childhood programs, the need for training and mentorship will rise, as will the need to test what works.

Other forms of experimentation in this area will be critical. As the Cooney Center and Stanford University task force (which produced the Take a Giant Step study) suggested, all of the national research agencies—from the Institute for Education Sciences, National Science Foundation, and National Institute of Health—have a role to play in conducting ongoing research that will inform professional practices in integrating technology for purposeful early learning. That report had two valuable additional recommendations we wish to reiterate. The task force recommended new funding.

- **Create a strategic inventory of R&D initiatives.** We need to know more precisely what is being done to modernize the field of teacher education and professional development for teachers of young children. The federal government, in collaboration with universities, regional labs, and private sector partners, should determine what research has been done and is being funded on the use of digital media in teacher education and professional development. Data collection should be coordinated by an entity at the U.S. Department of Education. The information gathered would allow the identification of knowledge gaps and form the basis for a government-wide strategy to support digital media R&D to benefit teaching and learning.
- **Build new incentives for public and private investment in infrastructure that supports R&D design collaborations.** Development of faster and cheaper multimedia channels of distribution is needed in order for professional development designs to propagate.

Important first steps have been taken to secure high-speed broadband access in most schools, with a priority on reaching low-income communities. An expansion of the E-Rate program to include preschool classrooms would also help foster research and development on professional practices that work. Other needed infrastructure should include greater support for digital media and learning research that connects design partners such as public media, university labs, libraries, and technology firms with local practitioner.

(Barton et al., 2011)

Conclusion: Media Mentors and the Class of 2030

In our recent book, *Tap, Click, Read: Growing Readers in a World of Screens* (Guernsey & Levine, 2015), we opened with this image:

Spotlight on Tap, Click, Read

It's graduation day, 2030. High school students and their families are filling into stadiums and auditoriums around the United States ... It seems like only yesterday that these students were babies. They arrived in the world at a time of immense change in how people communicated and learned—days that began to include smartphone apps, on-the-fly video making, instant photo sharing, YouTube ... and more. Some of these students have become careful, focused readers with skills in filtering, creating, and making sense of the continual streams of information coming their way. Guided by a community of parents and educators who recognized the potential of new tools and mentors they have become uber readers, literate in a way almost unimaginable in the days before they were born.... (but) others are flailing. Some didn't make it to this graduation moment at all. Never given consistent attention and disconnected from tools and teaching strategies that could help, they have failed to master the habits of mind and the requisite skills to succeed in a global and digital age. This waste of potential will have been, tragically, wholly preventable.

(Guernsey & Levine, 2015)

Today's young children—the high school graduates of 2030—are the citizens and workforce who will attempt to solve the problems our generation has left in their path. And yet, so many face obstacles. Not only are two in three fourth graders struggling to read proficiently but there are also few opportunities for their teachers to go beyond basic reading skills and teach children to be creators of and critical thinkers around digital media. In an era wherein reading and actively communicating in order to understand ever more complex phenomena such as climate change, economic globalization, and cooperative security are the responsibility of every citizen, we hope that a new paradigm of early literacy development will be developed, starting now. We call our formulation "readia," an intentional blending of traditional reading competencies with digital media capabilities. Or to state this more precisely, we must deploy media more intentionally in the service of learning.

As this chapter has suggested, media mentorship is an important, but missing, component in the necessary modernization of early literacy programs. We have argued that both policy and practice will need to lead a deliberate shift to support newly designed professional development programs, to fund rapid iteration action research, and to apply new program designs that prioritize equity and the needs of America's increasingly diverse learners. Media mentors—the adults who mediate the new nested environments of the more complex ecological system that every child encounters today—are among the most important pillars to prepare the class of 2030 for success. Indeed, they are perhaps the most vital leaders in confronting a vitally important challenge: To help all children gain a deeper understanding of the highly networked world in which we all live.

References

Allen, L, & Kelly, B. B. (Eds.). (2015). *Transforming the workforce for children birth through age 8: A unifying foundation*. Washington, DC: National Academies Press. http://iom.nationalacademies.org/Reports/2015/Birth-To-Eight.aspx

Barron, B., Cayton-Hodges, G., Bofferding, L., Copple, C., Darling-Hammond, L., & Levine, M. H. (2011). *Take a giant step: A blueprint for teaching young children in a digital age*. New York: Joan Ganz Cooney Center at Sesame Workshop.

Berdik, C. (July 2015). The best screen time. *Slate*. www.slate.com/articles/technology/future_tense/2015/07/tech_goes_home_program_teaches_computer_basics_to_low_income_parents_and.html

Biancarosa, G., & Griffiths, G. (2012). "Technology tools to support reading in the digital age." *The Future of Children, 22*(2), 139–160.

Campana, K., Mills, J. E., Capps, J., Dresang, E. T., et al. (forthcoming). Early literacy in library storytimes: A groundbreaking study of measures of effectiveness. *Library Quarterly*. Chicago, IL: University of Chicago Press.

Campbell, C., Haines, C., Koester, A., & Stoltz, D. (2015). *Media mentorship in libraries serving youth*. Chicago, IL: Association for Library Service to Children. www.ala.org/alsc/mediamentorship

Guernsey, L. (2014). *Envisioning a digital age architecture for early education*. Washington, DC: New America. www.newamerica.org/education-policy/envisioning-a-digital-age-architecture-for-early-education/

Guernsey, L., & Levine, M. (2015). *Tap, click, read: Growing readers in a world of screens*. San Francisco, CA: Jossey-Bass.

Jenkins, H., Purushotma, R., Weigel, M., Clinton, K., & Robison, A. (2009). *Confronting the challenges of participatory culture: Media education for the 21st century*. Cambridge, MA: MIT Press. Retrieved from https://mitpress.mit.edu/books/confronting-challenges-participatory-culture

Katz, V. (2014). *Kids in the middle: How children of immigrants negotiate community interactions for their families*. New Brunswick, NJ: Rutgers University Press.

Katz, V. S., & Levine, M. H. (2015). *Connecting to learn: Promoting digital equity for America's Hispanic families.* New York, NY: Joan Ganz Cooney Center at Sesame Workshop. www.joanganzcooneycenter.org/wp-content/uploads/2015/03/jgcc_connectingtolearn.pdf

Kirkorian, H. L., Pempek, T. A., Murphy, L. A., Schmidt, M. E., & Anderson, D. R. (2009). The impact of background television on parent–child interaction. *Child Development, 80,* 1350–1359. doi:10.1111/j.1467-8624.2009.01337.x

Lapierre, M. A., Piotrowski, J. T., & Linebarger, D. L. (2012). Background television in the homes of US children. *Pediatrics, 130*(5), 2011–2581. doi:10.1542/peds.2011-2581

LEAD Commission. (2013). *Paving a path forward for digital learning in the United States.* http://leadcommission.org/sites/default/files/FINAL%20LEADComm_PavingPath_Report_091713a.pdf

Lee, J., & Barron, B. (2015). *Aprendiendo en Casa: Media as a resource for learning among Hispanic-Latino families.* New York: Joan Ganz Cooney Center at Sesame Workshop. www.joanganzcooneycenter.org/wp-content/uploads/2015/02/jgcc_aprendiendoencasa.pdf

Levine, M. H., & Gee, J. P. (2011). *The digital teachers corps: Closing America's literacy gap.* Washington, DC: Progressive Policy Institute. http://progressivepolicy.org/wpcontent/uploads/2011/09/09.2011-Levine_Gee-The_Digital_Teachers_Corps.pdf

Mills, J. E., Romeijn-Stout, E., Campbell, C., & Koester, A. (2015). Results from the Young Children, New Media, and Libraries Survey: What did we learn? *Children and Libraries: The Journal of the Association for Library Service to Children, 13*(2), 26–35.

Neuman, S., & Celano, D. (2012). *Giving our children a fighting chance: Poverty, literacy, and the development of information capital.* New York: Teachers College Press.

Rideout, V. (2014). *Learning at home: Families' educational media use in America.* New York: The Joan Ganz Cooney Center at Sesame Workshop. www.joanganzcooneycenter.org/publication/learning-at-home/

Takeuchi, L., & Levine, M. H. (2014). Learning in a digital age: Towards a new ecology of human development. In A. Jordan & D. Romer (Eds.), *Media and the well-being of children and adolescents.* New York: Oxford University Press.

Resources

- *Envisioning a Digital Age Architecture for Early Education,* New America Policy Brief, March 2014 www.newamerica.org/downloads/DigitalArchitecture-20140326.pdf
- *Getting a Read on the App Stores: A Market Scan and Analysis of Children's Literacy Apps,* Sarah Vaala, Anna Ly, and Michael H. Levine, Joan Ganz Cooney Center, 2015 www.joanganzcooneycenter.org/publication/getting-a-read-on-the-app-stores-a-market-scan-and-analysis-of-childrens-literacy-apps/
- *Pioneering Literacy in the Digital Wild West: Empowering Parents and Educators.* Lisa Guernsey, Michael H. Levine, Cynthia Chiong, and Maggie Severns, Campaign for Grade-Level Reading, 2012 http://gradelevelreading.net/wp-content/uploads/2012/12/GLR_TechnologyGuide_final.pdf

- *Screen Time: How Electronic Media—from Baby Videos to Educational Software—Affects Your Young Child,* Lisa Guernsey, 2007 www.lisaguernsey.com/screen-time.htm
- *Transforming the Workforce for Children From Birth through Age 8: A Unifying Foundation,* Institute of Medicine and National Research Council of the National Academies http://iom.nationalacademies.org/Reports/2015/Birth-To-Eight.aspx

Learn More...

- Tap, Click, Read www.tapclickread.org
- InTEL, Integrating Technology in Early Literacy Map http://atlas.newamerica.org/tech-early-literacy
- Guernsey, L., & Levine, M. H. (2015). Pioneering Literacy in the Digital Age. In C. Donohue (Ed.), *Technology and Digital Media in the Early Years: Tools for Teaching and Learning* (pp. 104–114). New York: Routledge, and Washington, DC: National Association for the Education of Young Children.
- Joan Ganz Cooney Center at Sesame Workshop www.joanganzcooneycenter.org
  - *Families and Media Project* www.joanganzcooneycenter.org/initiative/the-families-and-media-project/
  - *Apps en Familia,* 2016 www.joanganzcooneycenter.org/wp-content/uploads/2015/08/jgcc_appsenfamilia.pdf
  - *Aprendiendo en Casa: Media as a Learning Tool among Hispanic-Latino Families,* June Lee and Brigid Barron, 2015 www.joanganzcooneycenter.org/publication/aprendiendo-en-casa-media-as-a-learning-tool-among-hispanic-latino-families/
  - *Connecting to Learn: Promoting Digital Equity for America's Hispanic Families,* Vikki Katz and Michael H. Levine, 2015 www.joanganzcooneycenter.org/publication/connecting-to-learn-promoting-digital-equity-for-americas-hispanic-families/
  - *Family Time with Apps: A Guide to Using Apps with Your Kids,* 2014 www.joanganzcooneycenter.org/publication/family-time-with-apps/
  - *Learning at Home: Families' Educational Media Use in America,* Victoria Rideout, 2014 www.joanganzcooneycenter.org/publication/learning-at-home/
  - *The New Coviewing: Investigating and Designing for Joint Media Engagement,* Lori Takeuchi and Reed Stevens, 2011 www.joanganzcooneycenter.org/publication/the-new-coviewing-designing-for-learning-through-joint-media-engagement/
- Lisa Guernsey and New America www.newamerica.org

- ○ Tech and Young Children: U.S. Dept. of Ed Elevates Need for Guidance and PD, *New America EdCentral,* September 14, 2015 www.edcentral.org/tech-young-children-u-s-dept-ed-elevates-need-guidance-pd/
- ○ Common-Sense, Science-Based Advice on Toddler Screen Time. Finally! *Slate,* November 13, 2014 www.slate.com/articles/technology/future_tense/2014/11/zero_to_three_issues_common_sense_advice_on_toddler_screen_time.html
- ○ A Cautionary Tale of Pediatricians, Parents, and Facebook, *Slate,* February 19, 2014 www.slate.com/blogs/future_tense/2014/02/19/facebook_depression_scare_offers_a_cautionary_tale_of_pediatricians_parents.html
- ○ *How True Are Our Assumptions About Screen Time?* NAEYC Families, September 2012 http://families.naeyc.org/learning-and-development/music-math-more/how-true-are-our-assumptions-about-screen-time
- ○ EdTech for the Younger Ones? Not Without Trained Teachers, *Huffington Post,* NoSSsvember 17, 2011 www.huffingtonpost.com/lisa-guernsey/edtech-for-the-playdough-_b_1097277.html
- • Tech Goes Home www.techgoeshome.org

Index